Brothels,
Bordellos, &
Bad Girls

Brothels, Bordellos, & Bad Girls

Prostitution in Colorado, 1860–1930

Jan MacKell

Foreword by Thomas J. Noel

UNIVERSITY OF NEW MEXICO PRESS
ALBUQUERQUE

First paperbound printing, 2007.
ISBN-13: 978-0-8263-3343-8

Library of Congress Cataloging-in-Publication Data
MacKell, Jan, 1962-
    Brothels, bordellos, and bad girls :
    prostitution in Colorado, 1860-1930 /
    Jan MacKell; foreword by Thomas J. Noel.
    —1st ed.
    p. cm.
    Includes bibliographical references and index.
        ISBN 0-8263-3342-7 (cloth : alk. paper)
    1. Prostitution—Colorado—History.
    2. Prostitutes—Colorado—History.
    I. Title.
    HQ145.C6M33 2004
    306.74'082'09788—dc22
                        2004011784

Cover photographs: (*front*) 1905 postcard;
(*back*) Ida Mulle's publicity photo
Images courtesy of Jan MacKell
Design and composition by Melissa Tandysh

To the ladies and their undying spirit

Contents

Foreword

꧁꧂

By Thomas J. Noel

Prostitution thrived in Colorado's male-dominated pioneer era, especially in the mining towns. The 1860 U.S. Census for Colorado Territory lists 32,691 males and 1,586 females. With twenty men competing for each woman, it is not surprising that some women were, to put this delicately, recycled.

Delicacy, humor, respect, and compassion are among the merits of Jan MacKell's *Brothels, Bordellos, and Bad Girls: Prostitution in Colorado, 1860–1930*. Although other authors have flirted with Colorado's commercial sex, Jan provides a detailed overview. Jan, a Cripple Creek historian and preservationist, has spent time researching, supporting, and interpreting the state's only National Register brothel museum, the Old Homestead in Cripple Creek. For Pearl DeVere's operation there, Jan even unearthed the probate records listing Pearl's red silk underskirt, sealskin coat, and Persian silk dress.

Jan has been researching these elusive women for the last fifteen years, prowling among the manuscript censuses, Sanborn maps, property records, marriage records, and probate court records. She spent days in the basements of dusty country courthouses with spiders crawling in her hair. Such persistence allows Jan to offer rich detail on shady ladies who rarely used their real names or even stuck with the same professional name for long. She tracks many of them to their graves, through their declining years filled with abuse, disease, narcotics, and violence. Once a "girl" became old or pregnant or just plain tired, her career was often over. Yet some of these resourceful women, as Jan points out, defied the odds and became successful and happy.

Jan's research uncovers touching tales like that of a baby raised in a brothel to become a boy who always played in his yard alone. When a compassionate neighbor asked him over to play with her children, he replied, "No, my mother is a whore and says I am to stay home." Prostitutes relished chances to be with children, Jan finds. Children, for one thing, did not ostracize them. These women, often lonely and abused and depressed, also took comfort in pet dogs and cats who also were non-judgmental and always affectionate.

Upscale cathouses such as Cripple Creek's Old Homestead and Denver's House of Mirrors commemorate the high end of the skin trade. There, visitors paid handsomely for a fine dinner, wines, cigars, and music before heading upstairs. "We'd take our evening gowns right off as soon as we could," recalled one high-class parlor worker. "We didn't want them to get messed up or torn or anything, for sometimes a man . . . would try to start taking off our gowns himself, and we'd have to beat him to it."

Pricey prostitution parlors that have been preserved are far different from the miserable little one- or two-room cribs where many women conducted business. Such cribs are much harder to find, although Telluride's Popcorn Alley is one surviving example, now recycled as low-income housing.

Whoredom has attracted more folklore than fact. Even the most prized Colorado artifacts—such as the brass brothel tokens manufactured by the late Fred Mazzulla—are fraudulent. They are not even replicas, just figments of Fred's imagination. One giveaway to this hoax is the "Good for One Screw" type verbiage stamped on these brass checks. Nineteenth- and twentieth-century prostitutes used better language than many twenty-first-century schoolgirls. Ladies of the lamplight preferred euphemisms to four-letter words. Laura Evens, the long-lived, much-interviewed Salida madame, was typical in insisting that her girls never talk loudly or lewdly.

Loose women have generated a loose history. Many a wannabe historian and tour guide, if short of local color and confronted by an antique hotel, saloon, or even a house turned to commercial uses, will brand it an old whorehouse, a carelessly used term that tends to stick. Proving that commercial sex happened in a century-old building, of course, is a hard charge to disprove—or prove.

Most communities officially outlawed prostitution to appease the moral element yet tolerated red-light districts confined to a less desirable part of town. Brides of the multitude were good for business and for municipal revenues. Whenever a town became cash strapped—which happened as often then as now—officials could raid the red-light district and fine the madams. To increase revenues, simply raise the fines or increase the number of raids.

A few towns strove to be hooker free. Colorado Springs, even then, was a self-righteous, godly place that banned the world's oldest profession. Nearby Colorado City, however, welcomed the laughing ladies of easy virtue and provided the booze and brothels that Colorado Springs outlawed. So Colorado Springians could ban their vice and enjoy it too.

In this fresh look at many heretofore obscure fallen angels, Jan MacKell concludes that many of these women wanted to be unknown. They did not want to embarrass their families. Whatever else Colorado's lost ladies lost, they did not lose their humility.

Preface

※

The intention of this book is not to romanticize, poke fun at, or degrade the long-departed prostitutes of Colorado. It is not meant to point fingers, accuse, or reveal embarrassing information. Rather, I have chosen to recognize one of society's most unappreciated and misunderstood classes: women who, generally through no fault of their own, sold their own bodies and risked their lives simply in order to survive. I have tried to right the wrongs and, if possible, vindicate the thousands whose lives have been forgotten, written off, laughed at, and so poorly represented.

This has been a fifteen-year-long project, a fascination and very nearly an obsession with knowledge about Colorado's red-light ladies. In these pages, I have attempted to look closely into their lives and minds. It's been an intriguing journey of never-ending questions. What did they think? What were their favorite pastimes? What circumstances enticed them into their careers? Did they enjoy what they did? What were their aspirations?

How strong these women must have been. They were in the most despised profession possible. They battled for their place in society and struggled with guilt over what they were doing on a daily basis. They risked relationships with their parents, siblings, and children, often paying the very high price of being shunned by their families and friends. The chance for a relationship with anyone outside of their profession was minimal, and the odds of ever compensating for their mistakes were slim indeed.

My research has revealed a startling variety of women from all walks of life engaged in prostitution. They were not limited to any one way of life, upbringing, or inclination. Their dispositions vary greatly, from true nymphomaniacs to fine upstanding girls, from drug-addicted urchins to proper, teetotaling businesswomen. They all had dreams, hopes, and desires. And they were brave enough to gamble on prostitution in order to achieve their goals.

The reader should note that there is no insult intended in the use of ethnic slang words in this book. In the time of which I write, African Americans were commonly referred to, even by themselves, as blacks, darkies, coloreds, Negroes, and niggers. In the days before political correctness, such terms were in common use, with few taking offense to them. The use of such proper nouns as Nigger Mollie, Hannah the Jap, or French Marie appear as they were recorded.

It is not my intention to offend descendants, friends, or anyone else associated with anyone mentioned in this book. There are many people out there who are proud of their heritage, no matter how shameful it may have been during their ancestor's life. When madam Anna Ryan's granddaughter saw "Annie," her mother, and her sister on the screen while

Fig. 1. An unidentified prostitute, dressed in typical lingerie of the nineteenth century.

(From the author's collection.)

watching a documentary about prostitution, she was both amazed and amused—even after learning that Anna once spent jail time for killing former police officer Maurice Lyons. "What [Annie] did has nothing to do with the person I am today," the woman said. On the opposite end of the spectrum, Ida Grey's grandson was disheartened to learn she may have worked as a prostitute at Cripple Creek's Old Homestead in 1896 and refused to believe it, explaining that the grandmother he knew was a "fine, religious woman." In fact, many women were just that once they were able to marry and get out of the profession.

Admittedly, identifying possible prostitutes has included a minimal amount of guesswork, and there may be some women who are mistakenly included. I sincerely apologize to anyone offended. But the past is just that, and no amount of denial will ever change it. People are often shocked and disappointed to discover that Grandma was a prostitute, and understandably so. But Grandma had a name and a life, and it is more cruel to deny her memory than it is to recognize her as an integral and colorful character in Colorado's fascinating history.

Acknowledgments

⁂

So many people and organizations assisted me in this long journey. The writing of this book would not have been possible without their assistance. Penrose Public Library of Colorado Springs with its city directories, newspaper files, and census records has been absolutely invaluable. The same goes for the Tutt Library at Colorado College, McClelland Library in Pueblo, the Canon City Library, the Woodland Park Library, Franklin Ferguson Library in Cripple Creek, the Cripple Creek District Museum, the Salida Regional Library, the Denver Public Library, the Stephen Hart Library at the Colorado Historical Society, and every courthouse and city hall in these cities.

Many people have been of immense help and inspiration during the writing of this book. They include, but are certainly not limited to, Eleanor Smith, my mother, mentor, and best friend; Erik Swanson, director of the Cripple Creek District Museum; Harold and Lodi Hern and Charlotte Bumgarner of the Old Homestead Parlor House Museum; Chris Clausen of BPOE #316 in Cripple Creek; Mary Davis and her wonderful staff at Penrose Public Library in Colorado Springs; Lee Michels, who loves Laura Bell as much as I do; Leland Feitz and Paul Idleman of the Old Colorado City Historical Society; Richard Marold of the Cheyenne Mountain Heritage Center; Tom Noel for providing so much insight and for getting me into this fun and wonderful mess; Thayer Tutt of the El Pomar Foundation; Donna Nevins of Salida; Kim Tulley; Missie Thomas Trenary; Cliff Dvorak; Sally Johnson; Mary Sanders, Ohrt Yeager; and everyone else who ever put up with me spinning stories about "my girls."

In retrospect, I would also like to thank some people who inspired me in my writing. They include Jimmy, Victor, Dawn, and Tricia; my dad, Wally Smith; Irene Smith; my paramour and best friend, Buck Gibbons; Bob and Julia Trout, who love their former red-light neighborhood and home with all their hearts; and all of my friends who have joined me in my fascination with the red-light ladies.

Chapter One

Red-Light Districts

✿

Special thanks to St. Margaret of Cortona,
the patroness saint of fallen women.

The term *red-light* has long been used to describe districts of prostitution. In America, its origins date from the days when railroad men left their red signal lanterns outside the brothels while paying a visit to a lady of the evening—so they could be found in an emergency. The sign of a red lantern on the porch became known as a way to identify brothels, which often appeared as legitimate homes or businesses on the outside. And, true to its romantic shade, the color red was used by many a prostitute in her decorating schemes. Many red-light districts got their start alongside railroad tracks, where numerous saloons already abounded. There, railroad employees and visitors alike could stop for a pleasure visit.

In the West, red-light districts became especially popular among lonely miners and other men who came to seek their fortunes sans their families. As early as 1870, ordinances were passed in the city of Denver prohibiting prostitution. Apparently, the new laws were of little avail. The *Rocky Mountain News* of July 23, 1889 commented that saloons were "the most fruitful source for breeding and feeding prostitution." In 1891 the Colorado General Assembly passed a law prohibiting women from entering saloons or being served liquor in Denver.[1] Nevertheless, most brothels did serve alcohol—also known as nose paint, tonsil varnish, and tongue oil—freely and at very high prices. Bottles of wine could sell at five hundred times their cost, thereby covering other losses. In Denver, brothels served beer in four-ounce glasses at $1 each. In comparison, one could purchase a schooner of beer in other parts of town for just a nickel.

1

Expensive or not, it was well known that almost anything could be obtained where the red lantern hung.

Many red-light districts served as their own private communities. Within their boundaries, prostitutes worked, ate, slept, confided in each other, fought with and stole from one another, and established rank among themselves. In these small and often forlorn-looking neighborhoods, women hoped, dreamed, and tried to see through the dimness of their futures. Their place of employment was also their home, where they were treated for illness, looked after the sick, and dressed the dead. Drug overdoses and alcohol poisoning, both intentional and accidental, were common. Most experienced girls and madams knew how to handle funeral arrangements. Even if the family of the dead could be found, relatives often refused to claim the body.

Within the prostitute's home, her immediate "family" consisted of her coworkers and her boss. Jealousy and competition, however, were just as likely to rear their ugly heads among women within the same house or district. More than a few soiled doves sought friendship and comfort in some of their customers. Often male companionship was the only hope a prostitute had for a lasting friendship of any kind. Sometimes women were fortunate enough to marry their consorts, but woe to the woman who became pregnant with no prospective husband. Her inconvenience put her out of work and cost the madam money. Abortion was always an alternative, but not a very pleasant one. Toxic poisons could be used to induce abortion but could easily prove fatal for the mother as well. Backroom abortions, performed by unskilled midwives, could also have disastrous results. Women who chose to give birth raised their babies in the brothels, pawned them off on relatives or friends, or sent them away to school—if they lived. One of Leadville's back alleys was so well known for the number of dead infants found there it was named "Stillborn Alley."[2] Daughters of prostitutes were sometimes trained by experienced professionals to follow their mothers into the business. One of the most notorious brothels in Denver during the year 1882 was kept by a madam, her daughter, and two nieces.

No matter its legalities, prostitution was in demand and flourished wherever men were willing to pay for it. The average "trick" cost anywhere from 50¢ to $10, depending on the girl or the house. In the more elite parlor houses of the city, a customer could expect to pay $100 or more for an all-night stay. The price also largely depended on the availability of women in any given camp or city. Women who managed to ply their trade with only a few competitors could often make enough to retire within just a few months.

Brothel tokens were introduced as an easy form of payment in many bordellos and parlor houses. Also called love tokens or brass checks and thought to be of Greek origin, such coins usually came in the shape of today's fifty-cent piece or dollar gambling token. Variations included oval coins, buttons, business cards, or even slips of paper. Not all brothels used checks, but many did. The checks kept the girls and the customers honest. The practice of using such tokens worked something like this: the customer purchased his token or tokens directly from the madam. Upon finding the woman he wanted, the customer in turn gave the token to her. At the end of the night, the girl returned the tokens she had received to the madam. This prevented the girls from making their own cash deals in the privacy of their rooms. It also prevented customers from taking advantage of the house. Tipping was usually allowed, however, permitting the girls to have a little pocket money. A popular claim among sources in Cripple Creek is that some girls could turn in as many as fifty tokens per night. Some of the smaller denominations, such as dollar tokens, could be used in slot machines as well. Such forms of payment remained in use as late as World War II.

Brothels did not usually lack either notoriety or popularity once they were established. For those new to town, however, and especially in larger cities, forms of advertising were limited. Soliciting in the newspapers would often have been out of the question even if prostitution were legal. Most papers pounced on the girls' misfortunes, exploited their actions, jeered at their attempts to improve their situations, and displayed only mild sympathy when they died. Therefore, brothels had to resort to unusual methods for attracting customers. Business cards with a brothel address, some with what was considered vulgar language for the day, could be passed discreetly to prospects or even slipped into their pockets without them knowing. Some of the less expensive forms of advertising included discount nights, hiring bands to parade the streets and solicit, or driving new girls in a buggy around town. "Virgin auctions" were also widely advertised to attract more business.[3]

In larger cities like Denver, a directory of dance halls, gambling dens, and brothels was easily obtainable if you knew whom to ask. Called Blue Books or Red Books, these handy directories were a skewed version of the social registries passed out among elite societies. In the early days, "Blue Book" was construed to mean "Blue Blood." Many a madam plagiarized the "Blue Book" title in hopes that wealthy men would consult the books looking for acceptable houses of business and find their brothels instead. In time, the Red Books were published as a tongue-in-cheek alternative. Ultimately, the illegitimate Blue Books and Red Books of any city's seamy underside directed travelers and newcomers to established pleasure resorts. They also helped those unfamiliar with the city to avoid trouble with seedier establishments.

Fig. 2. Denver's Red Book gave specific details about the city's brothels. Only well-off madams could afford such advertising.

(Courtesy Colorado Historical Society.)

The 1895 *Travelers' Night Guide of Colorado* was unique in that the booklet advertised brothels statewide, with scenic photographs of the state interspersed throughout. The sixty-six-page guide was conveniently made to fit in a vest pocket. Among the advertisers in this book were Pearl DeVere of Cripple Creek, Bell Bristol and Lucille Deming of Colorado City, Nellie Clark of Grand Junction, Clara Ogden of Lake City, Gussie Grant of Telluride, and Jennie Rogers and Georgie Burnham of Denver.[4] The ads contained within such directories were free to be bold by the standards of the day. Messages such as "Twenty young ladies engaged nightly to entertain guests" and "Strangers Cordially Welcomed" told wayward visitors of the best houses to go to for fun. Advertisements were rarely brazen or crude; prospective customers were told what they needed to know in polite verbiage. Occasionally working girls competed by taking ads out against each other, accusing certain other houses or girls of bad business practices or highlighting other uncomplimentary aspects.

Elite parlor houses often requested letters of recommendation from satisfied customers, which they displayed for new prospects. Occasionally engraved invitations were sent to prospective clients for grand openings or special parties. Sometimes the girls would wear their fanciest dresses on the streets as a form of advertising. Other times madams took their employees on excursions to nearby mining camps. Under the guise of a "vacation," the girls could drum up new or temporary business. In 1911 and 1912 the Cripple Creek prostitute register records a number of women, such as Maxine Murry, Mazie Paterson, Katie Price, Laura Scott, Dora Willison, and others, who appear to have been only visiting from Denver for a week or two before returning home. Quite possibly, these women were "on loan" from their Denver bordellos or even scoping out business opportunities in Cripple Creek.

Lower-class brothels advertised more freely. A common pitch was for the girls to sit, invitingly dressed, in second-story windows and call to prospects down below. In the cribs, usually located in the poorer section of the district, women were not beyond leaning out of their doorways inviting passersby to "C'mon in, baby." During the 1880s and 1890s in Denver, open soliciting was legal for many years. Horse races down main streets, water fights to show off their wares, and public pillow fights were even more brazen methods of advertising. When the come-ons grew crude, soliciting was outlawed and curtains were required on all red-light windows in many towns. Accordingly, "accidental" holes were ripped in the curtains, allowing passersby their own private peep show. A more drastic measure of advertising was "hat snatching." A girl would grab a man's hat from his head and escape into the brothel with it. The hapless male would then attempt to go inside and retrieve his hat without falling victim to the pleasures within. In Central City, the refined Wakely sisters, Flora and Louise, were known to grab passing miners and dance with or sing to them in order to lure them inside the theater where they performed.

The prostitute went by several other names. She was known as the soiled dove, lady of the evening, jewelled bird, fallen angel, shady lady, that other woman, lady of the lamplight, frail sister, *fille de joie, nymph du pave*, the fair Cyprian, the abandoned woman, scarlet woman, painted hussy, fancy girl, bawd, good-time Daisy, trollop, strumpet, harridan, woman of the town, wanton woman, moll, norrel woman, erring sister, and—least attractive—hooker, slut, and whore. And there were other terms: *carogue* was another word for harlot, specifically, "a woman who, in revenge for having been corrupted by men, corrupts them in return." During the early 1800s, *blowens* were prostitutes or women who cohabited with men without the sanctity of marriage.[5]

The average prostitute was about twenty-one years old, although some were as young as thirteen or as old as fifty. No matter her age, the prostitute's ultimate goal was to make money fast, marry well, and become socially acceptable. At the very least, she desired to become a courtesan or mistress to a very rich fellow who might marry her someday. Being a courtesan required being beautiful, intelligent, educated, and sophisticated. Achieving such wit and charm took training and practice. According to Lawrence Powell:

> Most also were required, in the upscale sporting houses, to learn to play a musical instrument, take singing and elocution lessons, comportment lessons, and imitate the high fashion mandates of society. They had to be able to pass for a governess or companion to a rich man's child or elderly parent. If they succeeded, they were sometimes housed in an unmarried man's home. In any case, they had to be presentable in order to travel with wealthy patrons and obtain the coveted role of mistress versus chatelaine. Madams ran "charm schools" which mimicked the schools for young wealthy daughters of society.[6]

A girl would be lucky indeed to land in such a prestigious position. Meanwhile, she worked hard and late, generally preferred drugs to fattening alcohol, and did what she could to make a life for herself. In her spare time she cleaned her wardrobe and linens, read, did needlework, or gardened. A good number of shady ladies also became quite adept at card games, since it helped pass the time between customers and made for better entertainment when playing against clients. Cats and dogs made suitable companions for prostitutes. A favorite pet was the French poodle, because the little dogs were easy to keep in small quarters. Often her pets were the only loyal friends a girl had.

Prostitutes in general hoped to find freedom and wealth quickly and perhaps even enjoyed their job at the start, with the impression that not much work was required. Younger girls earned less than their older, more experienced counterparts, but they learned quickly that if they stayed too long in one place they risked being labeled old-timers. Jennie Bernard, for example, was noted as paying fines for protitution in 1896. In 1912 Jennie surfaced in Cripple Creek looking for work. By then she was a good sixteen years into her profession and was likely moving more and more often as her looks and talents faded. To avoid moving constantly or falling into disuse, a working girl had to make her money and get out of her career as quickly as she could. Many did not, and only a small percentage got out of the profession and went straight before their career ruined them altogether.

Denver prostitute Belle Grant was one who got out. In her day, Belle was notorious and known to become violent when drunk. Her talents at knife fights and shoot-outs were no secret in town. During the winter of 1887, Belle telegraphed another prostitute named Lil, who was living in Aspen. The girls decided to move to Salt Lake City together. At Pueblo, however, Belle had the inexplicable urge to disembark and stay the night. When she went to bed later that evening, Belle later claimed, she received a visit from the ghost of her mother, who sat on the bed, placed her hand on Belle's head, and told her that if she continued on her wayward path the two would never meet in heaven. The next morning, Belle lost no time in sending Lil on to Salt Lake City while she herself returned to Denver, where she began hanging around the churches and taking in sewing. She eventually went to work for the Salvation Army.

Belle Grant's story is unusual in that she successfully saved herself from prostitution. If she had chosen to remain in her career, she probably would have aspired to become a madam. Many madams were prostitutes who were no longer attractive but had vast experience in the business. A few were employed as "parlor ladies" for dance hall owners. Madams oversaw, owned, or controlled most aspects of their business, from fancy parlor houses to dance halls and down the line to lower-class cribs. Their goal was to make money, and lots of it. Acting as sophisticated and discreetly as possible to avoid trouble with the law was essential. Some madams were so discreet that even their girls did not know the customers' names.

Despite their bad reputations, most madams stayed on the good side of the law by donating to local charities, schools, hospitals, and churches. Many took in the sick, the poor, and the orphaned. Most helped find employment for their jobless friends. They also contributed involuntarily by paying monthly fines or fees required by the court, and their building rent was higher than that of any legitimate business in town. In Salida, for instance, madams were fined as much as $100 monthly, and their girls paid $25 and up. Almost all city councils passed laws prohibiting prostitution, but timely payment of fines for breaking those laws usually assured a madam her business was safe.

Because of their many financial obligations, madams worked to maintain excellent credit. Good standing at the bank was important should any problems occur. Some madams kept a "ceremonial" husband for legal and financial reasons. Such men were usually longtime friends or lovers who could be trusted. Their job was to vouch for their "wife's" reputation, sign legal papers, serve as bouncers, and generally help the madam out of any unpleasant messes.

Men were rarely prosecuted for their participation in the prostitution industry, but there were exceptions. In 1874 a Mr. Baron of Pueblo answered charges of being drunk, visiting a Mexican house of ill fame, and assaulting the occupant—for which he paid a total of $10 in fines. And in 1886 local newspapers in Silverton reported on a local ball where, after escorting their respectable companions home, many of the men returned for a second dance hosted by ladies of the demimonde. "The indignation of the respectable ladies of our city," commented the paper, "is just."[7] The *Boulder County News* voiced similar sentiments in 1888 after reporting on several local boys from good families who were arrested for visiting a brothel. "If young men have no more self-respect or respect for their parents or friends than to seek such low resorts, the whole community shall be made acquainted with the fact so they may be treated accordingly."[8]

If a prostitute collided with the law by disturbing the peace, fighting, being on the street at the wrong time, swearing, or being intoxicated in public, her madam had to answer for her. If the madam was unavailable or unwilling to bail her out, the prostitute usually could not pay her own fine and had to work out her debt in jail: doing time, cleaning, or even trading sexual favors for her freedom.

The prostitute's wardrobe consisted of evening wear, afternoon "costumes," and lingerie. Additionally, the girls required plenty of powder, other cosmetics, and perfume. Since many prostitutes could get no credit, they were forced to purchase their personal items through the madam and were therefore always in debt to her. Most girls paid their own room and board, purchased their personal beverages, and disbursed about half their fee to the madam.

Prostitutes were also expected to obey house rules, which their madams oversaw with a firm hand. A few madams could be cruel or violent, making sure their girls were too indebted to them or too scared to leave or failing to care for them when they fell sick. When a Tin Cup prostitute calling herself "Oh Be Joyful" expressed her desire to marry a local rancher, her madam, Deadwood Sal, refused to give up the girl's contract. In desperation, the rancher and his friends rescued Oh Be Joyful in the dead of night, and the two were married in a cabin on the hill above town before galloping off to live at the rancher's spread.

At the opposite end of the spectrum, it was not uncommon for madams to have to evict, sue, or even swear out complaints against their girls and others. Boulder madam Frenchy Nealis sued saloon keeper James Nevin to reclaim her furniture from an apartment above his bar in 1877. In 1882 Mollie May of Leadville charged Annie Layton with stealing a dress. In turn, Annie accused Mollie of running a house of ill fame, and Mollie retaliated by revealing that Annie was employed as a prostitute. Ultimately, all charges were dropped. In 1885 Silverton madam Mable Pierce filed a complaint against employee Bessie Smith for welshing on a loan and stealing back her own clothes, which she had used for collateral. Within a week, Mable sued Jessie Carter for the same offense. A few months later, Mable also sued Jessie Carroll for disturbing the peace. In 1897 a Creede madam known as Mrs. Joseph Barnett, alias Ardeen Hamilton, shot and killed employee Kate Cassidy. Hamilton admitted to the shooting, but claimed self-defense. And as late as June of 1905, Helen Ward suffered during raids by Colorado City authorities, when a former employee named Annie Rock (probably Annie Rook), testified against her after quarreling with the would-be madam. Ward spent six months in the El Paso County Jail for conducting a disorderly house, despite her compliant guilty plea. Rock was charged with mayhem, but the outcome of her case is unknown.

In spite of the occasional skirmish, a good madam served as a surrogate mother to her girls. Because of their lifestyles, most call girls were ill tempered, frequently depressed, given to drinking, or addicted to drugs. It was the madam's job to pacify her girls as much as she was able and protect them from the law, clergy, and rough customers. In Trinidad, a Madams' Association was formed to provide protection and care for the girls. This respected organization followed guidelines resembling a union and included a convalescent home for those who became ill. Trinidad, like Cripple Creek, required a health card issued by an approved physician in order for girls to work. This rule was also practiced in Colorado City, Silverton, and many other towns in Colorado. In Salida, Laura Evens was well known for caring for her girls, including getting them regular health exams and finding them other employment when they no longer made suitable prostitutes.

Naturally, those madams who best cared for their workers also had the fanciest brothels in town. Called parlor houses, these aristocratic businesses were more likely to appear in prime locations within larger cities. City directories usually listed them as boarding houses, but anyone familiar with the city knew what they really were. The average house employed anywhere from five to twenty working girls, plus servants, a musician, and a bouncer. The naughty ladies employed there were required to be talented, attractive, and classy. According to a prostitute named LaVerne who worked for madam Laura Evens (sometimes spelled Evans) in Salida, "Miss Laura never wanted us girls to talk loud, and we were always taught to watch our language. We parlor house girls never used four-letter words."9

The decor of most parlor houses was lavish and fine to suit its wealthy customers. The average parlor house contained several bedroom sets, furniture, and other accoutrements necessary to the business. In Silverton in 1899, Dottie Watson's house consisted of seventeen floor carpets, one stair carpet, nine bedroom sets with springs and mattresses, two sets of parlor furniture, four heating stoves, twenty-one window shades, and an eighteen-by-forty-inch mirror. Arriving guests were generally shown to the parlor, or perhaps a music room or a poker parlor, and invited to partake of a variety of entertainment with wine, gambling, music, dancing, and dining before the couples retired upstairs.

If a client did not have a special woman in mind, the madam could select one for him. An alternative to this practice is today illustrated at the Old Homestead, now a museum in Cripple Creek. There, girls disrobed and paraded one at a time through a closet with a glass door. The gentleman could then see each lady for himself and pick the one he liked.

Regular customers could establish credit, but patrons who did not have credit were required to pay up front. Established clients were catered to, since they were usually wealthy and powerful men in the community. Not all customers, however, were gentlemen. As LaVerne of Salida explained, "We'd take our evening gowns right off as soon as we could. We didn't want them to get messed up or torn or anything, for sometimes a man . . . would try to start taking off our gowns himself, and we'd have to beat him to it."10

Working women in the parlor houses were fed nourishing meals, dining on red meat and lots of milk to keep them healthy. After all, their jobs required strength and stamina. Each new customer meant bathing, fresh clothing, and a change of sheets (some girls would place a strip of canvas at the foot of their bed, so the customers' boots or shoes would not soil the linens). Occasionally girls were "rented out" to stag parties or other events requiring strenuous travel. A first-class parlor house never opened on Sunday, thus giving the ladies a chance to rest and catch up on their personal chores. The parlor house lady was generally well to do, as long as she retained good employment. In Cripple Creek, purchasing mining claims or stocks was as fashionable as buying a new dress.

So close were parlor ladies to the upper echelon that often they made fewer attempts to mask their identities than their lower counterparts. Some brothels in Denver, such as Anna "Gouldie" Gould's house, actually kept photos of their girls on file. Most prostitutes preferred not to be photographed and identified as working girls, but in Gouldie's case the practice served several purposes. Upon receiving a discreet phone call or message from uptown hotels, Gouldie could dispatch runners with the pictures and

Fig. 3. By yesterday's standards, pornography such as this was considered lewd and often illegal. Judging from the makeup of this unidentified girl, the photograph probably dates from between 1910 and 1930.

(From the author's collection.)

allow the prospective customer to select the girl of his choice. Photographs were also handy for advertising purposes, and they served as proper identification in case of trouble with the law or death.

Pornography was a whole other matter. Photographs of a sexual nature were a valid means of advertising for both the girl and the photographer. Exhibitionists certainly flourished in the 1800s and beyond, and much pornography of the day reveals a variety of poses from artistic to vulgar. Back then a photograph of a woman in the nude, no matter how artistic, could be considered pornographic in nature. A good many parlor house girls jumped at the chance to have themselves photographed wearing no more than a scarf or lacy lingerie. In cruder photographs the subjects appear to have been poorer girls who could be persuaded to pose for a few dollars or drinks. In more than a few instances, some prostitute pornography includes women who appear to be drugged, humiliated, or downright frightened, and the sexual acts they portray are vulgar even by today's standards. So it was for women who could not control the camera, simply because they did not rate parlor house status.

Unfortunately, many women lacked the talent and good looks required for employment in a parlor house. Others were habitual troublemakers or too old to work in a parlor house. Any girl who failed to live up to her madam's expectations was unceremoniously shown the door. A few were unfortunate girls who had been recruited in Europe or China with promises of wealth and success in America. Upon arriving in the United States, they became indentured servants to a brothel owner. In the case of Chinese women, many were sold as slaves before they even left China. Even more girls were solicited in eastern cities to come out West, with the guarantee of high wages and a good life. Pimps, saloon owners, and dance hall managers could often be found waiting at the train or stage station for girls who had answered their advertisements in eastern newspapers. More often than not, the newcomers found themselves in a strange town with no money, at the mercy of those who had promised them such a good life.

Girls who were recruited elsewhere or could not make the grade in a parlor house worked in common brothels. These houses of prostitution were not as nice, not as reputable, and often not as clean as parlor houses. A brothel, or whorehouse, was housed in anything from a canvas tent to a rented apartment above a gambling hall. Brothels housed in their own buildings usually had saloons. Their employees ranged in age from sixteen to thirty-five and came from a variety of backgrounds. Brothel women earned less (approximately $10 per customer) but served more customers than their higher-up counterparts. They were also more vulnerable to drug and alcohol abuse, violence, and disease. Common brothels experienced high turnovers among the girls, who moved on, were fired, or were forced to find new employment when the brothel closed down.

Dance hall girls, also known as "hurdy-gurdy girls," worked in saloons and entertained customers with song, dance, and skits. Some also doubled as prostitutes in rooms above the saloons. In Cripple Creek, most dance halls had a small bar in front, beyond which was a railing with a gate. The girls would await their partners beyond the railing, while a "caller" enticed men to pick a girl and dance. The caller acted almost as a pimp, commanding the girls to attract more customers if business was

Fig. 4. Although dance hall girls did not always work as prostitutes, they were often persecuted as such. Many dance hall girls were portrayed as just another pretty face, as illustrated on this 1905 postcard.

(From the author's collection.)

slow. The customer paid the bartender a quarter or so, which included the price of the dance and a beer. Dance hall girls received about a dime of the customer's quarter for their share, but they earned most of their money in tips. After the dance, the men and their partners would proceed to another bar, located in back of the hall. Hard-sell customers could be invited to the "wine room" to imbibe further before being seduced. The girls' actions were rigidly controlled. They were not permitted to linger at the front bar but could usually talk a customer or two into going to a rented room upstairs. Many saloons had one-room cribs behind or on the side of them.

Most dance halls of this sort were within the legal limits of the law. As the *Ouray Times* commented in 1881, "If a dance hall is well managed, and kept in a proper place, and the prostitutes are not allowed to parade the streets and back alleys, we see no reasonable grounds for complaint, but when they get to scattering here and there . . . and use vulgar and obscene language . . . it is high time that there should be some action taken to stop such nuisances. Fire them out."[11] If a dance hall remained on the right side of the law, however, it could be a fairly profitable business.

It is important to note that not all dance hall girls were prostitutes. Some were employed strictly as hostesses, entertainers, singers, and dancers. Many dance hall girls were merely aspiring actresses or performers with no desire for the lives they led. Socializing with actresses, however, was frowned upon in decent society, making it difficult for such women to procure any real gainful employment.

More than a few famous performers began their careers this way. Among them was Ida Mulle, one of a number of actresses portrayed in provocative poses in photographs issued by Newsboy Tobacco Co. in the late nineteenth century. The casual observer of Ida's photo may believe she was less than a talented actress. But apparently Ida was fairly successful, starring in the Boston Theater's production of *Cinderella* and meriting mention in several publications about American theater and screen actresses.

Others were not so lucky; they were mostly young, unmarried immigrants or the wives or widows of poor miners. No matter their background, however, many dance hall women were eventually swallowed up by the seamy world they lived in, ever fearful that their work as prostitutes might lower their status to that of the crib girl.

Crib girls lived in smaller houses or shacks, sometimes designed as tiny row houses. Like dance halls, cribs were more prominent in small towns and

IDA MULLE.

Fig. 5. Ida Mulle's provocative publicity photograph did much
to enhance her career. Note the kitten in Ida's lap;
many actresses, dance hall girls, and prostitutes had pets.

(From the author's collection.)

military or mining camps when the West was still quite young. Eventually every city had its share of undesirable cribs. Their occupants were an unfortunate lot. Usually they were prostitutes who had outgrown their usefulness in the larger brothels due to health or age. Often their initial goal was to be self-employed and assured of privacy, but these dreams rarely came true. Instead, the average crib girl paid high rent to a madam or landlord. Her profits usually went to a pimp, lover, or some other undesirable overlord in her life. Domestic violence broke out often among couples who worked as a pimp and prostitute. The law often turned their backs on those who beat prostitutes, while the public felt that the "whores" got what they deserved. Too often the death of a working girl served as a grim reminder to others of what brutal and unsafe lives they led.

Streetwalkers were an even poorer class of prostitute. Their accommodations usually consisted of run-down hotel rooms or apartments. Streetwalkers were more likely to be unhealthy and unclean, and they earned much less than their fellow prostitutes. Their one advantage was more freedom, since their lack of any permanent address made them harder for the law to track down. But their plight was twice as bad as those in the upper classes. The streetwalker's chances of survival were slim. Usually she was destined to sink lower still, to the status of a "signboard gal." These were girls who were washed up, untalented, ugly, or sick. Often they lacked a place to call home, sleeping in back streets, alleys, and gutters. Business with signboard gals was conducted wherever a quick few minutes of privacy could be found, sometimes behind a large street sign or billboard—hence the name. In Trinidad, one signboard gal conducted business behind a billboard at Santa Fe and Main Street. Another worked on top of a former butcher's block behind a building. Signboard gals charged much less, often no more than a trade for drinks, drugs, or food. Their lives were miserable, with no hope for enhancing their future.

While any prostitute could fall into one or more of the categories listed here, the careers of most tended to be consistent with their backgrounds. Some came from poor or abusive homes, and some came from middle- and even upper-class families. Those who grew up in poverty were slovenly and unskilled, while women who were raised properly and with educations usually succeeded at making much money in their profession. In Colorado City, for example, Laura Bell McDaniel was from a working-class family who lived and worked in the same town as she. Educated and allegedly beautiful, Laura Bell succeeded in running several prosperous brothels in Salida, Colorado City, and Cripple Creek.

Blanche Burton also operated in Colorado City and was the first madam in Cripple Creek. Uneducated, Blanche was duped in at least one mining scheme in Cripple Creek but ran a successful business. In 1894 Blanche moved back to Colorado City, where over time she became a recluse. While Laura Bell McDaniel and Blanche Burton were diverse in background and lifestyle, they shared at least two common bonds: both women were in a profession disapproved of by society, and both probably wished they were doing something else.

Chapter Two

Life as a Harlot

The Passing of Faro Dan

Cactus Nell in the gaudy gown
Of a dance hall vamp in a border town
Had tried her wiles on a man who seemed
To read her smiles as he stood and dreamed
And he paid no heed to the tell-tale leer
Of the brothel queen as she lingered near
But turned and looked to another place,
Removed from the glare of her painted face.

The she-thing paled with a tang of hate
At the slight implied by the measured gait
Each step seemed telling as words might say
He despised her breed and the tinseled way
And she raged within as the dance hall clan
Observed the move of the silent man
And she made a vow that the man should pay
For the public slight—in the brothel way.

A whispered word and hurried plan
Was told in the ear of Faro Dan
Then Nell wandered out on the dance hall floor,
Then stopped a bit as an idler would
Quite close to the place where the stranger stood
And Nell, with the hate of her creed and race
Stepped close and spat in the stranger's face.

The silence fell and the place was still
Like a stage that was set where the actors kill
And the stranger stood and calmly viewed
The taunting face of the woman lewd
Then his eyes were turned till they rested on
Her consort near, with his pistol drawn
Then he slowly grinned and turned his head
To the brothel queen, where he calmly said,

"I reckon girl there's been a day
When a mother loved in a mother's way
And prayed, I guess, as her baby grew,
She never would be a thing like you
And so for her and the child she bore
I've pity gal, and I've nothing more."
Then turning again to Faro Dan,
"I'm calling you hombre, man to man."

The call was quick as a lightening flash
And the shots rang out in a single crash
And the stranger stood with a smoking gun
And viewed the work that his skill had won
Then walking slow to the dance hall door
He turned to the awe-struck crowd once more.
"I just dropped in from Alkali,
And now, I reckon, I'll say goodbye."
—Myrtle Whifford, 1926

Prostitutes came from all walks of life. Some escaped poor or negligent homes as young girls. Others were widows with children to feed or were unskilled in labor with no other hope for making a living. More than a few were lured into prostitution as a viable way to dance, drink, kick up their heels, and have a good time. Still others came from fine upstanding families from the East and were educated or talented musicians and singers.[1] Some, such as Mattie Silks of Denver, were simply looking to make some good money. "I went into the sporting life for business reasons and for no other," Mattie once said. "It was a way for a woman in those days to make money and I made it. I considered myself then and do now—as a business woman."[2] Mattie always claimed that she was never more than a madam and never worked as a prostitute.

In fact, more women approached their profession on a strictly business basis than is widely thought. One former customer recalled how most girls would remove only the essential clothing to transact their business and hurried their customers along. "When it came to the actual act, though, the routine was standard. . . . Then she'd wash you off again, and herself. Then she'd get dressed, without even looking at you. You could see she was already thinking about nothing but getting downstairs."[3] Brothels were in the business to make money, and their employees had to keep customers on the move.

Even more women turned to prostitution as an alternative to dull or abusive marriages. It was no easy matter, being married in the Victorian era. Given the harshness of the times—no electricity, backbreaking chores, a plethora of vices such as gambling, drinking, and drugs, and procreational rather than recreational sex, it is no wonder many marriages ended in divorce. The misery doubled with the death of a child, or if either spouse was given to beating the other. So, when Ed Harless's wife turned up missing in Victor, it was no real surprise to anyone except maybe Ed.

Fig. 6. Victor in 1900 sported a number of saloons, gaming houses, dance halls, and brothels scattered throughout the city.

(Courtesy Cripple Creek District Museum.)

The Harlesses first appeared in Victor in 1902. Ed was a miner at the Portland Mine, residing with his bride at 321 South 4th Street. But he apparently balanced his time between Victor and Denver, where he had another home. It was probably during one of his absences that Mrs. Harless unexpectedly packed her bags and caught the next train out of town. Ed went looking for her, much as any husband might do. He found her in Silverton, and the November 29 *Silverton Standard* reported what happened next. Harless had arrived from Victor the day before. According to the newspaper, he had been consulting a spirit medium in Denver regarding his wife's whereabouts. The clairvoyant informed Harless that he had to look no further than Silverton to find her.

Harless beat a path to Marshal Leonard's door in Silverton. After a short investigation, the good marshal led Harless to a bordello on Silverton's notorious Blair Street. As was the case with so many before her, the price of Mrs. Harless's freedom was to land in a strange town with no support. Prostitution was a viable way to get some cash, and the girls on the row had beckoned her in. The two men entered the room occupied by Mrs. Harless. As the marshal stepped to the window to let in some light, the woman let out a scream. The marshal turned in time to see the husband "drawing an ugly looking revolver." Leonard wrestled the gun away from the angry man and promptly deposited him in the city pokey. Harless was fined $50 and costs.

Women who left dull marriages for a more exciting life in the prostitution industry often failed to find the freedom they sought. The *Boulder County Herald* in 1881 reported on a young man from Kansas who found a female acquaintance from back home working in Boulder. The two were married, thus saving the girl from the clutches of prostitution. In 1884 the newspaper *Kansas City Cowboy* wrote about a woman who changed her mind after turning to prostitution: "A well dressed gentleman stepped into the dance hall and to his surprise found his long lost sweetheart, whom he had given up for dead. After wiping the tears away, the lover commenced asking how come she was living in such a place. The lovely unfortunate with dazzling eyes gazed up at him and said, 'Charlie, I don't know. It has always been a mystery.' The couple left on the late train for Pueblo where they will be joined in the happy bonds of holy wedlock."[4]

Occasionally too, young girls joined the industry for no other reason than because they were wild. In 1899 the *Silverton Standard* reported on a boardinghouse waitress who stepped out for a break and wound up "drunker than a fiddler" at a local dance hall. "The event was but a

Fig. 7. The wild lifestyle of the average prostitute shocked and shamed her family, causing wounds that would never heal. A photo as revealing as this postcard from the 1920s would have given any mother heart palpitations.

(From the author's collection.)

repetition of the girl's old tricks," reported the paper. "She is young, her parents reside here and if they have no control over her she should be sent to the home for incorrigibles."[5]

No matter where they came from, most working girls counted on being banished and shunned by their families, who were naturally shocked and ashamed at their actions. If at all possible, the average prostitute launched her career far away from her hometown and lied about her job position in her letters back home. Stories of prostitutes whose families discovered their true occupations were so numerous that they inspired songs such as this:

Aunt Clara

Chorus
Oh, we never mention Aunt Clara,
Her picture is turned to the wall,
Though she lives on the French Riviera
Mother says she is dead to us all!

At church on the organ she'd practice and play
The preacher would pump up and down
His wife caught him playing with Auntie one day
And that's why Aunt Clara left town

Chorus

With presents he tempted and lured her to sin
Her innocent virtue to smirch
But her honor was strong and she only gave in
When he gave her the deed to the church

Chorus

They said that no one cared if she never came back
When she left us, her fortune to seek
But the boys at the firehouse draped it all in black
And the ball team wore mourning all week

Chorus

They told her that no man would make her his bride
They prophesied children of shame,
Yet she married four counts and a baron besides,
And hasn't a child to her name!

Chorus

They told her the wages of sinners was Death
But she said if she had to be dead
She's just as soon die with champaign on her breath
And some pink satin sheets on her bed

Chorus

They say that the Hell-fires will punish her sin,
She'll burn for her carryings-on
But at least for the present, she's toasting her skin
In the sunshine of Deauville and Cannes

Chorus

They say that she's sunken, they say that she fell
From the narrow and virtuous path
But her French formal gardens are sunken as well
And so is her pink marble bath

Chorus

My mother does all of her housework alone
She washes and scrubs for her board.
We've reached the conclusion that virtue's its own
And the only reward!

Oh, we never speak of Aunt Clara
But we think when we grow up tall
We'll go to the French Riviera
And let Mother turn us to the wall!

It's more exciting . . . Mother turn us to the wall! [6]

In most cases, the girls' backgrounds echoed their lifestyles in the industry. In about 1905, a sad-eyed mulatto woman named Dorothy "Tar Baby" Brown arrived in Silverton. Born in Chicago, Tar Baby had been raised in an orphanage. Despite being one of the toughest girls on the line at Blair Street, Dorothy eventually married Frank Brown, who was on the police force. An acquaintance recalled that the Brown household was filthy. Dorothy would roll her own cigarettes and flick the used butts onto the ceilings and walls. The Browns had one son, who died in an accident in 1954. Tar Baby died in 1971 at Durango.

In order to truly disguise their identity, many soiled doves sported one or more pseudonyms. Fake names and nicknames were common. They were used to elude the law, make a fresh start, or avoid undesirable people in a girl's life. In some cases, prostitutes planning to move on were actually able to bribe the local newspapermen, upon their departure, to print an "obituary." The demise of a girl's pseudonym would prevent any questions about her whereabouts, securing her safety from the law and others and allowing her to move on with an all-new identity.

Finding these women's real identities is a task that will never be complete. Cripple Creek's prostitute register for 1912 lists a Jessie Ford, along with her physical description and the listing of her birthplace as Des Moines, Iowa. She had recently come from Denver. Because her name is noted as an alias, however, Jessie's story may never be known. Another was Bertha Lewis, whose real name is not listed. Bertha arrived in Cripple Creek in January of 1912 from Denver. The only other known facts about Bertha are that she was born in Kansas, she was black, and she left town on March 10.

Because the majority of prostitutes used pseudonyms, tracking them from town to town was difficult for the law and others. An interesting coincidence that illustrates this fact is the number of women with the uncommon surname of "St. Clair" who appeared in Cripple Creek and later Colorado City. The 1896 Cripple Creek city directory lists one Eve St. Claire rooming at 335½ Myers Avenue. There was also an Ida St. Claire who roomed at 133 West Myers in 1896, working as a laundress. The 1900 directory lists Miss Irene St. Clair at 420 East Myers. Then in 1904–5, Jeanette St. Clair is listed in the Colorado City directory at 615 Washington. In 1907 yet another St. Claire, this one known as Miss Celia, resided at 341 Myers Avenue in Cripple Creek. The directories mentioned above rarely list any other St. Clairs, prostitutes or otherwise. Miss Millie Lavely is another puzzle. In 1900 she lived at 420 Myers Avenue. Five years later Millie was living at 315 Myers. The 1907 city directory shows no Millie Lavely, but does show a Miss Millie Laverty residing at the Old Homestead Parlor House. Whether any of these women actually shared a connection will likely never be known.

It was not always easy to conceal one's identity. The authorities certainly knew every alias of Bessie Blondell, a.k.a. Bessie McSean, a.k.a. Dorothy McCleave. In June of 1912 Bessie arrived in Cripple Creek and began sporting at 373 Myers Avenue. A native of Ohio, Bessie had last worked in Denver. On August 16, the city clerk recorded that Bessie had departed for Denver once more on the 7 A.M. train, adding the note, "From there she goes to El Paso, TX."[7] Blondell was Bessie's married name, and her husband had been convicted in El Paso, Texas, for smuggling. He was sentenced to two and one-half years at Levenworth Prison. Bessie was also under indictment for smuggling. Her ultimate fate is unknown. She may have wound up in New York, where a woman of her name died in 1981. And there were other women, such as Cripple Creek prostitute Sophia Green of Mackey, Idaho, who sometimes used the last name of her husband, Brockey Jones.

Choosing a pseudonym must have been a fascinating game for working girls, whose new names could mean taking on a whole new persona. Coming up with a fake identity had its challenges, and many girls obviously had fun with it. Witness such tongue-in-cheek names in Cripple Creek as Jack Williams, Dickey Dalmore, Jonny Jones, Teddie Miles, and Grace Miller, a.k.a. Grace Maycharm. Other names were symbolic or taken from local landmarks, ethnic origins, or even status symbols of the day. Vola Keeling, alias Vola Gillette, likely fabricated her new name in Cripple Creek from the nearby town of Gillett. Not at all surprisingly, Louise Paris was a French prostitute working in the French block of Myers Avenue in Cripple Creek. The name frequently denoted where the girl was from, as in the case of Colorado girls China Mary, French Erma, Dutch Mary, Irish Mag, Austrian Annie, Kansas City, and Denver Darling.

Other times a girl's nickname played on her talents. Names like the Virgin, Few Clothes Molly, Featherlegs, Smooth Bore, and Sweet Fanny let prospective clients know what they could expect from these women. Sometimes the girls chose their own pseudonyms; other times they were dubbed by their clients or other girls on the row. Many of those names, however, were not complimentary. Such women as Two Ton Tilly, Ton of Coal, Noseless Lou, and Dancing Heifer probably had little to do with fabricating their nicknames.

Other less romantic names included Dirty Neck Nell, Dizzy Daisy, Tall Rose, Greasy Gert, Rotary Rose, PeeWee, T-Bone, Rowdy Kate, Mormon Queen, Lacy Liz, and Nervous Jessie. Salida prostitute Lizzie Landon was also known as White Dog Liz. One of the most insulting names was imposed on Lottie Amick, a.k.a. the Victor Pig. Lottie had been living in Colorado since at least 1898, when she married one Oliver C. Chase in Colorado Springs. By June of 1911 Lottie was living at 342 Myers in Cripple Creek. On January 7 of 1912 she moved to Victor, where she probably picked up her degrading pseudonym. She returned to Cripple Creek in June and in May of 1913 departed for Colorado Springs.

And then there are a few names whose origins will never be solved, such as a pair of girls in Pueblo who called themselves the Hamburger Twins.

There is little doubt that many girls had fun making up new names and using them to fool authorities, sometimes right under the law's nose. The Cripple Creek register of prostitutes for 1911 reports on two different women named Alice Clark. Both arrived on September 22 from Denver and both took up residence at 435 Myers. One was black and one was white. One was a year older than the other, and both had about the same build. The striking similarities noted for two completely different women lead one to speculate whether one or two officials took the descriptions— and which one of the girls was really Alice Clark.

It was also a common practice for prostitutes to use several different pseudonyms during their careers. Sometimes the name was duplicated, as in the case of two Pueblo women who were both named Dutch Kate. The first was found dead in 1876 with bruises on her body and her jewelry missing. The second Dutch Kate made the papers in 1882 for chasing a man up and down Union Avenue with a knife, "threatening to have his heart's blood." She eventually was incarcerated without further incident.[8]

Whatever her name, every prostitute strived to look and be at her best at all times, despite her hectic, hazy, and downright dangerous lifestyle. Dress was very important to prostitutes, whose vanity knew no limits and whose job was to look, smell, and feel good. Of her coworkers in Cripple Creek, dance hall girl Lizzie Beaudrie recalled: "Some of the other girls had short lawn dresses with a drop yoke and little ruffles on the bottom of the skirt. Not a girl wore a tight fitting dress or very much jewelry, and the girls all looked clean."[9]

Farther up the fashion ladder, Laura Evens recalled paying between $100 and $150 for her gowns in Leadville at Madame Frank's Emporium during the year 1895. "We wore heavy black stockings embroidered with pink roses," she remembered. "No short skirts and hustling in doorways like the crib girls."[10] Indeed, harlots in smaller, wilder camps such as the town of Gothic dared to wear dresses clear up to their knees. But the fancier girls would take any measure necessary to procure their fancy gowns. Once Ethel Carlton, wife of freighting and bank millionaire Bert Carlton of Cripple Creek, gave some of her old gowns to a servant to distribute among the poor girls in town. Later, as she gazed upon a wagon full of soiled doves going by, Mrs. Carlton recognized her cast-off dresses. Her servant, apparently, had taken the gowns right down to the row and sold them for a profit. Mrs. Carlton was said to be quite amused by the incident.

Fashion was at least as important among the red-light ladies as it was to those in decent society. Every inch of detail was carefully paid the utmost attention, as illustrated in Lizzie Beaudrie's detailed description of a woman she noticed standing at the bar for a drink one night at the Red Light Dance Hall: "She wore a velvet suit, a short, pleated skirt up to her knees, a white silk blouse with a sailor collar trimmed with narrow lace, long sleeves with turned back cuffs and a little Eton jacket to match her skirt. The skirt and jacket were trimmed with gold braid. The suit was black. She wore black stockings and spring heel patent leather slippers. Her hair was cut short and curled all over her head."[11]

If the women of the red-light district paid attention to such details, so did the general public—especially the media. In April of 1872 the *Pueblo Chieftain* gave a somewhat humorous account of a scuffle between Esther Baldwin and her girls and Sam Mickey, a Denver gambler. Upon depositing Baldwin into "a scuttle of coal," Mickey "followed up his advantage and went for the rest in rotation, and in less time than we have been writing it, the floor was covered with false teeth, false curls, false palpitators [probably false breasts], patent calves, chignons and other articles of feminine gear too numerous to mention."[12] The *Leadville Chronicle* noted a similar scuffle when reporting a fight between inmates of the Red Light and the Bon Ton: "The fight was short and bloody. The air was thick with wigs, teeth, obscenity and bad breaths."[13] Even Central City wasn't safe, when "[a] span of girls on Big Swede Avenue tried to kill each other night before last. They only succeeded in burning some dry goods and conflagrating a lamp."[14]

Hair, teeth, and facial makeup were other important facets of everyday life. Many women, such as Cripple Creek prostitute Marion Murphy, bleached their hair. Records on these women indicate that bleaching was a trend brought with such eastern beauties as Bertha LeRay of Chicago.

In the days before dyes and manufactured hair products, bleaching was a very dangerous process during which one could suffer burns to the skin as well as the eyes. Harlots such as the mulattoes Mary Buchanan and Lillian Bryant, who worked in Cripple Creek in 1911 and 1912 respectively, bleached their hair with most interesting results. In Lillian's case, the Chicago lovely's black hair was bleached to a wild red color.

An unfortunate fact that is easily forgotten is that many girls also had poor teeth, not having the luxury of a toothbrush or lessons on how to use it. Thus, many girls had missing, gold-filled, or gold-capped teeth. Cripple Creek prostitute Marie Brady had four of her upper front teeth filled with gold. Her coworkers Ruth Allen and Lillian Bryant had both gold crowns and gold teeth.

Once they were dressed in their best finery, the girls were ready to go to work. Whether they worked in a parlor house or a dance hall, part of their job involved socializing with customers in some sort of party atmosphere. Much of the time, however, their actions were rigidly controlled. If they lingered with a customer too long or engaged in too much conversation and not enough sex, they were reprimanded. Outrageous behavior was not permitted except in the lower-class brothels and bars. The Alhambra Saloon in Silverton posted strict rules for its dance hall girls:

1. No lady will leave the house during evening working hours without permission.
2. No lady will accompany a gentleman to his lodgings.
3. No kicking at the orchestra, especially from the stage.
4. Every lady will be required to dance on the floor after the show.
5. No fighting or quarreling will be allowed.[15]

The social life of a prostitute was minimal outside of the workplace. Children were a sight near and dear to many prostitutes simply because it was rare to see them and easy to procure their trust. Colorado pioneer Anne Ellis recalled a day her young son visited a house of prostitution quite by accident in Bonanza: "[A]t one time in my married life, their house was just back of mine on the mountainside. . . . once my creeping baby disappears, and I finally spy him, his yellow curls shining in the sunlight, crawling step by step up this flight, and I watch him to see he doesn't fall backward, letting him go, much to the disgust of my neighbors, but I know these girls can't hurt him, and he may help them."[16]

Cripple Creek resident Art Tremayne recalled that when he was a child in the 1920s, a visit to his step-grandmother's home required passing a local brothel. As the boy and his mother walked along, young Art noticed some women in the second-story window of a house waving down at him. Art waved back. "I thought they were the nicest people," he remembered. Art's mother knew better. Grabbing her son's hand, Mrs. Tremayne whisked down the street and out of sight of the shameful women.[17]

Such innocence endeared children to prostitutes. They were not as biased or judgmental as adults, and they were willing to run errands for the girls. Prostitutes often sent messengers and newsboys to buy their drugs for them at the local pharmacy. In the interest of discretion, the girls would send the boy with a certain playing card and money to the drug store. The pharmacist, upon receiving the card, knew what the girls were ordering. The boys usually received a good tip for completing the mission.

The hurt at being ostracized by society must have been great to many a prostitute, especially those who willingly donated to local charities, churches, and schools. In the mode of the day, the good deeds of the red-light ladies were unreciprocated, and the girls rarely received credit for their benevolent acts. City authorities sought to make an example out of Colorado City madam Mamie Majors by arresting her for maintaining a house of ill fame in 1905. Two friends, druggist Otto Fehringer and saloon owner N. B. Hames, bailed her out of jail along with Mamie Swift and Annie Wilson. Despite Mamie Major's pleas in court and testimony of her many good deeds, the district attorney painted a picture of a destitute, hardened, and horrible woman who was getting what she deserved.

Although prostitutes were generally banned from public functions, some theaters and other public facilities did reserve special sections for them. The girls were required to enter by a less conspicuous door, and their reserved seating was usually in the back of the theater, out of public view. The girls generally attended such functions with each other, as no decent man wanted to risk being seen in public with them. In the mountain town of Montezuma, a local madam known as Dixie was allowed to attend baseball games so long as she remained seated at the end of the stands and away from decent folk. Perhaps to spite them Dixie, whose real name was Ada Smith, usually showed up for the game dressed in her best. Moreover, she boldly did her shopping at the Rice grocery store in Montezuma. Initially only Mr. Rice would take her orders. Eventually her proper and businesslike manners paid off, and the rest of the family began waiting on her as well. Of special note was

Dixie's habit of buying milk by the case to feed the stray cats and dogs around town.

Friendships among the girls on the row were important for several reasons. For one thing, establishing friendships lessened the chance of getting into fights. Also, it was rare to associate with people who were not in the profession. One exception was the unique relationship between a proper lady named Mindy Lamb and the notorious Mollie May of Leadville. One night in 1880, Mindy's husband, Lewis, allegedly committed suicide in front of Winnie Purdy's bordello. The only witness was a bully Lewis had known from childhood, former marshal Martin Duggan. Duggan had just attempted to run over Lewis with a sleigh he was delivering to Winnie, and it was widely suspected that Lewis had not committed suicide at all but was actually shot to death by Duggan.

It was said Mindy swore revenge on Duggan, promising him: "I shall wear black and mourn this killing until the very day of your death and then, Goddam you, I will dance upon your grave."[18] A few days later Mollie May stopped Mindy on the street. "You don't know me," she told Mindy, "but I wanted to tell you that what happened to a decent man like your husband was a dirty rotten shame and I'm really sorry for you."[19] The two women became friends, often having a chat right in front of Mollie's place. Not surprisingly, Mindy's family was unaware of the friendship until she insisted on attending Mollie's funeral in 1887.

Women who made lasting friendships on the row felt lucky indeed. Laura Evens recalled fondly her friendship with Etta "Spuds" Murphy, whom Laura affectionately called Spuddy. The two apparently met in Leadville in 1895. Laura liked Etta's business sense immediately. "Spuddy saved most of her [money]. Sewed $100 bills in her petticoat."[20]

Laura extended a rare protective tenderness toward Spuddy. Part of her benevolent feelings was sympathy. "She was putting her brother through medical college," Laura later remembered, "and when she went back east to attend his commencement he refused to recognize her. Now, wasn't that a rotten thing to do?"[21] Laura and Spuddy parted ways in about 1896. Laura went to Salida, while Spuddy departed for Pueblo. For Laura there were many great memories of being in Leadville with Spuddy. She once recalled the night in 1896 she and Spuddy rented a sleigh drawn by a horse named Broken-Tail Charlie. After a cruise around Leadville, the women drove the sleigh right into the famous Leadville Ice Palace. "Broken-Tail Charlie got scared at the music and kicked the hell out of our sleigh and broke the shafts and ran away and kicked one of the 4 × 4' ice pillars all to pieces and ruined the exhibits before he ran home to his stable."[22]

Another time Laura and Spuddy managed to rent two chariots from the Ringling Brothers Circus, which was in town, in exchange for an "elephant bucket" of beer. The ensuing race down Harris Avenue ended when Laura crashed her chariot into a telephone pole. One of Laura's customers saved her from arrest. In fact, Laura's male friends in Leadville were many. Once during labor strikes, as union men blocked entrance to a mine, Laura showed up under the guise of visiting a friend who had not been allowed to leave. She was permitted to enter. What the guards didn't know was that she was smuggling the payroll for nonunion miners under her skirts. Her effort was rewarded by a dinner invitation to the mine owners' home plus $100.

A third story of Laura's escapades was recounted by the lady herself to Fred Mazzulla in 1945. In 1909 Laura escorted five of her girls and a musician to Central City for a party. "One evening, after a successful game of poker, one of the players, tho't to revenge for his losses, to humiliate me by mentioning—how us poor unfortunates were ostracized from decent society (which at that was least of our thoughts) stated, 'he would like to escort me to the lodge dance.'" Incensed, Laura bet the man $50 that she could attend the dance in a disguise so discreet that nobody would recognize her. The bet was on, and Laura showed up at the dance—dressed as a nun. Upon pretending to faint as a means of leaving the dance, Laura lost no time in collecting her money from her escort. "Imagine my friend's surprise," she wrote, "when even he did not recognize me in this costume as I had succeeded in going to a Ball that I was ordinarily ostracized from."[23]

Laura Evens's clients often came to her rescue. Many prostitutes made loyal friends out of their favorite customers, a varied lot from all walks of life. A good many of them were miners and young single men, but they could also be millionaires, business owners, laborers, city officials, and even law enforcement officers, husbands, and fathers. In Denver Jennie Rogers's house was well known as the place where local lawmakers retired at the end of their workday. Then as now, men gave virtually unlimited reasons for visiting houses of prostitution. In a day and age before such pastimes as watching sports, attending strip-tease joints, and eating at franchises like Hooters, visiting a brothel was socially acceptable in most male circles. Single men who yearned for companionship were frequent customers, and more than a few of them probably shopped for wives.

Married men, however, also were known to frequent brothels, if only pursuing the clichéd idea that they enjoyed cheating on their wives.

Husbands had other reasons for seeking intimacy elsewhere, largely due to their wives being disinterested or uncomfortable—both physically and emotionally—when it came to having sex. During the Victorian era, the personal toilet of a woman was a complicated one indeed. Daily dress, no matter the weather, involved yards of petticoats, slips, pinafores, pantaloons, stockings, bustles, and corsets. All were skillfully hidden beneath dresses made of heavy material. In short, Victorian dress was downright uncomfortable. The wearing of tight corsets could cause severe shortness of breath—hence the term *fainting couch,* given to lounges designed for one to fall back or lie upon. In some cases corsets caused internal injuries to the organs, and could even be used to induce an abortion. One store catalogue even advertised an instrument devised to push organs back where they belonged by inserting it into the vagina.

These were days when premenstrual syndrome, menopause, lack of estrogen, and other issues with the female anatomy were hardly recognized. To make matters worse, recreational sex was forbidden by society. Periodicals and books of the time warned against the evils of intercourse, frightening young girls into believing they would go mad or become depraved—just for having natural feelings. Sex was a forbidden subject, and many adolescents grew up without benefit of a talk about the birds and the bees. Proper girls were brought up believing sex was bad, the exception being to produce children.

Even if a woman felt up to having sex, lack of reliable contraception was an issue of major importance. Mothers who already had large broods certainly didn't need another mouth to feed. The number of women who died during or after childbirth was alarming in the days before advanced medical practices. One had to be careful, but methods of birth control were limited. Douches of vinegar and water, or sponges inserted into the vagina after sex were thought to wash away or absorb semen (in fact, they probably helped push the semen into the womb). Other homemade contraceptives were fashioned with cocoa butter or Vaseline or diaphragms made from hollowed-out lemon or orange peels or beeswax. Poorer women believed squatting over a pot of steaming water or other liquid after sex would help fumigate their internal organs. Some husbands refused to buy condoms, first made from animal membrane and later from synthetic rubber. Others refused to let their wives practice contraception at all. Thus many wives withheld from having sex altogether, leaving their husbands in frustration. (One 1908 advertisement by the Butcher Drug Company of Colorado Springs sold electric vibrators for "vibratory massage" for $25. The ad features a photograph of a young woman in a nightgown holding the device, which leads one to believe that women were probably able to access other means of gratification.) It was an ailment common to everyone, from the poorest to the richest.

With no Internet, only sporadic mail service, and nary a telephone to be found, many businessmen were required to travel extensively and often. Their visits to brothels in the cities they visited were likely less discreet. But men were also known to visit bawdy houses in their own hometowns, where it was often more difficult to keep a secret. If their wives discovered these indiscretions, the recrimination could range from divorce to no reaction whatsoever. A woman with a husband who visited the occasional whorehouse was better than a woman with no husband at all—except that the fear of contracting venereal disease might put an end to marital sex once and for all.

Marshall Sprague relates the tale of a wife who seemingly ignored her husband's infidelity for a good portion of their marriage. One evening, as the couple dined at a Cripple Creek hotel during their golden years, the wife decided to put an end to her own questions about whether her husband had ever visited a house of ill repute. This was accomplished simply by having a note delivered that read, "How wonderful to see you, Jack dear! I am waiting in the bar! As always, Hazel V." The "V" stood for Vernon, as in the same Hazel Vernon who had run the Old Homestead and caused many a wife concern. Sure enough, the husband took the bait. "The old fellow read the note, blushed, mumbled 'My broker's on the phone' and scurried off," wrote Sprague, "eyes alight and looking 30 years younger."[24]

Because many men who frequented sporting houses, saloons, and gambling dens were upstanding citizens by day, newspapers often neglected to mention their names in articles about skirmishes and incidents. Witness a *Boulder County Herald* article from 1882, describing two men who overimbibed at a house of ill repute. "Accordingly Marshal Bounds and assistant Titus went to said house and arrested X and Y," reported the paper, with no other clue to the men's identities. Another article by the same paper in 1884 identified another male violator only as "R."[25] Likewise, authorities did a fine job of losing paperwork, scribbling out names, and disposing of mug shots, especially those of prominent or wealthy men. If the news was scandalous enough and the men were no more than common miners or from lower-class homes, the papers had no problem naming everyone involved.

Sheriffs and deputies were not exempt from having their names published, since in doing so the newspaper could point fingers and thus assist in cleaning up the city. In some towns, however, even well-known lawmen kept their own brothels. But the wealthy, politicians, and other important figures in society could usually count on the papers to keep their names out of it. Besides, newspapers and the general public usually found fault with the prostitutes involved, since it was at their dens of vice that the incidents usually took place.

It could not be said that prostitutes did not aid in keeping their customers' identities unknown. Some houses of prostitution were so secretive about their prominent customers they gave them masks to wear. The masks were usually made of leather or cloth with cutout eye and mouth holes, and sometimes beards made from real hair. The faces were painted, complete with rosy cheeks and eyelashes.[26] Often girls could service the same clients over and over again—without ever knowing their names. Even if the girls knew who their customers were, they were forbidden from seeing them, let alone acknowledging them, outside the red-light realm.

Although some women worked solely as dance hall girls, they were treated the same as prostitutes by decent society. Some resentment surely built up between prostitutes and their less sinful dance hall counterparts, many of whom never sold their bodies for sex. Just the same, gals such as Tillie Fallon, a dance hall girl in Cripple Creek in 1912, were lumped in with the baddest of girls by authorities. In 1899 the *Cripple Creek Citizen* reported on a dance hall girl named Blanche Garland who committed suicide with chloroform at the Bon Ton Dance Hall. Although Blanche was not a prostitute, the newspaper spilled forth details about the girl's life, much as reporters would brazenly reveal the facts about a prostitute in order to humiliate her to her family and friends. Blanche was about twenty years old, had had trouble with her lover the previous evening, and had parents who lived in town. Blanche had formerly been married to William Garland, who had died in 1896 from wounds received in the Spanish-American War.

Naturally, most girls aspired to marry their favorite customer. Mattie Silks of Denver recalled that some of her girls had married their clients and that most of them were satisfied with the union. "They understood men and how to treat them and they were faithful to their husbands. Mostly the men they married were ranchers. I remained friends with them, and afterwards with their husbands, and I got reports. So I knew they were good wives."[27]

If she couldn't marry a good man, the best a girl could hope for was to make friends with one or more of her customers. Cripple Creek dance hall girl Lizzie Beaudrie recalled an evening when everyone suddenly disappeared from the dance floor and she heard several gunshots outside. One of the gunmen walked into the hall and expressed some surprise at seeing Lizzie standing alone.

"Say, you, didn't you hear me shoot?" he said.

"Yes sir, but you weren't shooting at me, were you?" Lizzie replied.

"Well, why didn't you run and hide like the rest of them?" the man asked.

"I wasn't afraid. No, I guess not. So I couldn't run." Lizzie answered.

The man befriended Lizzie, commenting, "you are the only girl who ever spoke a civil word to me."[28]

The woman who managed to actually secure a lasting relationship with a customer was one lucky girl indeed. More often than not, however, women suffered in relationships with men who were alcoholic, addicted to drugs, or violent. Many male partners were no more than pimps who saw the chance to make money at a woman's expense. In 1889 Emma Moore was working for Ella Wellington in Denver. Emma was the wife of C. C. McDonald, who managed variety shows. When McDonald traveled to Montana, Emma fell ill and moved in with Abe Byers, who brought her back to health but began abusing her. Emma returned to work at Ella's, but at one point the police were called because Byers threatened Emma's life.[29] On December 23, 1896 a black man named Clarence Williams was apprehended in Poverty Gulch for fighting with his white mistress. Both were arrested and fined $5 each.

Domestic violence was shockingly commonplace in red-light districts throughout Colorado. Newspapers in Silverton were rife with stories of abuse by both women and men. In 1892 prostitute P. Jenny was under a doctor's care after a skirmish with a miner. In 1897 a woman known as Flossy stabbed a man who had offended her. In 1900 a jealous customer named Ten Day Jack Turner shot a man who was courting his favorite prostitute. After the shooting, Turner went to the brothel of Lillie Reed and clubbed her on the head. Also in 1900 George Lynch was arrested for smashing a mirror over the head of prostitute Sydney Davis.

Lizzie "Liddy" Beaudrie recalled seeing a woman named Jewel who had been in Cripple Creek since the early 1890s. One side of her face was stunningly beautiful; the other side was hideously scarred from face to neck from a knife fight with a jealous wife. Lizzie was shocked by the abusive treatment she witnessed, even though she herself was a victim. From approximately 1898 to 1904, Lizzie (née Ellson) worked as a dance hall girl in Cripple Creek. Born in 1882, Lizzie had lived with her grandmother and uncle somewhere in the East until the age of fourteen. Both "were very kind to me, and I never in all my life had a cross word spoken to me, or a hand raised in anger."[30]

That all changed in 1896, when Lizzie met Louie Beaudrie, an amusement park employee who literally followed her home and began stalking her. Lizzie found his charms irresistible. "I fell madly in love with him and him with me," she later wrote.[31] Thus began Lizzie's relationship with an abusive older man who, as it turned out, lived with his mother. The two never married, but Louie often introduced Lizzie as Mrs. Louie Beaudrie. He also told her grandmother and uncle they were married.

At first Lizzie found him handsome, polite, and a good singer. Then Lizzie lost her virginity to Louie and got pregnant. "[Louie] got medicine and made me take it and saw that I did, and soon I was alright," she said of her first abortion.[32] Lizzie was destined to have three more abortions and subsequent miscarriages. As time went on the relationship became more stormy, between Lizzie's temper and Louie's jealousy. Lizzie caught Louie cheating on her several times. Louie beat Lizzie when she returned from an innocent visit with her friend Myrtle. He also once shredded a dress she was wearing with a knife.

Eventually Louie went to Cripple Creek, sending for Lizzie sometime in 1898. The two took a room on Bennett Avenue, and Louie played piano in the saloons at night. Occasionally he took Lizzie out. Of Cripple Creek, Lizzie remembered, "There were a few stores, a bank, some restaurants, some drug stores and lots of saloons. The street was lit up and I liked it."[33] Soon Louie began taking Lizzie to dance halls, nestled in the heart of the red-light district. Lizzie described her first look at Myers Avenue in 1898: "We stood on the corner. I looked across the street. I saw a row of houses with women sitting in the windows. They had low neck and no sleeve dresses. A light shown above them and some were smoking cigarettes."[34]

Before she knew it Lizzie was employed at Crapper Jack's, which she politely referred to in her memoirs as Cracker Jack's. Her boss was Jack, and she quickly made friends with a coworker named Rose. Lizzie gave all her money to Louie. The two lived and dressed well, and Louie gave Lizzie a ring made from an opal tiepin and a gold watch purchased in Cripple Creek. These brief expressions of love, however, continued to be interspersed with occasional beatings.

Fig. 8. Crapper Jack's, shown shortly before Lizzie went to work there. Among the girls pictured here is Lottie Amick, a.k.a. the Victor Pig.

(Courtesy Cripple Creek District Museum.)

One night in 1902, Lizzie caught Louie with a blonde around his neck at his place of work. After a big row and Louie's promises of love, Lizzie was sent back home for a visit. She returned in about 1903, just after her twenty-first birthday. Louie refused to let her go back to the dance halls, offering to move with her to Pueblo instead. Shortly after the move, Louie went to find work in California. Left behind in Pueblo, Lizzie eventually ran into a friend from Cripple Creek who informed her that in her absence Louie had married the blonde girl she'd caught him with.

Lizzie returned to Cripple Creek immediately and confronted the woman, Jenny Nelson Beaudrie, at the Beaudrie home. Lizzie remembered that Jenny looked frightened upon seeing her. Lizzie pressed her advantage by being rude but left after ascertaining that Louie wasn't there. When Lizzie found Louie and confronted him, he spurned her with cruel words, claiming he had never loved her. Afterward Lizzie began drinking heavily. Her friend Rose had to talk her out of turning to prostitution. In 1904 Lizzie married a former customer known as Soapy and moved to Creede, where she lived until her death in 1960 at the age of seventy-eight. In 1944 Lizzie wrote her memoirs of her days as a dance hall vixen. Soapy, to whom Lizzie was married for over forty years, likely had no idea of the manuscript his wife secretly penned. Soapy died in about 1951. As for Louie, he later returned to his hometown and died there.

Lizzie's story was not uncommon. On the whole, society in general turned its back on such goings-on. Newspapers, with their sensationalistic journalism, just made things worse. The *Cripple Creek Times*, for instance, made light of the 1904 case of "Slim" Campbell, an anti-union miner in Cripple Creek who "brutally murdered a woman of the half world" after his release from jail during the 1903–4 labor wars. "He was allowed to make his escape by the sheriff."[35] In 1910 the *Pueblo Chieftain* poked fun at Miss Pearl Stevens, a drunken prostitute who called for the justice of the peace to come "pinch" Pete Froney for her after the saloon owner beat her. Much to the public's amusement, Pearl swore out a warrant for Froney's arrest but canceled it two hours later.

Occasionally, however, even the newspapers sympathized with prostitutes, such as in the sad 1905 case of Silverton dance hall girl Mable Kelly, who was beat and kicked nearly to death by pimp Frank Anderson. "He should be given the limit of the law," declared the paper, adding that upon completing his sentence Anderson should be run out of Silverton and tarred and feathered if he returned.[36]

The other extreme of such relationships resulted in many a heartbreak for prostitutes hoping to marry their customers. In 1876 the *Boulder County News* reported on Lena Rosa, an inmate at Sue Fee's brothel. Lena became despondent after receiving a letter from her lover in Georgetown casting her off. That night, even as another customer slept beside her, Lena rose and took an overdose of morphine. The newspaper commented that thirty-year-old Lena had left behind a nine-year-old daughter who was living in St. Louis. Lena's success at suicide was countered in 1882 by the saving of Frankie McDonald, an employee of madam Sue Brown. Frankie had also attempted suicide over a young man who refused to return her affections by taking morphine and laudanum. The act was repeated by Boulder prostitute Mamie Myers in 1889.

Not all girls allowed themselves to be victims. A resident of Central City recalled walking up forbidden Pine Street as a little girl and spying a scantily dressed prostitute dangling a silver crucifix over the front rail of her porch. Below was a prominent male citizen of the town, on his knees, begging her to give it back to him. And in 1867 the Central City *Tribune* commented on Moll Green and Elmer Hines, who were on trial for a murder committed at Green's house. Apparently the woman had just recently got out of jail for assaulting a man. Arrests for loud parties, lewd language, and even vandalism were also the norm during this time.

Laura Evens put up with very little. Her brass checks supposedly read, "Eat, Drink, Go to bed or Get out." Once she knocked her paramour, a man named Arthur, through a window for dancing too much with another woman. Of the incident, Laura recalled that "his head got stuck in the plate glass and like to cut his throat." She also willingly admitted, "When Arthur and I got mad at each other we'd fight with knives, and I've got scars where he cut me up. I loved that man."[37] Laura Evens may just have been the exception to the rule when it came to defending herself against rough customers. Laura's employee LaVerne recalled there was never a male bouncer at Laura's place, but if a customer got too rough as many as eight girls could offer assistance in subduing him. For this reason, Laura's girls never locked the doors to their rooms when they had a client.

Others took measures to defend not only themselves but also their own. Two harlots from Lake City serve as an example. One day Jessie Landers from Clara Ogden's Crystal Palace on notorious Bluff Street took a shot at a man who was forcing his attentions on her. The shot missed, hitting the girl's fiancé instead. Other sources say the fiancé was talking to a pimp and that Jessie shot him on purpose. Either way, Jessie was tried and convicted of murder. During her four-year sentence, she contracted tuberculosis. Upon her release, she returned to Lake City. Clara Ogden had long departed, but Jessie lived out her short life in Lake City. On her deathbed, the girl asked the Reverend M. B. Milne of the Baptist church to conduct services for her. He agreed. Shortly afterward the girl died, and her body was prepared for the funeral. At the church, however, one of the trustees refused to open the doors and admit the funeral party. The services were held elsewhere, with Milne keeping his promise and even accompanying the party to the cemetery. Later, the church trustee who had refused admittance was followed and horsewhipped by two women from

Bluff Street. There were several witnesses, but none would testify as to what happened.

If a girl could not rely on friends within her job position, she sometimes could rely on family. A surprising number of women entered into the profession via their mother, an aunt, or perhaps a sister. Birdie and Mae Fields were sisters who practiced prostitution in Colorado City in 1896. Likewise, when twenty-two-year-old Jewel Lavin arrived from Denver to work in Cripple Creek in September of 1911, she was accompanied by a twenty-year-old sister named Myrtle. Both girls left town on January 2, 1912, but returned within a few days of each other in February. In September the sisters departed again for Denver. Only Myrtle returned later that month and resumed working in Cripple Creek.

The family of a prostitute included children born to her while she was in the profession. Most women dreaded the idea of hindering their work with a pregnancy, and steps were taken to avoid such an inconvenience. According to Laura Evens's employee LaVerne, men sometimes brought rubbers with them, or they were provided by the girls, who insisted on using them. Douching was probably the most common form of birth control, concocted from solutions like bicarbonate of soda, borax, bichloride of mercury, potassium biartate, alum, or vinegar. Another popular method was a contraceptive made from cocoa butter with glycerin, boric acid, and tannic acid.

When these methods failed, pregnancy was dealt with on a case-to-case basis. Many women had their babies, but abortions could be induced with dangerous substances such as ergot, prussic acid, iodine, strychnine, saffron, cotton rust, or oil of tansy. Unpleasant and even perilous as it was, abortion was an attractive alternative to bearing a child for many. In March of 1895 in Cripple Creek, Mrs. Lucinda E. Guyer was on trial for causing the abortion-related death of Myrtle Coombs. A resident of Cripple Creek since at least 1893, sixty-year old Mrs. Guyer allegedly worked as a laundress and was located within a few blocks of the red-light district. Mrs. Guyer's attorney, a Mr. Goudy, pleaded insanity, but Lucinda was sentenced to one year in the Colorado State Penitentiary. Upon her release, Lucinda returned to Cripple Creek.

Children in brothels were more common in the lower-class houses. When Boulder madam Sue Fee died from her drug habits in 1877, she left behind a son guessed to be about four or five years old. The Denver census for 1880 lists three women, Ella Cree, Hellen McElhany, and Miss Doebler, as having a collective six children between them. Likewise, four-year-old

Elizabeth Franklin was living with her mother, Mary Franklin, in 1900 at Colorado City. Little Elizabeth, whose sibling had died, lived in her mother's workplace, Anna Boyd's bordello, at 625 Washington. In Trinidad, Margarita Carillo had a three-year-old Italian boy living at her brothel. The census notes the boys' parents were deceased.

Being raised in a brothel was not the easiest childhood to bear. The children often had little contact with the outside world, relying on the confines of the brothel for entertainment, education, care, and feeding. Because so many prostitutes were illiterate, their children tended to be illiterate as well, since sending them to public schools was often out of the question. Brothel children were more likely to be teased or bullied, and some schools refused outright to admit them. Their unstable home lives, as well as their tendency to relocate along with their mothers, made for poor attendance. Also, many prostitute mothers lacked the knowledge or inclination to send their children to school, or they were afraid of retribution from school authorities—such as having their children taken from them—if they did.

Without an education or chances for advancement outside of the bordellos they were raised in, most children faced dim futures with limited career opportunities—unless they learned the brothel or barroom trade. Daughters of prostitutes were sometimes, but not always, trained to follow in their mother's footsteps. Mrs. Annie Ryan is one of many who began a family operation in Cripple Creek with her three daughters before moving to Denver. Such actions were generally highly frowned upon by authorities and society, especially in situations involving preteenage girls. In 1876 the *Daily Rocky Mountain News* reported on Mary "Adobe Moll" Gallagan. A raid at Mary's Denver house revealed an eleven-year-old and a thirteen-year-old who were "employed" as prostitutes. The latter was a little black girl who had lost both arms and a leg in an accident.[38] Just a year later, the newspaper reported that a Mrs. Whatley had a fifteen-year-old daughter who had been a prostitute for three years. She also employed a twelve-year-old who told authorities she had been with men at Whatley's.

Rescuing these poor children was often the goal of crusades led by the Women's Christian Temperance Union and even police officers themselves. In 1880 the *Pueblo Chieftain* told the account of a sixteen-year-old Alamosa girl rescued from the brothel of Nellie Moon. The girl was talked out of continuing her budding profession by South Pueblo deputy sheriff Patrick J. Desmond.

At times the horror of placing their children in such dangers scared some prostitutes straight. On October 6, 1898, the *Cripple Creek Morning Times* reported on Robert Penton, who was found guilty in Colorado Springs of the murder of Dan Mills at Mills's saloon in the Cripple Creek District town of Goldfield. Penton had apparently confessed to Nell Taylor, whose husband, Bob, had held up the Florence & Cripple Creek Railroad back in 1895. It was Nell, a sometime prostitute, who had turned her husband in and guaranteed his conviction. A second man indicted along with Penton, Moore, was convicted of raping Nell's daughter earlier in the year. Presumably, Nell was trying to make a clean start for herself.

Besides sexual assault, children and teenagers were also subjected to the drug and alcohol use that was present in every bordello and parlor house. Depression ran high among the girls, many of whom became addicted to such vices to escape their problems. Many standard medicines contained potentially lethal doses of such drugs as laudanum, morphine, cocaine, opium, or alcohol. Wyeth's New Enterius Pills, Feeley's Rheumatic Mixture, and Godfrey's Cordial all contained morphine. Laudanum, a liquid form of opium, was applied to sprains and bruises or consumed straight from the bottle. Combinations of morphine and cocaine relieved colds. Visiting opium dens in the back of Chinese laundries or brothels was also a popular pastime.

Another deviant behavior was constant exposure to, or participation in, crime. During her career, a prostitute was likely to be arrested not only for violating ordinances against prostitution, but also for fighting, stealing, public drunkenness, or even murder. Fighting was very common among prostitutes. The *Pueblo Chieftain* in August of 1872 reported: "Yesterday a couple of abandoned women at the Hotel de Omaha had a misunderstanding that culminated into a regular street fight. They rolled and tumbled in the mud, pulled hair, fought, bit, gouged and pommeled [*sic*] each other and filled the air with blood curdling oaths. None of the police officers were on hand to interfere. It was a disgraceful spectacle and a strong illustration of the morals on the banks of the Arkansas."[39] In 1880 the *Boulder News and Courier* commented on a scuffle at Mrs. Brown's in lower Boulder that "resulted in the complete demolition of one of the ladies, whose head came in contact with an empty beer bottle."[40] And in 1899 the *Cripple Creek Citizen* told of Julia Belmont, who "carved up" Maggie Walsh at the Bon Ton Dance Hall. "The surgeons took several hours to sew up the gashes in the face." Julia, a fellow dance hall girl, was spurred to violence when she saw Maggie dancing with a favorite customer.[41] The same thing happened in Denver that year, when Minnie Gardner stabbed Nellie Thomas. Minnie had spied Nellie with her husband, Ed, and followed the couple to an opium den.

Newspapers enjoyed capitalizing on such scenes. In 1886 the *Silverton Standard* made the most out of a fight involving Dutch Lena and Irish Nell, who duked it out and were subsequently arrested. In June both Lena and Nell teamed up with Minnie "the Baby Jumbo" to beat up another girl known as Oregon Short Line. Lizzie Beaudrie also experienced violence in the dance halls. One night she had a fight with an employee named Grace, who came after her with a knife. Grace ended up with two black eyes, cuts on her mouth, and several bruises. Prostitutes were certainly not beyond killing. Denver newspapers were rife with similar incidents.

Most clients had to worry about stealing more than violence at the hands of prostitutes. Some girls learned to bite diamond lapel pins, buttons, and other small gems from their customer's jackets and shirts. Some brothels became known as "panel houses," wherein a woman would lead her victim into a room. Suddenly a man would pop out of a hidden panel, pass himself off as an enraged husband, and extort money from the surprised stranger before escorting him unceremoniously from the premises. Or that same panel might be used to sneak into the room and steal the victim's money while he slept or was otherwise engaged. Sometimes there was merely a sliding panel in the back of a closet. "Panel workers" would then remove the man's wallet and take just enough money from it not to be noticed before putting it back. "Creepers" accomplished the same thing by sliding stealthily across the floor to the man's clothes while the girl kept him busy. "Hook artists" used a rod and hook to lift the clothes into reach.

Prostitutes could also often be coerced to steal by their gentlemen friends or pimps. In 1885 Maggie Moss, a seventeen-year-old Denver prostitute, assisted her partner of three years to rob a bank. If they knew they might receive a beating for not making enough money, some girls were not beyond stealing to satisfy their pimps. At other times the girls raided each other's trunks or even collaborated on a crime together. In 1891 Denver prostitutes Blanche Morgan, Ardell Smith, Mattie Fisher, and Mollie White were arrested for successfully conspiring to kill William Joos with an overdose of morphine so they could rob him of $55.

Some crimes committed by prostitutes were no more than acts of vengeance. Men who were identified as spreading venereal disease were singled out, if they could be found. Catching such debilitating maladies was one of the worst fates a working girl could suffer. Over-the-counter remedies such as Naples Soap, the Boss, Armenian Pills, Big, Bumstead's Gleet Cure, Hot Springs Prescription, LaFayette Mixture, Red Drops, and Unfortunate's Friend seldom offered successful results. Mercury was used to cure syphilis but could just as easily prove fatal.

Laura Evens showed her employees how to check their clients for venereal disease before having sex. The procedure basically consisted of pinching the base of the penis with thumb and forefinger and squeezing while sliding one's hand to the top. If a telltale gray mucus came out, it could be assumed the client was infected. One customer recalled how a girl approached him and "seized my genital organ in one hand, wringing it in such a way as to determine whether or not I had gonorrhea. She did this particular operation with more knowledge and skill than she did anything else before or after."[42]

The girls took further precautions by washing their customers with soap and water. If a man had venereal disease the girls had to refuse him. After each transaction the girls washed first the men and then themselves, a practice that seems to have been common in most houses. In those days venereal disease was taken fairly lightly by the general public, probably because it was so rampant. Some men were even known to joke or brag about having "the clap" and spread rumors about where they got it and from whom. To the prostitute, however, venereal disease was serious business.

The public health care system was terribly primitive by today's standards, but a few cities in Colorado took steps to improve the situations of sick prostitutes. In 1881 the Ladies's Benevolent Union opened Pueblo's first hospital for the homeless. Part of the care included helping prostitutes to reform. Nellie Brown was one success story in 1890, although shortly after her reformation she died at the tender age of fourteen of unknown causes. In Cripple Creek, Frankie Williams and Edna Lewis are both noted in the city police register as spending some time at Mrs. Mattie Bidwell's rooms at 243 East Myers in January of 1912. In April Edna was noted as "back on row." As for Frankie, the girl worked briefly at the Old Homestead and at 435 Myers Avenue but died on June 1. Mrs. Bidwell's may have actually been a recovery house. Many ill prostitutes also ended up at St. Nicholas Hospital, cared for by the Catholic Sisters of Mercy.

Sadly, a large number of prostitutes succumbed to their reckless lifestyles and poor care. In January of 1896, nineteen-year-old Ruth Davenport constituted the saddest of cases in Cripple Creek. Newspapers reported how the girl lay dying above Mernie's Dance Hall, deathly ill with pneumonia. Below, it was business as usual, with music and dancing to the "Monterey." When Ruth died later that evening, the dance hall closed for the night and the revelers went elsewhere. The newspaper reported that Ruth had come from Central City the previous October. It was also said she came from a good home in Denver but was driven away on account of her wild ways. Beyond that, no other information was given.

In 1899 one of Silverton madam Molly Foley's girls, May Rikard, died after a night of combining alcohol and morphine. Girls of the row solicited donations for her burial. Less is known about the deaths of girls like Goldie Bauschell, who was twenty-nine years old when she came to Cripple Creek from California. Several aspects about Goldie pointed to the hard life she had led: she weighed in at 205 pounds, had smallpox scars on her face and a bullet scar near the front of her head. Goldie died on August 14, 1911. The cause of her death and place of her burial are unknown.

Suicide also ended many a life. Many girls favored drinking carbolic acid, which produced a quick but agonizingly painful death. When Cora Davis attempted suicide in Boulder in 1881, she used strychnine. The tragic picture of a soiled dove committing suicide was less than glamorous. Police reporter Forbes Parkhill recalled accompanying a policeman to Mattie Silks's place on New Year's night in 1913. Mattie silently led the men upstairs to the room of a girl named Stella, who was writhing and sobbing in agony on her bed after taking a dose of poison. The girl wore only a pair of silk stockings, despite the fact it was twenty-one degrees below zero outside. As the men carried Stella downstairs, she threw up on Parkhill and ruined his suit. There was no ambulance available; the men loaded her into the police car and delivered her to the county hospital, where she died the next day.

And there were other methods. Goldie was a resident of the Crystal Palace in Colorado City. In May of 1891 she attempted suicide by jumping from a second-story window. She was seriously injured but survived the fall, and whether she attempted to take her life again is unknown. In March of 1892 two of Mattie Silks's girls, Effie Pryor and Allie Ellis, were found lying nude together after a double suicide attempt via morphine. Effie was saved, but Allie died. Another alternative was taking pills, such as in the 1913 case of Nora McCord at Salida. On her deathbed, Nora declined to give her real name or that of her relatives.

For as much as they aspired to do themselves in, prostitutes were often quick to help others in need. The tragic and well-known story of Silver Heels, the Colorado dance hall girl whose aid to miners during a smallpox epidemic resulted in the scarring of her own beautiful face, is a case in point. So many yarns have been spun about the story of Silver Heels that the truth seems lost to history. Similar stories have been found in other parts of the United States. Most recently, author Tara Meixsell romanticized Silver Heels's story in a fictionalized novel of the same name. In Colorado only Mt. Silver Heels, located north of Fairplay, as well as a namesake creek and even a mine with its short-lived camp, attest to her ever existing at all.

According to most stories about Silver Heels, she was a beautiful dance hall or parlor house girl who hauled her petticoats into the Fairplay Mining District sometime between 1861 and 1870. Various writers have placed her at the district towns of Alma, Fairplay, Dudley or, more often, Buckskin Joe. There, she appeared at Bill Buck's saloon or "stepped daintily from the stagecoach which brought her to the mountains."[43] According to Kay Reynolds Blair, a manuscript by Albert B. Sanford in the Colorado Historical Society identifies Tom Lee as the man who tried to set the record straight about Silver Heels. According to Lee, the stage may have come from Denver, and upon disembarking the lone young woman seemed "lost and confused."[44]

So who was she? A 1963 *Denver Post* article theorized that her real name was Gerda Bechtel and that she hailed from Letitz, Pennsylvania, but had changed her name to Gerda Silber. The writer, Robert W. "Red" Fenwick, also asserted that the name Silber was really the girl's pseudo-surname, bastardized to make her colorful nickname.[45] In Blair's version by Sanford, Silver Heels next was taken under the wing of a local saloon and gambling hall owner, Jack Herndon. Upon being escorted to the best house in town, the home of Mr. and Mrs. Mack, Silver Heels fainted. While being cared for by Mrs. Mack, Silver Heels revealed her life story, which Mrs. Mack never told to another soul. Mrs. Mack's discretion endeared her to Silver Heels and they became good friends. Before long, according to Blair, Herndon found out her true name was Josie Dillon.[46]

Whoever she was, Silver Heels was said to be beautiful beyond comparison. Many a miner fell madly in love with the beauty, and it was said that some would walk for miles just to look at her. One or more of her paramours allegedly bestowed the gift of silver-heeled dancing shoes upon her, thus her colorful pseudonym. Indeed, Silver Heels in her beautiful shoes "could dance faster and more gracefully than anyone."[47] She also soon became a favorite of the town children, and in the version that has her living with the Macks she would often order candy from Denver and entertain the children in the afternoons. Furthermore, Silver Heels was an "angel of mercy," according to a miner named Henry Maher who was interviewed in 1938 at the age of eighty-five. Not only did she nurse the sick, but she was also willing to grubstake miners.[48] To top it off she had a good nature and was always nice to folks.

In the story by Blair, it wasn't long before Silver Heels was engaged to one of the local miners, possibly Jack Herndon. Jack and Silver Heels and the Macks all pitched in heroically to raise money, food, and clothing for victims of the Chicago fire of 1871. In the end Silver Heels was the star at a benefit to raise money, her music and dance studies serving her well. On her feet were her signature slippers, which in this version were not a gift of the mining men. The benefit raised $1,750, more than the other nearby camps had raised altogether.

Of course, most versions of Silver Heels's tale have her most famous heroics taking place during a smallpox epidemic.[49] Silver Heels stepped forward to help those with the virus when others wouldn't. Many people fled in terror, and even a telegram to Denver yielded only two or three additional nurses. Silver Heels made a makeshift hospital out of the dance hall formerly owned by her lover, and by some miracle apparently arranged to pay everyone's doctor bills herself.[50]

During this time, according to Blair's first version, Silver Heels's fiancé was one of the first to die. Interestingly, Sanford's version claims Josie did not contract smallpox. She and Jack left for Denver, married, and returned to Buckskin Joe. There they were given a huge reception, built a new home, and had a baby named Marion Lee Herndon. When Jack's father died in Kentucky about a year later, the couple gave their land to Tom Lee and departed forever. A survey group that visited the area sometime afterward were told to name the mountain nearby Silver Heels after their heroine.[51]

Blair's version by Sanford is probably the least known of the Silver Heels legends, even though it seems most sensible. But sensible can be boring, and every other tale about her has her catching the dreaded smallpox. The good citizens of Buckskin Joe nursed her back to health and though she survived, she was pockmarked for life. What happened next is anybody's guess, based on the various sources of this story. In one version, Silver Heels was forced to continue working alongside women like Jeannette Arcon in the dance halls of Buckskin Joe, Alma, Fairplay, Park City, and the nearby town of Montgomery, wearing a heavy veil to disguise her scars. Fenwick wrote that after a time she announced she was moving to Denver to marry "an old friend."[52] In Denver she resided for a time at a hotel before disappearing forever.

In another version, Silver Heels was so ashamed of her newfound ugliness she either left town or became a recluse. In some versions, her disappearance was discovered after a group of miners solicited $5,000 as her reward for aiding the sick and found her cabin empty when they went to give it to her. According to Max Evans, a heartbroken admirer painted her face on a barroom floor somewhere in town.[53] Other writers have ended

Fig. 9. The portrait of this young lady was found painted on the kitchen floor of a former saloon owner's home in Cripple Creek.

(Courtesy Cripple Creek District Museum.)

this tale with the most romantic part: years after Silver Heels left town, a woman wearing a heavy veil over her face was seen walking through the cemetery in Alma. In some versions she is dressed in fine clothes. In other versions she is weeping and escapes before anyone can get close enough to identify her.

A few authors have even speculated that Silver Heels was none other than Silver Heels Jessie of Salida. When smallpox hit the town, madam Laura Evens ordered a local physician to issue nurses' uniforms to her girls so they could aid the sick. Jessie, who was in Laura's employ, was given the duty of nursing a minister's wife. The minister was so grateful he offered Jessie a job as housekeeper and companion to his wife. The girl modestly declined, saying, "Now that my job is done, I'll be on my way back to Miss Laura's on Front Street."[54] The minister, who had no idea the young nurse was a prostitute, was shocked. Eventually Silver Heels Jessie married one Earl Keller and moved to Gunnison. Though she died in Gunnison in 1954, Jessie's wish to be buried in Salida was granted. The city showed its lack of prejudice against prostitutes by allowing Jessie to be buried in the city cemetery.

Despite all the mixed-up versions of Silver Heels's story, the girl ultimately epitomized the harlot with the heart of gold. Only a handful of prostitutes, however, ever really received thanks for their good deeds. Maggie Hartman of Lake City was one such woman. When a miner came down with pneumonia at the nearby mining town of Sherman, it was Maggie who offered to go nurse the snowbound man. After a week in the cold and desolate cabin, Maggie also became ill. Rescuers got her as far as George Boyd's cabin before another storm came up. Ultimately one of the good women of the town, Mrs. Mary Franklin, had Maggie brought to her home, but she died anyway. The Reverend George Darley of the Presbyterian church not only spoke over Maggie's services, he also visited her former house of employment and shook hands with each of the girls.

And there were others. In 1891 the *Silverton Standard* chastised the general public for its lack of compassion. It seemed a young woman named Mrs. Gallagher was suffering hardships after the birth of her third child, with no help or support from her husband. In the end only the ladies of the row came to her aid, providing food and assistance. Another time, a former resident of Montezuma reappeared in town after going through some hard times. The town threw a benefit for her, only to witness her entering a saloon with a disreputable character before making her way to the red-light district. A local stage driver was instructed to immediately escort the girl out of town to the train depot at nearby Dillon.

During the 1918 flu epidemic, many prostitutes worked as nurses, and during the Depression in the 1930s they were known to leave food at the backdoors of respectable homes without thanks or credit. Dixie, the Montezuma madam, joined her girls to care for the town's single men during the 1918 flu epidemic. In later years, Dixie also took food to prospectors who were growing old as Montezuma's mines played out. And in Breckenridge, a retiring madam agreed to sell her house to a large family with several children. The husband succumbed to flu before the transaction was completed, leaving the widow destitute. After the funeral, the madam quietly surrendered the deed without expecting a penny, with no one ever the wiser to her benevolent act. In another version of this tale, the heroine harlot was Minnie Colwell, a popular madam along the road to the Wellington Mine. It was said Minnie used her savings to buy a house for a family with five or six children that was destitute after a fire. That Minnie was publicly thanked for her good deed is doubtful. No matter the good deeds its practitioners performed, prostitution was a thankless profession.

Chapter Three

In the Beginning There Was Denver

ॐ

The miner came in '59
The prostitute in '61
And between the two,
They made the native son!
—Old western proverb

The miners in the 1859 Pikes Peak or Bust gold rush arrived in the new West primarily alone, without female companionship. Many had left their families behind, hoping to bring them out later once gold was found and riches were secured. For many a man, Denver, and its surrounding country, was a desolate, lonely place. Pioneer Albert Richardson remembered how he and his comrades sorely missed the presence of a lady in their midst. "We were all in the habit of running to our cabin doors in Denver on the arrival of the ladies," he said, "to gaze upon her as earnestly as at any other natural curiosity."[1]

In 1860 the ratio of men to women in Colorado was sixteen to one. In California Gulch near Leadville alone, there were 2,000 males and only 36 females. South Park boasted an amazing 10,519 men to 91 women! Most members of the gentler sex were well admired, respected, and obeyed. In their absence the men, desperate for companionship, held dances anyway and designated "female" dance partners by tying ribbons or handkerchiefs on their arms. If by some miracle a woman did attend a dance or other social gathering, she could rely on being treated with the utmost kindness despite wearing out her dance slippers with dozens of partners. Married men were fully expected to permit their wives to attend such social gatherings rather than keeping them at home.

To keep other men from feasting their eyes upon the rare and coveted female was considered downright rude.

The prostitutes of the early West were making themselves known, however. Following the gold booms of the West could prove especially successful for the gal who knew how to move quickly and ply her trade. Denver's very first "white" prostitute was said to be Ada LaMont, a nineteen-year-old beauty who married a young minister and came west with him in about 1858. Lo and behold, midway through the trip the minister disappeared, along with a young lady of questionable character. Ada arrived in Denver alone—but with a whole new outlook on her situation. "As of tomorrow," she said, "I start the first brothel in this settlement. In the future my name will be Addie LaMont."[2]

More women of vice were quick to follow. A leader of the demimonde in 1861 and 1862 was Lizzie Greer, a successful beauty who had many admirers, an expensive wardrobe, and plenty of diamonds. In general, however, Denver newspapers and authorities do not appear to have paid much attention to the illegal vice of prostitution in the early days. Their complacent actions were balanced by those in Central City, located due west high in the mining country. Central City was the site of the first real gold boom in Colorado in 1859. Surprisingly, however, the prostitution industry found it hard to flourish there at first. In 1860 a brothel in nearby Nevadaville was cleaned out by irate citizens. Six years later, another den of sin in Central City suffered the same fate.

Indeed, ousted ladies from other parts of Colorado found little shelter in Central City. An 1864 news article in the *Miners Register* complained heavily of a Madam Wright, who had been operating for some time on respectable Eureka Street directly below the Methodist church. The wicked woman had recently been arrested for larceny. Most interestingly, however, the *Register* did concede that it was possible to permit prostitutes to operate in any given city. "Perhaps such creatures should be permitted to live in a community," admitted the writer, "but they certainly ought to be severely treated for their offenses against morality and law, and compelled to remove to some remote locality where their presence will not be so annoying."[3] With time, Central City at last fell victim to the same vices as every other mining town in the state, even as newspapers and city authorities threatened to close them down as early as 1868. The proper folks in town were always quick to voice their disapproval of the red-light district and even banned those who patronized brothels or dance halls from other social events. One of these was Pat Casey, a miner who eventually struck it rich.

In his wealth, Casey retaliated against the puritans of Central City by loading up his favorite fancy girls each Sunday and driving them past the churches just as services were letting out.

When journalist James Thomson visited Central City in November of 1872, he described in his diary a Saturday night outing: "The prostitutes' ball at ——. Four fellows in four-bedded attic, three with girls at one time. The prize for the best dancer. Girl who had got it four times, refused it 5th. Went and undressed save stockings and garters. Danced wonderfully for five minutes, music playing, hall crowded. Then 'Here's the leg that can dance, and here's the arse that can back it up!' Redressed and danced with the others till daylight."[4] After several years of unsuccessfully trying to establish themselves in town, Central City's naughty girls migrated to Gunnell Hill above town instead. For years, Central City's red-light district enjoyed its lofty position while looking down on the city from the end of Pine Street, just a few blocks from the Catholic church. There the girls were free to service miners from both the Galena Mine and the Coeur d'Alene Mine above them. Downtown, places like the Shoo Fly Variety Hall still prospered.

The best remembered of Central City's shady ladies is madam Lou Bunch, a three-hundred-pound delight whose presence in town surely could not be missed. But there were others. May Martin was one girl who practiced in Central City. Others included Della or Lizzie Warwick, Jane Gordon, Mae Temple, the "elegant courtesan" Ruby Lee, and Ada Branch, known alternately as the Big Swede. Ada's house and wardrobe were among the fanciest in town, and Pine Street was alternately known as Big Swede Avenue in 1880. Cora Fish was one of Ada's employees. Other girls of Central are all but forgotten, with hardly a name to remember them by. A warehouse near downtown, however, is said to still bear graffiti from higher times: "Myrtle crib #13—wow. Sweetheart."[5]

One of the earliest comments on prostitution first appeared in Denver papers in 1874. An article reported on a local tavern called the Cricket, which was "ablaze last night with festivities. There was a dance from 1 A.M. to sunrise with liquor pouring freely throughout the night." Prostitutes present at the gathering included Belle Deering, Sadie Bent, Eva Hamilton, Elva Seymour, Kittie Wells, Laura Winnie, Gertie, Cora, Jennie Logan, Emma Marsh, Dutch Nellie, Mormon Ann, Frankie, and Annie.[6]

Just two years later, the first truly notorious madam of Denver arrived. Her name was Mattie Silks, and her appearance was so renowned that at least one folk song immediately surfaced about the illustrious prostitute and some of her more famous cohorts:

Fig. 10. Central City at the turn of the century. The red-light district was eventually located on Pine Street, the highest road on the left in this photo.

(From the author's collection.)

Mattie Silks and Fanny Ford
Drank theirs from a gourd,
Poker Alice she smoked a cherout;
Lily Langtree, they say,
Had been led astray
By the juice of forbidden fruit.[7]

Mattie was just twenty-nine years old when she arrived in Denver. Born in New York or possibly Indiana, she began her first brothel in Springfield, Illinois, in about 1865 at the age of nineteen. Next, Mattie attempted to run a brothel in Olathe, Kansas, but was run out of town. Wisely, she decided to spend her winters working in Kansas City while working the cattle-town circuit during the summer months. It was also said Mattie worked as a freighter between Missouri and Colorado before opening up for business

Fig. 11. Despite her portly appearance, Mattie Silks was
described as blonde and beautiful, with a resemblance to Lily
Langtry. The dress she is wearing in this studio portrait was
said to be replicated from Rubens's portrait of Marie de Medici.

(From the Mazzulla Collection, courtesy Colorado Historical Society.)

in Dodge City, Abilene, and Hays City, Kansas. A sign on her parlor house there read, "Men taken in and done for."[8] After hiring four girls in Kansas, Mattie headed for Colorado and traveled by stagecoach and freighter wagon around the Pikes Peak region, visiting a number of mining camps. Her vehicles contained a "portable boarding house for young ladies," which was actually no more than a canvas tent attached to a wagon. The bordello did, however, include a canvas bathtub.[9]

By 1873 Mattie was in Georgetown, where she operated one of five brothels on Brownell Street. While there, she married Casey or George Silks, a faro dealer from Pueblo. The couple may have had a child together. The two eventually separated, perhaps because Mattie's lover, a fireman named Cortez D. Thomson, was also living in Mattie's brothel. When Mattie arrived in Denver in 1877 Cort was still with her, having left behind his wife and daughter in Georgetown. It must have been love, for Mattie was willing to put up with Cort's drinking and gambling habits. She often gave him money, and it was said that despite two terrible beatings Cort gave Mattie, she loved him too much to leave him. Mattie Silks was certainly not the angel she aspired to be, however. The March 28, 1877 issue of the *Rocky Mountain News* reported Mattie was fined $12 for drunkenness, which she paid. In August it was said that Mattie challenged madam Katie Fulton to a duel over Cort. Folklore claims that when the women took their shots, they both missed—save for a bullet that went astray and struck Cort in the neck. He lived, and even pledged to be faithful to Mattie.

The *Rocky Mountain News* reported a different story: Katie and Mattie had an argument after a footrace in which Cort was victorious and for which Mattie won $2,000. During the argument, Cort punched Katie in the face and knocked her down. Katie's friend Sam Thatcher was knocked down as well. Then Katie was knocked down again and kicked in the face, which broke her nose. After the fight broke up, Cort took off toward town in his buggy. A carriage soon pulled up beside him, and a shot from said carriage hit him in the neck. Katie left town for awhile but in September returned to Denver, where she had another fight with Mattie. This time Mattie punched Katie, knocking her down and injuring her nose again.

No doubt Mattie was a feisty little vixen, but it was certainly no trouble for her to set up shop. She was described as blonde with blue eyes, clear skin, and a striking resemblance to actress Lily Langtry. Besides her good looks, Mattie quickly gained a good reputation for excellent service and pretty, honest, high-class girls. Under her regime, the girls paid Mattie room and board starting at $5 per week and split their earnings with her. Mattie's first brothel, which she purchased for $13,000 from Nellie French, was at 501 Holladay Street, now known as Market Street. Mattie's elite business cards were shaped like an oyster shell—a grand treat for Denver dinner tables in the Victorian era. In addition, Mattie rented or operated in the buildings on either side of her brothel and prospered there as well.

Over the next four years, Mattie's competition grew steadily. Women like Lizzie Greer slowly fell to the wayside. In fact, the *Denver Republican* took due notice when Lizzie's looks and talents began fading. By 1881 Lizzie had lost all of her money and admirers and had turned to alcohol to drown her sorrows. The newspaper noted she had been living for years in back alleys and along riverfronts, purchasing liquor when she could and eating out of the garbage bins of local restaurants. She was last noted as being found sleeping in a lumberyard and taken to the county hospital. The paper commented that her end was not far off. After her death, which probably occurred in January of 1881, the sight of Lizzie's ghost lingering near the undertaker's parlor was the subject of *Rocky Mountain News* stories as late as 1885.

In 1882 there were approximately 480 prostitutes working in Denver. In those times, two-room cribs on the row were rented to prostitutes for $15–$25 a week. White sections of the red-light district were called "dollar houses," with the parlor houses of Denver costing $5 and up per trick. The black sections—located beyond 21st and Market Street—were called "two-bit houses," reflecting the price paid for time with a prostitute. Thus a girl had to turn fifteen or even as many as fifty tricks per week just to make her board.

There is little doubt that Mattie Silks ruled with an iron fist. Some said she carried an ivory-handled pistol with her, concealed in a special pocket of a gown she had replicated from Rubens's portrait of Marie de Medici. But stagecoach driver Martin Parsons remembered that Mattie "didn't carry a gun in her clothes . . . for she didn't have to. She could control people by her voice, but then, they were spending money, and after all, that's what she wanted."[10] Mattie also provided food to those who were down and out. Sometimes she even sheltered them in the tent she had formerly used as a brothel. It seemed as though everyone trusted her. Admirers and even Mattie herself liked to boast—wrongfully—that she was never declared a prostitute in any arrest record or Denver newspaper.

Mattie's biggest competitor was Leah J. Tehme, or Leah Fries, better known as Jennie Rogers. Jennie actually spelled her name "Leeah," and once she told local police her real surname was Calvington. Born to Mr. and Mrs. James Weaver, Jennie was said to hail from Pittsburgh and may have been married to a doctor at one time. The union proved too dull for Jennie, and she allegedly ran away with a steamboat captain named Rogers. After living in St. Louis for a few years, Jennie arrived just two years after Mattie in 1879. She purchased her first house on Holladay Street for $4,600 in 1880. There, it was said, the chief of police from St. Louis would come to visit, and Jennie even had a portrait of him hanging in her brothel.

In fact, Jennie's St. Louis paramour did more than pay the occasional visit. A story was widely circulated in later years that the police chief decided to assist Jennie in opening her Denver house of ill fame by blackmailing one of Denver's leading citizens. Apparently this man's first wife

Fig. 12. Jennie Rogers when she was quite young, sporting her ever-present emerald earrings. Later in life, she wore glasses and looked much more studious.

(Courtesy Colorado Historical Society.)

had pulled a disappearing act, and the gentleman next married into a wealthy Denver family. Jennie's St. Louis friend and other political adversaries began circulating the rumor that the first wife had been murdered and even buried the skull of an Indian woman found on the plains in the man's backyard. Next the St. Louis officer and two other men called at the man's home posing as investigators, conducted a search, and dug up the skull. The surprised tycoon knew he was innocent, but he also knew that such a scandal could ruin his political career. Accordingly, the man "donated" $17,780 to Jennie for a new house. Jennie's St. Louis friend disappeared, and the matter was forgotten until it was related years later by someone who remembered the story.

Jennie was a tidy, astute, and almost studious-looking woman who knew her business. But she also had a temper. In about 1889 Jennie married Jack Wood, a bartender at the Brown Palace Hotel, who was fourteen years younger. It was said Jennie shot Wood in Salt Lake City a few months later when she found him in the arms of another woman. When police asked why she did it, she exclaimed, "I shot him because I love him, damn him!"[11]

Jennie maintained a friendship with her competitor, Mattie Silks. When Denver adopted an ordinance requiring prostitutes to wear yellow armbands, Mattie and Jennie agreed to have their girls dress in yellow from head to toe and parade all over town. The ordinance was repealed. For a short time Mattie and Jennie enjoyed their spot at the top of Denver's red-light district.

There were complications in Jennie's life, however. Even the elite Jennie Rogers, known for her fine dress and excellent horsemanship, could not avoid the occasional brush with the law. In 1880 she was arrested along with madam Eva Lewis for racing their horses through town. The pastime seems to have been popular among prostitutes, as two other girls were seen doing the same thing on Boulder's Pearl Street in 1880. (Incidentally, some say that Pearl Street was actually named for a prostitute. Others say it was named for a respectable woman who was an early pioneer.) In 1881 Jennie made the papers after her horse slipped on some ice and she fell to the street in the middle of the red-light district. Three years later, the classy madam was sentenced to ten days in jail for vagrancy and for taking morphine. The arrest did little to limit Jennie's ambitions, however. In 1884 she built her own three-story brothel on Market Street with three parlors, a ballroom, a dining room, and fifteen suites.

Shortly after Jennie's new house of pleasure was complete, Cort Thomson, whose ex-wife had just died, and Mattie Silks were united in matrimony in Indiana. When the couple returned to Denver, Mattie found herself with yet another competitor, Belle Barnard (a.k.a. Birnard). Belle had her beginnings as a prostitute in Cheyenne, Wyoming. At the age of twenty-nine she gave birth to a daughter, Grace, whom she later claimed was a niece. By 1885 Belle had a stately, two-story brick brothel at 518 Holladay Street. (When the name of Holladay was changed to Market, the address changed to 1952 Market Street.)

Two years after marrying Mattie, Cort received a telegram saying that his daughter, presumably the one left behind in Georgetown, had died during childbirth. Her surviving baby daughter needed looking after. Mattie convinced Cort to adopt the child rather than put her in an orphanage, and it was said Mattie willingly purchased her ranch on the eastern plains at Wray as a suitable place to raise the girl. There are several mysteries surrounding the child that Mattie and Cort took in. Once, when Mattie took in an abused little girl, police arriving to take the girl back to her mother discovered another five-year-old named Theresa Thompson. It was speculated that Theresa may have been a daughter of Mattie and Cort, or even perhaps a child by Casey Silks who was adopted by Cort. Or she could have been Cort's granddaughter, for whom Mattie purchased the ranch at Wray. The ranch served other purposes as well, namely as a place to keep Mattie's twenty-one racehorses.

Throughout the mid-1880s, Mattie continued to bask in Denver's limelight. It was said that Mattie once agreed—under pressure from Denver's chamber of commerce and also Cort—to serve as a courtesan to the president of the St. Louis Railroad. Her mission was to convince the tycoon to extend his railroad to Denver. For a month Mattie and the railroad magnate posed as husband and wife while touring California. Ultimately the endeavor was unsuccessful, although the chamber did pay off a $5,000 note for Mattie in return for her efforts.

In 1887 Mattie purchased two connecting brothels at 1916 and 1922 Market Street for $14,000 as well as other real estate around Denver, including a brothel at 2019 Market Street. She also kept two or three call girls in uptown Denver hotels to run appointments she made for them. Mattie's girls were well cared for, receiving two meals a day and half of their earnings in return for paying room and board. Mattie's good business sense saw her through some tough times in Denver; during the winter of 1887–88, 179 women were arrested for prostitution. Much to the dismay of the Women's Christian Temperance Union, many of these women were jailed right along with male prisoners, guarded by male jailers. The

WCTU convinced the city council to secure a matron for its female prisoners. The permanent position went to Sadie Likens, the second matron police officer in the nation.

In about 1889 Jennie Rogers built what was to become the infamous House of Mirrors at 1942 Market Street. She also married Jack Wood, the lover she had once shot. Over time, 1942 Market Street became one of the most prominent establishments in Denver's red-light district. The Circus, a three-story brothel that also housed Jim Ryan's saloon, was located across from Jennie's place. Sadie Doyle, one of Jim's employees, later recalled a night in 1901 when she was thrown in jail. Later that night, after her release, the jail caught fire. Fay Stanley's parlor house was just down the street. Other famous red-light establishments of Denver included Ruth Jacobs's Silver Dollar Hotel, Miss Olga's, and Mamie Darling's.

There were twenty-seven rooms in all at the House of Mirrors, including a kitchen, ballroom, four parlors, a wine room, and sixteen bedrooms. The front parlor was furbished in mirrors from ceiling to floor. A single bathroom, luxurious for the time, serviced the house. Under Jennie's ownership, suites in the house were said to be well stocked with fancy furniture, commodes, slop jars, rockers, lace curtains, and even writing desks. Known for her love of grand and eccentric things, Jennie also had five stone faces adhered to the facade of the building, including a bust of herself at the top. There has been intense speculation about who the other faces represented, including a story that they depict those involved in the blackmailing of the rich man who gave Jennie the money for her house. But the truth about them will likely never be known. The exterior decor also came complete with fancy scrollwork in a variety of mysterious designs.

Another notorious brothel could be found at the Navarre, formerly the Brinker Collegiate Institute for young ladies wanting to learn "customary Christian virtues."[12] Known as the Hotel Richelieu in 1890, the stately hotel, saloon, and gambling hall had fallen into the hands of gamblers Ed Chase and Vaso Chucovich during a poker game. Chase and Chucovich renamed the place the Navarre after a sixteenth-century French king, Henry of Navarre, and added prostitution. Belle Malone and Mary Paxton were among the working girls at the Navarre, which also welcomed visiting girls from nearby brothels if no other girls were available.

Mattie Silks's troubles with Cort Thomson escalated in 1891, when she caught him with prostitute Lillie Dab of Leadville. Mattie sued for divorce but then forgave Cort and withdrew the suit. In the uproar, Mattie may have just plain missed out on Jennie Rogers's plans to sell the House of Mirrors. Madam Ella Wellington got it instead, and with it she automatically became a part of Jennie and Mattie's elite circle. When the madams and bar owners of Denver cooperated to produce the *Denver Red Book* in 1892, Ella was a prominent advertiser. The *Denver Red Book* was published just in time for the grand opening of the ritzy Brown Palace Hotel across the street, which allegedly had an underground rail system or tunnel running to the notorious Navarre.

As the most brazen of directories, the *Denver Red Book* listed ads for the Arcade Bar on Larimer, Silver State Cigars, Schlitz, and the Walhalla Club Rooms. Prostitutes listed therein included Blanche Brown, Belle Birnard, and Minnie A. Hall. Belle Birnard advertised fourteen rooms, five parlors, a music and dance hall, plus twelve boarders. Jennie Holmes outdid Belle with twenty-three rooms, three parlors, two ballrooms, a poolroom, and thirteen boarders. But madam Minnie Hall at 2045 Market Street took the prize with thirty rooms, a music and dance hall, five parlors, a Mikado parlor,[13] and twenty boarders. Minnie had purchased her house from Sybil Field. When the only known copy of the *Red Book* was found on the floor of a streetcar and eventually donated to the Colorado Historical Society, it was noted that two pages were missing. The missing pages might have contained advertising for Mattie Silks and the Navarre as well as other well-known hot spots.

Ella Wellington, Mattie Silks, and Jennie Rogers continued to prosper during 1893, despite the repeal of the Sherman Silver Purchase Act. Originally, the Sherman Act was meant to assist the public by requiring the U.S. government to purchase silver in order to boost the economy. The plan was simple enough, but did not pan out as well as expected. When Congress repealed the act and the government stopped buying silver, thousands of silver miners—including millionaire H. A. W. Tabor of Leadville and Denver—went broke overnight. As the silver boomtowns quickly depleted, hundreds of families flocked to Denver. A good number of destitute women approached Jennie Rogers for work. Jennie put them up in respectable boarding houses, but refused to let them work for her or anyone else. As money allowed, she gradually sent them home to their families instead.

Jennie's kind act was no doubt overshadowed by the shocking and tragic suicide of Ella Wellington in 1894 at the House of Mirrors. The former wife of Fred Bouse (or Bowse) of Omaha, Ella had forsaken her confining life as a wife and mother of two adopted children and run off with one Sam Cross. After Cross apparently left her in Salt Lake City, Ella had made her way to Denver in 1889, taken on the name Wellington, and gone into business in the red-light district. After purchasing the House of Mirrors from Jennie Rogers, Ella spared no expense in her advertising and business cards and seemed to be doing quite well.

On the evening of July 27, 1894, Ella was in attendance at her brothel, wearing a silk gown and a $2,000 necklace as well as several ruby and diamond rings. Ella's regret at leaving her husband became painfully apparent when some old friends of the former couple unexpectedly paid her a visit. Fred was remarried, they said, and was very happy. So were the children. The news was too much for Ella, who began babbling, "I too am happy, O so happy!" Then she abruptly started upstairs, exclaiming, "O I am so happy! So happy that I'll just blow my goddam brains out!" Upon reaching her bedroom, Ella did just that. Arapahoe County clerk William R. Prinn happened to be lying in Ella's bed at the time and later gave his statement to the coroner.

Poor Ella's story does not end there. After a funeral procession that took every available carriage in town, Ella was buried at Riverside Cemetery. Her most loyal admirer, Frederick N. Sturges, slept on top of her grave for several nights and purchased a plot next to Ella's. Within three weeks the heartbroken Sturges overdosed on morphine. In his pocket was a picture of Ella with a note written on the back: "Bury this picture of my own dear Ella beside me."[14]

The death of Ella Wellington seemed to be the beginning of several unlucky incidents in Denver's red-light district. The most prominent was a series of mysterious murders of prostitutes. Three murders in particular caught the eye of authorities, possibly because of their similarities: a towel had always been stuffed in the victim's mouth, and there was never a sign of forced entry. Thus the girls were assumed to have fallen victim to one of their customers.

The first woman to die was Lena Tapper, who was strangled in her home on Market Street in September. Next twenty-three-year-old Marie Contassot was strangled to death on October 28. Despite the deceased's swollen purple face, eyes bugging from their sockets, and the presence of a rope nearby, the coroner listed Marie's cause of death as unknown. Marie was from France, having come to America with her sister Eugenie some years before. In Denver Marie worked for Charles Chaloup, a Frenchman who served as her pimp. The number one suspect in Marie's death, however, was her beau Tony Saunders. Alternately known as Tony Sanders and

AN UNHAPPY QUEEN.

Startling and Tragic End of Ella Wellington's Life.

A BULLET SENT CRASHING THROUGH HER HEAD.

A Queen of the Denver Demi-Monde Dead on Her Bed from a Pistol Bullet—She Had Passed a Riotous Night, in Which Her Past Had Been Recalled by the Visit of Men Who Had Known Her as a Wife and Mother—Remorse of Keenest Character Seized Her as the Lights Paled Before the Sun—the Lights Paled Before the Sun—An Inquest To-Day.

Ella Wellington, queen of the Denver demi-monde, was found dead in her room a few minutes after 6 o'clock yesterday morning. A bullet from a 32-calibre revolver had been fired into the back of her head above the right ear. The aim had been true. The bullet took a downward course in crashing through skull and brain and lodged behind the left ear. Death had followed it surely and quickly.

When found the life had passed out of the body, gaudily robed with lace and expensive finery. Ella Wellington chose as her death clothes a close fitting silken garment with point lace falling from the sleeves and skirt. A necklace valued at $2,000 was about her neck, and her fingers were covered with rings set with diamonds and rubies. The bed was curtained with damasks and the finest lace, and throughout the room everything indicated that the occupants had lived in luxury, sinful as it may have been. Her life's blood had bespattered the silken gown and stained the white bed and downy pillows.

At 1942 Market street high revelry reigned all Thursday night. The place

THE SUICIDE.

Fig. 13. Ella Wellington committed suicide wearing a silk and lace gown, a $2,000 necklace, and diamond and ruby rings. Even wealth and success could not prevent some prostitutes from taking their own lives.

(Courtesy Colorado Historical Society.)

Antonio Santpietro, Saunders led a double life as both a Denver police-man and a pimp on Market Street. Marie had just moved in with Saunders a week before. After repeated questioning, however, Saunders was released.

Next police focused on Chaloup and Eugenie. Marie and Eugenie had been due to inherit a large sum of money from a relative in Paris, and Chaloup and Eugenie had just recently returned from a trip to France. Chaloup had also purchased property in Paris. Furthermore, friends and neighbors of Marie claimed her sister and Chaloup had planned to acquire the inheritance and leave Marie with nothing. Eugenie refused to deny or confirm any of the rumors. Chaloup claimed Marie had received $2,000 in property and jewelry from him and produced a signed receipt from her that released him from any further obligations to her. Neither Chaloup or Eugenie were charged with the murder.

Marie Contassot merited burial in Denver's Riverside Cemetery. After her original interment, Marie's body was moved to a plot purchased by Eugenie. Her grave was decorated by a large tombstone and a life-sized angel. The heartening inscription read:

> We regret the loss of our sister
> All of her family and friends
> Pray for her.[15]

In the wake of Marie Contassot's murder, Mattie Silks had iron bars installed on the windows of her brothel. By now the girls of the row were frightened, and Denver newspapers spread panic with headlines declaring "Jack the Ripper" was in town. They also dubbed Market Street "Strangler's Row." Despite upgraded security in the red-light district, a third murder happened in November, when Kiku Oyama was also found choked to death. After Oyama's murder, the better-class parlor houses shut down or shortened their business hours for a time. Most of the lower-class, one-room crib girls could not afford to cease business and were forced to remain open. Police began taking a harder look at murders that happened in the red-light district, but there were no more murders immediately after the death of Oyama.

At least two other unsolved murders are documented in Denver's red-light district. One was the killing of a black prostitute named Nettie Clark in the late 1890s, but Nettie's death was probably not associated with the killing sprees of 1894. In 1903 yet another woman, Mabel Brown, was stran-gled in her home on Market Street. Again the killer was never caught, but

Fig. 14. In a rare act
of sympathy, Denver's
Riverside Cemetery
willingly accepted
Marie Contassot's
body for burial.

(Courtesy Buck Gibbons.)

by then the murders of 1894 were only a faint memory on fast-moving
Market Street.

In about May of 1895, the House of Mirrors came back to Jennie
Rogers's ownership. A couple of years later, Jennie and Mattie Silks were
only slightly overshadowed by another Denver prostitute, Verona (a.k.a.
Fannie) Baldwin. In 1883 in San Francisco, the British beauty had made
big headlines after she shot her millionaire cousin, E. J. "Lucky" Baldwin,
in the arm. Verona claimed Lucky had sexually assaulted her while she was
teaching school at his expansive ranch. Baldwin survived, about which
Verona commented, "I ought to have killed him. Yes, I ought to have killed
him at the ranch."[16] Verona was just twenty-three years old at the time.
Three years after she was acquitted due to Lucky's refusal to testify, Verona

sued her cousin for child support. Afterward he successfully committed her to an insane asylum. She fought him, along with the general public, and was released.

In the late 1890s Verona arrived in Denver and purchased a house at 2020 Market Street. Her life in Denver appeared to be fairly uneventful, the exception being an 1898 newspaper article, which reported that Verona had taken in a young girl calling herself Mary Anderson. Mary, fresh off the train from Wyoming, was seeking employment at various brothels. Escorting her was a strange woman who had approached her at the employment office and talked her into becoming a prostitute. Madam Baldwin, however, upon seeing the girl was truly innocent and a virgin at that, convinced Mary to return home and notified the police to put her on the next train home. This they did, paying for the ticket themselves. Verona was in business in Denver for over twelve years. She eventually retired and died in the 1940s.

In 1898 Mattie Silks and Cort Thomson followed up a tour to Great Britain with an excursion to Alaska, where Mattie opened a temporary brothel in Dawson City. The endeavor lasted only three months due to Mattie's aversion to the cold weather, but it was said she netted $38,000 for her efforts. Upon returning to Colorado, Cort continued with his wild ways while Mattie got back to business. In April of 1900, after several weeks of debauchery involving alcohol, opium, and the celebration of his birthday, Cort Thomson died sitting in a rocking chair at the Commercial Hotel in Wray. Mattie was by his side, and she paid for his funeral costs. What became of the child Mattie and Cort were raising is unknown, but most historians say Mattie adopted her. Some speculate the girl was then educated in some faraway school and raised to become a respectable woman.

Jennie Rogers also suffered hardships. Jack Wood had died in 1896 at the age of thirty-eight. Competition along Market Street was ever growing, with prostituties like Mildred Ackley and Pearl Adams joining the ranks. The year 1902 proved to be even more stressful: Jennie's beloved dog died, and she was diagnosed with Bright's disease. To escape her woes and pressure from authorities, she temporarily moved to Chicago, where she opened another brothel. There she met a politician named Archibald T. Fitzgerald, a man twenty years her junior, whom she married at Hot Springs, Arkansas, in 1904. Shortly afterward Jennie returned to Denver for the funeral of prostitute Lizzie Preston, a much-admired colleague who had also been a friend of Mattie Silks. Back in Chicago, she found out

Fitzgerald was still married to someone else, left him, and came back to Denver for good in 1907.

In Denver Jennie forgave Fitzgerald. She lived at the House of Mirrors but periodically made short excursions with him to Arkansas. She died on October 29, 1909, having willed her estate to her sister and a niece and nephew. She was buried in Denver's Fairmont Cemetery under the name Leah J. Wood, next to her first husband, Jack. Fitzgerald contested her will and claimed half of her estate. He eventually settled for $5,000 in cash, jewelry, and some property in Illinois.

In 1910 or 1911 Mattie Silks purchased the House of Mirrors for $14,000. Mattie immediately moved in with her longtime housekeeper, Janie Green, and commissioned a local tile worker to inlay her name, "M. Silks," on the front step. It was like putting a final, victorious stamp on the red-light district. At last, Mattie Silks was the reigning queen of Denver's tenderloin district.

Chapter Four

How Colorado City Came to Be

꾨

All about Rahab

Of Jerico's Rahab, we've read the report
That she made her living with amorous sport,
She concealed on her roof both of Joshua's spies—
(Is it possible they became clientele guys?)
Down a rope of red drapes, they fled from her shack;
Then to their camp, they sneaked their way back.
To Joshua they said: "We got some good dope;
But we cut a deal that you'll honor, we hope.
You see, there's this bimbo who hid us at night;
Please keep her household safe from the fight.
She'll hang a red curtain right on her wall;
Our boys must not mess with that whorelady's hall!"
So her signal was honored—fortuitous drape!
And Joshua's rowdies went elsewhere to rape.
Now that is the reason, to this very day
Crimson curtains are hung where hookers do play.
                              —Charles F. Anderson

The Pikes Peak gold rush of 1859 created a stir not just in Denver but in other parts of the state as well. Hundreds of prospectors and merchants were making their way to the gold fields on the western slope of Colorado, often encountering angry Native Americans in their quests. The trails south of Denver included Ute Pass, an ancient Indian trail that skirted the base of Pikes Peak near today's Colorado Springs. Prospectors J. B. Kennedy, Dr. J. L. Shank, and D. M. Slaughter, the first men to stake claims in South Park, were later killed by Indians near Kenosha Pass. Even as late as 1869, Major James B. Thompson noted two hundred Utes who had a winter hunting camp near today's Cripple Creek. Throughout the winter of 1874–75, Ute leader Ouray camped near Florissant with six hundred other Utes.

Despite a few skirmishes with Indians, however, white settlers continued migrating into the Pikes Peak Region. The trail from Colorado City actually began at the opening to several canyons comprising Ute Pass, and it wasn't long before a town formed to furnish supplies for travelers heading west via the pass. When it was first established in 1859, Colorado City was every bit a notoriously rough western town. Long before Colorado Springs came along with its antiliquor laws and elite citizenship, Colorado City sprouted as a thriving supply town. The place was a virtual melting pot for easterners who swarmed the state in search of gold. All the required elements were present: ramshackle houses, churches, a school, hotels, and saloons. The first tavern was opened in 1860 by John George. Accordingly, Colorado City's population grew to include enterprising merchants, faithful families, hopeful miners—and prostitutes. There is no doubt that the soiled doves who flocked to Colorado City saw golden opportunities. Trains and

Fig. 15. Colorado City shortly after it was founded. Within a year of its inception, the town had at least one saloon.

(From Special Collections, courtesy Pikes Peak Library District.)

freighters stopped daily on their way to the gold fields, initially bringing lots of single and lonely men. In those early days, the business was hardly regulated, and these women had the freedom to work and live where they chose.

In 1861 Colorado City was made the capital of Colorado Territory. A series of courthouses were built in an effort to turn Colorado City from a blue-collar, transient town into a first-class city. The most notable of these was a courthouse located inside of what was known as Doc Garvin's cabin. The tiny, one-story log cabin was originally located at 2608 West Colorado Avenue, but has been moved several times in the last century.[1] Colorado City aspired to become the state capital, but its efforts were in vain. Visiting politicians were less than impressed with the rough and wild city. The capital was moved to Denver, and in 1873 the new, elite, and ostentatious city of Colorado Springs managed to win the county seat. Founded by Quaker William Jackson Palmer, Colorado Springs sought to be the "Saratoga of the West," with fancy homes, nice hotels, and a variety of tuberculosis sanitoriums, which were all the rage among suffering easterners. Furthermore, Palmer's wife, Queen, talked her husband into outlawing liquor houses within the city limits. It stood to reason, then, that Colorado City should excel where Colorado Springs did not. A variety of activities, from prize fighting to prostitution to drinking to dancing, went on at all hours around what is now the 2500 block of Colorado Avenue.

In fact, much of Colorado City's new commerce was generated by Colorado Springs. Although residents and authorities in Colorado Springs frowned on Colorado City, many of the former's residents were regular patrons of "Old Town," whose saloons and sporting houses were quickly growing in number. Do-gooders in Colorado Springs tried to blame the Colorado Midland Railroad for bringing in undesirables and encouraging the saloons, parlor houses, and Chinese opium dens in Colorado City. But the fact was Colorado City already had these elements long before the railroad came through in the 1880s. Plus, the town was sandwiched between Colorado Springs and Manitou Springs, so passage through Colorado City was absolutely necessary in order to access Ute Pass.

In an effort to mask the activities of Colorado Springs and Colorado City's more prominent citizens, tunnels were built from the Denver & Rio Grande Railroad tracks south of Washington (now Cucharras Street) that led to the gambling houses and brothels of Colorado City. Later, tunnels were also built from the north side of Colorado Avenue to the south side, so visitors to the casinos and bordellos could avoid being seen. From south-side gambling houses like Jacob Schmidt's at 2611 W. Colorado, the

Argyle block, and Geising & Perbula's Saloon, patrons like "Eat 'Em Up Jake" could slip out the back way and through a tunnel or a discreet hallway to the bordellos across the alley.

Oddly, the first twenty-five years of Colorado City's growth are rather obscure. The 1879 city directory shows a mere ninety-nine entries, perhaps due to the transient population. By 1880 Colorado Springs was fairly booming, but Colorado City was still not much more than a village with a few streets and no visible red-light district. That's not to say that some women did not ply their trade in the city limits, especially in 1884, when the population surged to four hundred souls. That year, there were four known saloons, operated by Henry Coby, Al Green, John Keller, and Charlie Roberts.

By 1886 saloon owners included N. Byron Hames, with his Hoffman House; Alfred Green; Dave Rees of the Windsor Café; John Keller, whose Ash Saloon also served as a general store; Charles Roberts; John Rohman; Jack Wade; and Larry Watts.

The Largest Stock of Old Goods IN THE WEST.

GREEN RIVER WHISKY, "The Whisky without a Headache."

"The Hoffman,"

N. B. Hames, Propr.

COLORADO CITY, COLO.

Tony Faust's Celebrated St. Louis Beer on Draught.

F. B. Rice & Co's Famous Mercantile Cigars.

Fig. 16. N. Byron Hames's Hoffman House was one of the fanciest saloons in Colorado City. City directories advertised the bar with colored inserts such as this.

(From the author's collection.)

In all, there were twelve to sixteen saloons. There were also two justices of the peace, who were apparently trying to gain some sort of order in rowdy little Old Town. One of the earliest attempts to close down gambling was noted in the November 26, 1887 issue of the *Colorado Springs Gazette Telegraph*, which unaccountably reported, "The gambling houses of Colorado City have re-opened and are now running full blast."[2]

Apparently, city authorities had already attempted unsuccessfully to shut gambling down. With all those saloons, more than a few prostitutes were surely present as well. One of the first prostitutes on record at Colorado City was probably Mrs. Isabelle Semple, who resided on Washington Avenue in 1886. Isabelle died in 1901. A more famous early madam was Minnie Smith, a.k.a. Lou Eaton, a sometime gambler who was well known throughout Colorado, including in Buena Vista, Creede, and Denver's Market Street, where she was known as both Lou Eaton and Dirty Alice. In Colorado City Minnie purchased a large old two-story house on the south side of Colorado Avenue. She was in her mid-thirties at the time and described as "a slender little woman, not good looking and a vixen when aroused."[3] Vixen was right; Minnie was well known for her terrible temper and was in trouble a lot during her short stay in Colorado City. Once she was brought in on charges of nearly beating a lawyer to death with the butt of a gun, and early magazines sported engravings of her horsewhipping a man she caught cheating at cards.

By 1888 the number of saloons in Colorado City had grown to twenty-three and included those run by such notable operators as T. R. Lorimer, Henry Coby, Byron Hames, and Alfred Green. A glassworks factory at Wheeler and 25th Street manufactured local liquor bottles. The population had swelled to fifteen hundred, mostly due to industry growth as the Colorado Midland Railroad took root and a number of factories appeared. Nearly thirty years after Colorado City's inception, the city fathers finally decided it was time to create such necessities as a police department and appointed city positions. Police magistrate Renssolear Smith oversaw the first of two city halls, which was built at 2902 West Colorado Avenue. By then shoot-outs, drunken brawls, and "good ol' boy" fights had become common sights, and horse racing up and down Colorado Avenue was a popular pastime.

In the midst of this uproar, a number of single women were living on Colorado Avenue. Many of their occupations are unclear but for that of Mrs. Bell McDaniel, better known as Laura Bell McDaniel. Within a year of her arrival, the enterprising woman had access to twenty-four saloons and only a handful of competitors. Laura Bell's sisters of the underworld included Miss Belle Barlow, Miss Daisy Bell, Miss Fernie Brooks, Mamie Maddern, Emma Wilson, and Hazy Maizie, a laudanum addict. In those early days of rampant prostitution at Colorado City, most of the women seem to have plied their trade along Colorado Avenue. When the Argyle block at 2603–2607 West Colorado was built in 1889, the downstairs was used as a saloon, with gaming rooms and retail establishments. Mr. Connell, the original owner, later sold the building, and the upstairs was divided into apartments and used by prostitutes.

As late as 1890, women such as Minnie Smith were still conducting business on Colorado Avenue. A number of single women, such as Miss Lizzie Thompson, Miss Kate Herzog, Miss Edna Ingraham, Mary Dean, Fannie E. Eubanks, M. J. Duffield, J. Erlinger, Miss M. H. Richards, and Daisy Johnson, however, began appearing on Washington Avenue (now Cucharras Street) one block south of Colorado as well. The 1890 Sanborn Fire Insurance maps do not show any "female boarding"—the early term for female-occupied brothels—on either Washington or the main drag, Colorado Avenue. A number of saloons on Colorado, however, are depicted as having rooms above them or behind them that might have served as brothels. Most conveniently, the Denver & Rio Grande Railroad had by then laid its tracks down Washington Avenue, providing much opportunity for prostitutes to do business with male travelers passing through town. Sanborn maps for 1892 show "female boarding" in two buildings each on the north and south sides of Washington Avenue between 1st and 2nd streets. Two other notable women on Washington, a physician named Mrs. N. Albrecht and a "colored" woman named Mrs. Conrad Alesatha, are worth mentioning because they too may have had something to do with the red-light district. Other girls, such as Miss Fernie Brooks, were living yet another block south on Grand Avenue.

The new police magistrate, J. J. Guth, was by now hearing a series of complaints from citizens about the growing red-light population. In late January 1890, the *Colorado City Iris* commented on saloon owner Byron Hames, who made a speech on behalf of prostitutes at a mass meeting. In the wake of Hames's speech, police responded by conducting raids in May. One arrestee was Mamie Maddern, who was operating out of a shack. Police arrested Mamie and several men. One of the men, Fred Thornton, later returned and, according to the newspaper, began to "frolic with Mamie." Customer Henry Pettis objected to this and shot at Thornton three times, hitting him twice.[4]

In 1891 there were finally enough established brothels in Colorado City to merit a listing in the city directory. The six bordellos were discreetly listed as boarding houses, and the directory also listed twenty-one saloons. One of the taverns was the Palace at 25th Street and Colorado Avenue, which listed Frank James, brother of Jessie James, as a card dealer. Frank was no stranger to the red-light districts of Colorado, having been written up in the *Boulder County Herald* in 1882 for brandishing a revolver in a Boulder bordello and

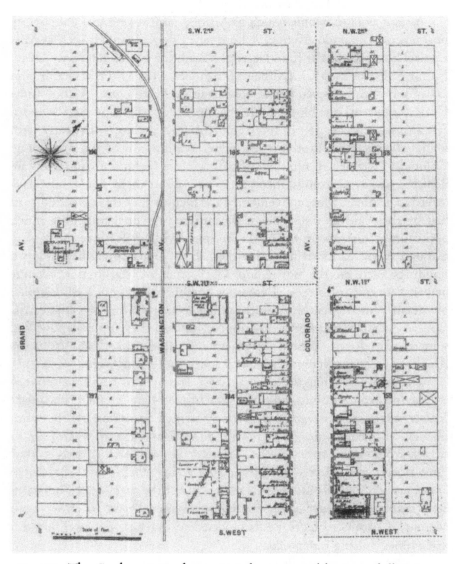

Fig. 17. The Sanborn map from 1892 shows several houses of ill repute, marked "F.B." for "female boarding," along Washington Avenue. Note the large number of saloons along Colorado Avenue.

(Courtesy Cripple Creek District Museum.)

making threats. After frightening several working girls, James was arrested and hauled to the cooler to rethink his actions. Other notable places in Colorado City included Byron Hames's Hoffman House at 2508 Colorado Avenue, the Nickel Plate at 2528 Colorado Avenue, the Bucket of Blood, located along Fountain Creek at 25th Street, and the Silver State at 2602 Colorado Avenue. Nearly every saloon in Colorado City stayed open twenty-four hours a day and usually had gambling upstairs.

The city authorities were no doubt up in arms over so many saloons and the disgraceful lack of decorum they displayed. Both the saloons and the brothels were quickly escalating out of control. In January of 1891 a girl named Clara who worked for Laura Bell McDaniel attempted suicide by taking eight grams of morphine. The newspaper predicted she would die, although she was being attended to by a physician. Little else was revealed about Clara, except that she had recently migrated from Denver and wore eyeglasses.

Later that month Minnie Smith made a trip to Denver under her pseudonym, Dirty Alice. She was arrested on the 24th for intoxication and released on the condition she would come right back and pay her fine. Instead Minnie disappeared and was thought to have gone to Creede, where she used her money from Colorado City to open a well-known sporting house. Then in May banjo player William Clark of the Crystal Palace went on a drinking spree. When he couldn't sleep, Clark took some morphine and overdosed. The physician called to his side misdiagnosed his malady as a "brain infection" and administered even more morphine. Clark died at the tender age of thirty.

The Crystal Palace was no doubt a rough place. The dance hall and brothel probably opened in about 1889 when Bob Ford, the killer of Jessie James, was dealing faro there. If the stories of both Bob Ford and Jesse James's brother Frank James working there at different times are true, they are mighty ironic stories indeed. By May of 1890 it was also known as the Crystal Palace Theater. Later it was also referred to as simply the Palace. On April 20, 1892, the *Colorado City Iris* reported on one Ed Andress, proprietor of the Crystal Palace. Andress was arrested for being drunk and disorderly and fined $10 and costs. Unable to pay the entire fine in cash, Andress threw in his watch. He was arrested again the next day for running a disorderly house. This time the fine was $58.05 and Andress lost his license.

Later that year city authorities decided to exercise more control over the red-light district by building a new city hall at 119 South 26th Street, literally around the corner from the district.

Fig. 18. Colorado City's second city hall was within a stone's throw of the red-light district. This photograph was taken in the 1980s, long after the city hall closed.

(From the author's collection.)

By then the sporting houses on Washington were so active that the original courthouse, four blocks away, was too far for the frequent police trips. Colorado City authorities realized that the city could make more money from fining brothels each month than it could by closing them. Accordingly, the city assessed fines for a variety of violations regarding prostitution—and began reeling the money in with a vengeance.

Still, arresting sinners proved a difficult job for Colorado City authorities. Many of the early town trustees and officers were saloon owners themselves. To make matters worse, most prostitutes had no problem paying a little ol' fine if it meant they could stay in business. The surge in prostitution in Colorado City during the 1890s alarmed city officials as well as the media. The *Colorado Springs Gazette* pounced on every chance to report on the goings-on in the district. When Bell Barker died of a morphine overdose in 1893, the paper reported that her Colorado City friends buried her "in good style" but that Billie Huffman, "the tin horn who was living with her," left the country.[5]

Similar sentiments were expressed about Minnie Smith. After Colorado City, Minnie had gone to Creede and then Cripple Creek. There, she allegedly ran a rooming house that was actually a parlor house over a saloon on Bennett Avenue. Unfortunately, forty-five-year-old Minnie was not distinguished enough for Cripple Creek, and the competition proved too tough for her. When Minnie committed suicide with morphine in Cripple Creek in 1893 or 1894, her body was brought back to Colorado City for burial. Minnie was actually buried in Evergreen Cemetery beside her first husband, Royster Smith. Allegedly, Minnie's grave mate on her other side was Bruce Younger of the Younger Gang. When Bruce sickened and died "an ugly death" in 1890, the underworld of Colorado City paid for his funeral and gave him the plot next to the Smiths. (No records of these burials appear to exist.) Minnie also left a considerable estate, but what became of it is unknown.

Drug overdoses, both intentional and accidental, were not at all unusual. In November another Crystal Palace employee, Oscar Bills, died from smoking opium. A Chinaman known as Kim Yonk was arrested in connection with the death because Bills had recently visited his opium den. Around the same time Miss Remee, a "variety artist" at the Crystal Palace, took morphine in a suicide attempt. She was saved but threatened to do it again. Finally, in January of 1894, a dance hall girl from the Crystal Palace was arrested for robbery and thrown in jail. Authorities had had enough and ordered the place closed, and proprietor C. N. Hamlin was fined $55 for keeping a disorderly house. Hamlin married one of his girls, Mrs. Hazel Levitt, just a few months later.

The Women's Christian Temperance Union, better known as the WCTU, was waiting for chances such as the closing of the Crystal Palace. In 1894 the WCTU submitted a petition to impose hours of operation on all saloons, bowling alleys, halls, and "other resorts." Only 152 people signed the petition, but city authorities had just begun. A widely publicized raid in 1896 was followed by a series of new ordinances: "Keepers of disorderly houses shall not refuse to admit officers. Officers may break doors and arrest with or without warrant." Getting caught in the act of prostitution was a $300 fine, with additional punishments for frequenting opium joints, houses of prostitution, or dance halls. Furthermore, music was not even permitted at houses of ill fame or saloons.[6]

The new ordinances went into effect almost immediately, but a raid in February netted only two girls and their visitors. In April of 1896 another police raid netted thirty-three arrests, plus two vagrants who stole a pair of clippers from a local barbershop. But still the girls came, and many stayed. Both Ida Anderson and Mary Franklin moved to Colorado City in 1896, staying as late as 1900 and 1906 respectively. Colorado City reacted to the influx of newcomers by passing even more new ordinances as misdemeanor offenses. They included laws against impersonating an officer, concealing weapons, nudity, indecent dress, cross-dressing, selling lewd or indecent books or pictures, public or private drunkenness, keno tables, faro banks, shuffleboards, playing bagatelle or cards, gambling, possessing gambling devices, and disorderly houses.[7]

Also within the new ordinances houses of ill fame were banned within three miles of the city limits. Houses of prostitution that violated the ordinance were fined $300. Prostitutes were fined $10–$50. Dance halls were assessed a $25–$100 fine. A new curfew was also imposed: 9 P.M. from March 1 to August 31 and 8 P.M. from September 1 to February 28 for anyone under the age of fifteen. Saloons, which were also still forbidden to play music, were not allowed to admit minors. Finally, saloons, tippling houses, and dramshops were to be closed from midnight to 6 A.M. and all day on Sundays. For a few years the new ordinances seemed to work, although Sanborn maps indicate the presence of more brothels on Washington Avenue and twenty-two saloons along Colorado Avenue.

Women Involved with Prostitution in Colorado City, 1900–1901[8]

Name	Address	Notes
Sybil Brooks	North side Washington between 6th and 7th streets	Died 1901
Hester Elliott	North side Washington between 6th and 7th streets	Madam
Nina Gibson	West side S. 7th Street— near Washington	
Anna M. Gillette	South side Washington between 7th and 8th streets	Domestic
Nellie Hill	710 Washington	
Hazel Lynam	North side Washington between 6th and 7th streets	Madam
Emma Williams	708 Washington	Cook

Chief of police George G. Birdsall, who was appointed in 1900, vowed that things would change. One of Birdsall's first moves was to prohibit gambling in 1901. But by then the shady ladies of Colorado City were running amok, aided by such prominent establishments in the district as the Anheuser-Busch Brewing Association at the southwest corner of 6th Street

Fig. 19. George Birdsall reigned as chief of police in Colorado City for over a decade and promised to clean up the town. Despite his efforts, however, Birdsall had a hard time chasing off the soiled doves of Colorado City.

(Special Collections and Archives,
courtesy Tutt Library, Colorado College.)

and Washington. Throughout the year, more and more girls showed up to ply their trade. Some left, some didn't. Business flourished as even more saloons and gambling halls opened. Even girls like Georgia Hayden, who had been in Cripple Creek since 1893 and was a favorite of mining millionaire Jimmy Burns, came to try their luck. Among the new girls were veterans like Laura Bell McDaniel and Mamie Majors.

By 1902 there were still twenty-seven saloons and more than thirty combined saloons and gambling halls. In addition, a large number of "dressmakers" and other single women were occupying either side of the red-light district on Washington Avenue. The brothels along Washington included the Union Hotel at 708 Washington, the Central Hotel at the northwest corner of Washington and 6th Street, and eight houses in the 600 block.[9] Prostitution was going strong in Colorado City.[10]

Chapter Five

Women of the Western Slope and Central Colorado

❧

Oh, the lust for mountain gold dust
Brought us lusty mountain men
Who through lust for mountin' women,
Quickly lost their gold again.

—E.L.

Harsh winters and precarious lifestyles awaited those ladies who dared venture through central Colorado and on to the western slope beginning in the late 1850s and early 1860s. Literally hundreds and possibly thousands of tiny camps and cities, some no more than two cabins big, abounded. A scattering of roads and trails led to these settlements, whose commodities may or may not have provided food, clothing, or medical help. Yet venture these women did, traipsing from camp to camp or city to city.

One of the earliest camps to provide sporting houses was Boulder. After its inception in 1858, the population fluctuated in accordance with gold discoveries nearby. From harboring nearly 1,000 citizens in 1859, the population had dwindled by the summer of 1860 to a mere 174 people. Unlike the ratio of men to women elsewhere, 43 of these inhabitants were female. The city was incorporated in 1871, and the town fathers adopted an ordinance against prostitution in 1873. At first Boulder's houses of ill repute were scattered throughout town. Soon, however, most of the houses were congregating at the end of Railroad Street or Waters Street (now Canyon Boulevard) between the 1900 and 2100 blocks. Reigning madams in 1877 included Julie "Frenchy" Nealis near the corner of what is now Broadway and Walnut. A Canadian lass named Susan Brown, possibly also known as

Mrs. L. Morrow, ran two separate brothels in the 1900 block. In the wee hours of the morning of January 30, 1878, one of the houses burned, causing a loss estimated between $2,400 and $3,500. The *Colorado Banner* noted that this was the seventh time Susan Brown had suffered a fire.[1]

Susan's seamy reputation was set in stone. She delighted in fighting one madam Mary Day in public, and the two women were suspected of setting fire to one another's brothels. The *Colorado Banner* reported in July of 1878, just six months after Susan Brown's fire, that Mary Day's bordello had also burned. Madam Day lost no time in confronting Madam Brown, and each accused the other of setting the respective fires. The ensuing scuffle left both women with black eyes and cuts, and Mary Day paid $19 in court costs for causing the fray. In fact, fire was a common misadventure in Boulder. When a blacksmith shop near the red-light district caught fire in 1879, the papers noted that a dozen women of the demimonde came to watch the conflagration.

By 1880 five bawdy houses were in operation, including the White or Bon Ton House. Built in 1867 and considered the second finest building in town, the Bon Ton was owned by a respectable Boulder family before being converted to a bordello in the 1870s. Twenty-five-year-old madam Susan Brown kept three girls: Bessie Pound, Alice Thomas, and Frances Vale. Her bordello was in full swing, and the illustrious lady's success even allowed her to build two respectable houses as rentals at 18th Street and Spruce in 1882. If Susan Brown was indeed Mrs. L. Morrow, she passed away on March 21, 1886. By then, local papers were voicing their discontent. "The first thing a person sees on lighting from the cars in Boulder," complained the *Boulder County Herald,* "and the last seen on getting on the train are these institutions of infamy."[2] In August three hundred respectable Boulder ladies signed a petition against the red-light district and presented it to city council.

Indeed, the city of Boulder seems to have been rife with shameful cases involving its prostitutes. A news item in 1881 told of two young ladies, on their way from a prayer meeting, who were accosted by a pimp from the row. After fleeing into a local store, the girls were escorted home by a Mr. Robinson. Their assailant was never caught. In 1886 a new brothel opened in what had been Boulder's first schoolhouse. The house burned in 1890. Knife fights at madam Mary Etta Kingsley's were common. Etta first appeared in Boulder in 1882 at the age of about thirty-three. In 1888 the marshal was called to Etta's house, where he found the large black madam wielding a ten-inch carving knife at another working girl and arrested both women. The divine Ms. Kingsley did have a soft side, however, and even purchased a burial plot for one of her girls, Mamie Price, after Mamie overdosed on cocaine in 1888. Etta died in 1902.

In 1884 black prostitute Mollie Gordon was brought to court with her white patron and charged with fornication. Both parties offered to marry in order to justify their actions. The idea of interracial marriage, which was deemed illegal, incensed the judge and both were fined. Neither Mollie nor her partner could pay and went to jail. Other antics in Boulder came in such feminine forms as Lottie Diamond, Grace Henderson, Rosa Hessey, Regina Hetrick, Mrs. William Locke, Nellie Meeks, Dot Nelson, Marie Paige, Mamie Pratt, Rae Rogers, Lot Williams, and a girl calling herself Mountain Pink (she was identified by newspapers as one Alf Powell).

Surrounding cities learned their lessons from Boulder. In 1881, two years after a fire that nearly wiped it out, the mining town of Caribou in Boulder County voted to outlaw gamblers and loose women from their new community. Most surprisingly, the law was easy to uphold, perhaps because Caribou was a most uncomfortable place to live anyway. The town was located at an elevation of nearly ten thousand feet, subject to one hundred-mile-an-hour winds, and suffered terrible snowstorms with drifts that could top twenty-five feet in height. Prostitutes plying their trade within the community of six hundred were easy to spot, and besides, there was no railroad to Caribou.

In answer to Caribou's new law, the shady ladies, gamblers, and saloon keepers relocated to the old mining town of Cardinal two miles south of Caribou. Known alternately as Cardinal City and New Cardinal, the revitalized town was a true "sin city" occupied specifically by saloon keepers and prostitutes for vices and pleasures of the flesh. From there, the girls could service those who made clandestine trips not only from Caribou but also from the nearby mining towns of Nederland, Blackhawk, and Central City. Between 1878 and 1883 there were some fifteen hundred people at Cardinal, some of whom had already been living there when the sinful outcasts of Caribou arrived. The business district included a post office, stores, and a boardinghouse.

Cardinal was just the beginning. Another early town was Breckenridge, now a ski and tourist mecca, established in 1860. Like Cardinal, Breckenridge was unusual in that its soiled doves were not located right in town; they were across the Blue River west of town. Those wishing to visit the Blue Goose, the Columbine Rest, the Pines, or any other house of prostitution had to cross the river to find them. Breckenridge was one of only a handful of towns whose red-light district flourished outside the city limits. Another was Hahn's Peak, whose Poverty Flats above town contained both saloons and brothels. At the northern city of Jamestown, prostitutes lived in an area alternately known as Lower Jimtown or Bummerville. Occasionally the women grew weary of their confinement and ventured to town. One resident recalled a day when the ladies of Breckenridge's red-light resort made a memorable trip to the city. "[T]hey hired a fancy rig from the livery stable and went for a wild ride up and down the streets. They stopped at saloons for fresh inspiration and descended upon the stores whence respectable shoppers fled. They were finally routed and returned to their domain by the sheriff and some hardy aides."[3]

On the western slope, Lake City was home to one of the earliest red-light districts in the region. The district was located on the south end of Bluff Street in an area known as Hell's Acre. Also known to frequent Hell's Acre were some of the roughest thieves and murderers around. The San Juan Central dance house was among the rowdiest in the state, owned by two outlaws named George Betts and James Browning who were eventually lynched for killing the sheriff. The goings-on in Lake City were typical for the time, but the red-light population was nothing compared to another western slope city, Silverton. No sooner had Silverton's post office been established in 1875 than a bevy of soiled doves began flocking into town. The first and best known of these was Jane Bowen, a.k.a. the Sage Hen, who first appeared in Silverton with her husband, William Bowen. William invested in mining, while Jane ran Silverton's first variety theater.

Within a year the Bowens had constructed a combination saloon, dance hall, and bordello called Westminster Hall after Jane's home in London. In a short time, however, the place became known as the Sage Hen's Dance Hall after Jane's colorful nickname. Jane Bowen's appearance in Silverton was followed by that of Alice Morris, who purchased the first recorded brothel in September of 1878. By 1879 Silverton had forty saloons and dance halls, twenty-seven gambling dens, and eighteen brothels. Gambling and prostitutes were available twenty-four hours a day. City ordinances that year included laws against prostitution that decreed bawdy houses were to pay $50–$300 per month and prostitutes $10–$100. The ordinances also assessed fines for any saloons or gambling houses allowing lewd women or prostitutes.

During the harsh winter months the fines lessened, as prostitutes migrated to warmer climates and certain saloons and hotels closed until spring. But the summer months saw houses of prostitution running full blast, welcoming such newcomers as Molly Foley. Born in Scotland, Molly first arrived in Colorado in 1864 and came to Silverton at the age of forty-two in 1880. There, she opened up shop as a madam and employed crib girls. Alongside her establishment were Alice Hanke's, who bought Alice Morris's old place, and Mrs. Ellen Murry's.

In the meantime, Jane Bowen built a new residence directly behind the Sage Hen. When Jane and William adopted an eleven-year-old girl, city officials barely seemed to bat an eye. In fact, the Bowen's respectable status in Silverton is not surprising. Like the neighboring town of Ouray, many early brothel landlords in Silverton were respectable citizens with families. Still, authorities in Silverton kept their eyes peeled for any wrongdoing, and on June 30, 1881, the *San Juan Herald* commented, "The brazen-faced effrontery shown by some of the Amazons of [Silverton] as exhibited upon the public streets and thoroughfares, is becoming a nuisance to every decent and respectable citizen."[4] Then in September, prostitute Bronco Lou was arrested for slipping a mickey into some miner's drink and robbing him of $350. Slowly but surely, the citizens of Silverton were becoming outraged at such bold antics.

The coming of the Denver & Rio Grande Railroad to Silverton in 1882 increased the influx of prostitutes as well as the general populace. Silverton's brothels varied from combination saloons and dance halls to tiny one-room cribs. The population at the time was three thousand and growing. Suicides also escalated; Mollie Durant was just one unfortunate who, after surviving a morphine suicide attempt, died a few days later of pneumonia. In 1883 Silverton had twenty-nine saloons and no fewer than 117 working girls. The numbers stayed steady through 1884. Most of the saloons lined Green Street, the main drag, but prostitution was limited to Blair Street one block southeast. More ordinances were enacted, including an attempt to confine dance halls and bordellos to one area. Some of the girls, it seemed, had been so bold as to build their brothels within a few doors of city hall. In answer, the Bowens moved their business out of the glare of the main street to their residence in the back and expanded the building.

More arrests followed. In 1884 prostitute Lizzie Thompson, alias Lizzie Fisher, was arrested just six months after arriving in town. Blanche DeVille, another chronic troublemaker, was arrested no fewer than four times for theft. Blanche's career, at least in Silverton, ended when she was injured after being thrown from a horse. In 1887, after a brief stint in Denver, that old-timer Molly Foley finally made the newspapers after she was arrested for some unknown crime but discharged due to lack of evidence. In 1888

Fig. 20. Silverton's notorious Blair Street was much subdued by the 1950s. Today the red-light district houses restaurants and shops.

(From the author's collection.)

Molly was in the news again, this time for having a fistfight with Lizzie Fisher. Molly was destined to make the newspapers several more times, including the mistaken report of her death in 1896.

Still, Silverton appeared almost saddened by the July 14, 1889 suicide of Nettie Lewis. Nettie, a slim brunette from an upstanding Washington Avenue family in Brooklyn, had been working for madam Minnie Strong in Silverton, having recently arrived from Denver. Nettie's first job in Silverton resulted in her termination, as she was described as being "not a good rustler and too much of a lady."[5] Minnie Strong's place did not serve beer, so one night Nettie purchased a bucket to share in her room with a client. During the course of the evening, Nettie told her customer she was in love with him. When the would-be suitor made no move to commit, Nettie took a bottle of carbolic acid from her trunk and drank it. Dr. Pascoe was summoned, but Nettie died within a few minutes. She was buried in Hillside Cemetery above town.

Jane Bowen's husband, William, died in 1891, but Jane carried on in the prostitution industry. Later that year she bought a new saloon and bordello called the Palace Hall and threw a grand opening ball that was attended by just about everyone in town. Unfortunately, Jane's hard luck was just beginning. In 1893 her newly arrived nephew died at the dance hall, leaving a wife and nine children back home in England. Two years later a misunderstanding with another of her nephews took a nasty turn when he was caught putting carbolic acid in food being served to Jane and her girls. Finally, in 1898, Jane's adopted daughter, Emily, committed suicide in Denver. After this last tragedy Jane went to England for a few years.

Meanwhile, another pioneer prostitute had arrived in Silverton. Her name was Matilda Wenden Fattor, appropriately enough—it was said that "Big Tilly" weighed between three hundred and four hundred pounds, and that she made annual trips to the Mayo Clinic for fat-reduction surgery. Born in Sweden in 1875, Tilly first arrived in Georgetown with her father in 1888. She moved to Ouray in 1893 before coming to Silverton, whose citizens quickly took to the big woman. Big Tilly's husband, Celeste Fattor, was said to be half her size. And there were others. In 1901 Mrs. Harry Morris, a.k.a Fly Frankie and Jimmie-the-Tough, was arrested for saying obscene things to "colored" prostitute Polka Derick. A year later Jimmie was assigned to scrubbing the jail for fighting. Some months later she was the subject of yet another skirmish in Durango.

When Jane Bowen returned to Silverton after her lengthy vacation in 1902, she found at least two more new faces in town: sisters Louisa and Marie Maurell, formerly of Ouray. The girls, who had arrived shortly after Jane's departure in 1898, had managed to build up a sizeable business. In 1902 Louisa built the Diamond Belle. It was two stories with a dance hall and twelve rooms. While the building was under construction, the women published a letter in the *Silverton Standard* defending their patronage of a Chinese restaurant. Such practices were frowned upon by citizens of Silverton, who were openly prejudiced against the Chinese. Prostitutes were more open-minded.

In 1904 pioneer Lizzie Fisher died of peritonitis after twenty years of doing business in Silverton. She too was buried at Silverton's Hillside Cemetery. Old and tired, Jane Bowen finally retired from the profession in 1905. Even the Maurell sisters suffered hardships. Soon after the Diamond Belle opened, a Frenchman began frequenting the brothel, since the girls were also French and spoke the language. Upon awakening one morning and finding his money missing, the man stabbed Louisa. The wounds were not fatal, and the Frenchman served twenty days in jail. The ensuing tension between miners and the Maurells resulted in slow business and fights between Louisa and her girls. A short time later, Louisa's piano player dropped dead from a heart attack brought on by drinking. After years of taking out loans to keep afloat, the girls finally sold out in 1907 and disappeared.

Such failures spelled success for Tilly Fattor, who purchased the Tremount Saloon in Silverton in 1907. Tilly served as both madam and bouncer of the bordello upstairs, which had fourteen rooms. Silverton native Earnest Hoffman, born in 1898, recalled that prostitution was still a viable industry in Silverton when he was a boy. "As for the women," he said of the Blair Street gals, "they were a social necessity in those days. You got to remember that almost all of the miners in those days were young and single."[6]

Indeed, whenever someone tried to do away with prostitution, local mine owners fought it, knowing that providing alcohol and women would keep their employees in good spirits. Silverton finally resorted to implementing the "foolproof" system of tracking prostitutes through the public health system. In Silverton rules appear to have been pretty strict, as the girls were required to have weekly, rather than monthly, health exams. Their clean bills of health were required to be hung on the wall in their rooms.

A Dr. Lynch was one of many physicians who took his turn at examining the ladies of the lamplight in Silverton. Initially the good doctor made house calls. But the infected girls, knowing of the doctor's impending arrival, would wash thoroughly in an attempt to pass the health exam. In time Dr. Lynch caught on. From then on the women were required to come to his office and wait at least an hour before being examined. Of course, the girls were required to pay their fine at the time of their exam, and it was said the city made so much off prostitution that their taxes were considerably lower than other towns in comparison.

One of Silverton's last notable prostitutes was Pearl "21" Thompson. Pearl operated the Mikado in Silverton along with another woman named Frances Belmont. Pearl kept a small dog, which she loved dearly. The local kids would kidnap the dog several times a year and hide it until a frantic Pearl offered a reward to find it. She never caught on to the scam. Pearl may have committed suicide; she died on February 13, 1928, at the age of thirty-six.

Near Silverton was Eureka, one of thousands of small camps that, for a time, blossomed into towns but never got very big. Eureka was just one of a handful of towns to benefit from Silverton's red-light district. The wicked ladies of Silverton even visited outlying boardinghouses at the mines, riding up to the precarious cliff-hanging structures in ore buckets. Van Huff, who moved to Eureka with his parents in 1902, recalled: "When the weather was good, three or four ladies used to come up from Silverton in a surrey all dressed in fancy clothes. They would go upstairs over the saloon and then go back to Silverton before night-fall." Huff also recalled there was only one "cat house" in Eureka, with one lady living there year round. At the time roughly two dozen families lived in Eureka. The house was a tiny log cabin that probably originally served as a miner's home.[7] Prostitutes like the one in Eureka could sometimes become acting madams during more prosperous times. Madam Dixie of the town of Montezuma, for example, hired two or three extra employees when area mines were doing well; during the lean times Dixie worked alone.

Farther north on the western slope was Leadville, which sported one of the wildest red-light districts in Colorado. Founded in 1878, the town had six dance halls within a year. The price of a dance then was 25¢, but some girls such as Maude Deuel of the Pioneer Dance Hall later remembered making as much as $200 a week. Much of Leadville's red-light district was located on the lower end of Harrison Avenue. There were also cribs on State Street and nicer brothels on West 3rd and West 5th streets. French Row, Coon Row, and Tiger Alley were located in the older section of town along State Street; the older places were more rundown and dangerous. Chestnut Street, which paralleled State Street, also contained several houses of ill repute. "I seldom go down that street," wrote Princeton graduate George Elder to his family in those early days, "but when I do I always notice [the dance halls] full and lots of music and noise."[8]

Most interestingly, French Row in its very early days was actually much more respectable than even some of the more elite brothels in Denver. The ladies there, most of whom did not speak English, were much cleaner and classier than their counterparts in Denver. The French ladies of Leadville rarely imbibed liquor, nor did they allow their clients to drink. Furthermore, they found profanity offensive and kept nice and tidy two-room cribs. They were also disgusted with American prostitutes, whom they regarded as drunken, disrespectful slobs. None of them planned to stay in Leadville longer than they had to.

The 1879 city directory shows Leadville had 4 banks, 4 churches, 10 stores, 31 restaurants, 19 beer halls, 120 saloons, and a whopping 118 gambling houses! Help-wanted ads for positions in the dance halls were quite bold. One read:

Leadville
Wanted: Fifty waiter girls!
High wages, Easy work,
Pay in Gold promptly every week.
Must appear in short clothes or no
engagement![9]

Another ad read:

Good steppers, make yourselves some money.
Fun galore! Fine clothing!
Nothing untoward which could tend
to affect a lady's sensibilities allowed at
The Golden Nugget Saloon.[10]

There is little doubt that few of these saloons were true to their word, prompting the *Leadville Daily Chronicle* to comment, "Men are fools and women devils in disguise. That's the reason the dance halls clear from one to two hundred dollars a night."[11]

Very early on, Leadville caught on to the fine process. The initial fee was $5 per house per month. Later the city charged madams $15 and prostitutes $5. The fines were due on the 20th of each month, and it was said the income constituted a large part of policemen's salaries. Therefore, the prostitutes were pressured when payments were late. Several of Colorado's more notorious prostitutes got their starts in Leadville. Names like Carrie Linnel, Frankie Paige, and Molly Price made the papers often. And there was Mollie May, sometimes known as Jennie Mickey. Born Milinda May Bryant to Thomas and Bessie Bryant in Illinois or Virginia, Mollie was said to have lost her virginity without sanctity of marriage as a young girl. Soon she had wandered west and was working as a prostitute and theater performer in Cheyenne.

By 1876 Mollie had a house of ill repute in the Black Hills of South Dakota. There, two brothers became embroiled in a brief gunfight over her. One shot at the other and missed, hitting Mollie. It was said the metal in her corset deflected the bullet, saving her life. It was also said that part of Mollie's ear was bitten off by prostitute Fanny Garretson when the two tangled over a man named Jim Brown. Earlier in her career, Mollie had also gained a bad reputation in Silver Cliff and Bonanza for running around with a man of questionable character named Bill Tripp. What is known for sure is that Mollie spent some time in Pueblo before migrating to Leadville in about 1879. In Leadville Mollie became a popular madam. She purchased a large house at 144 Main Street (now 3rd Street) and had the only telephone in town. The 1880 census notes Mollie had ten boarders and two male employees living at her house.

Within a year Mollie sold her house to the city of Leadville, which in turn used it for a city hall, of all things. Mollie's new brothel at 129–131

Fig. 21. Leadville's bawdy State Street was a flurry of activity in the 1800s. A good number of brothels were mingled with saloons, gambling halls, and other pleasure resorts.

(Courtesy Denver Public Library.)

West 5th Street in Leadville was among the finest houses in town, and silver millionaire Horace Tabor was said to be a silent partner in the business. One of Mollie's competitors was a madam named Sally Purple who had a brothel next to hers. One day Mollie May and Sally Purple got into a fight over, it was said, which of their birthplaces was the better place to hail from. Insults were exchanged between the two houses, then gunfire. The battle ended two hours later with no injuries. "Both parties are resting on their arms," chortled the *Leadville Democrat*, "and awaiting daybreak to resume hostilities."[12]

Mollie made the papers again in 1880, when a raid netted seventeen prostitutes on the row, and two young men jumped from a second-story window at Mollie's to escape arrest. In 1882 Mollie was the subject of yet another scandal when the rumor circulated that she was buying a nine-month-old baby named Ella from a couple known as Mr. and Mrs. Moore. The madam stayed silent until a local newspaper and several citizens voiced their concerns about her intentions. In May Mollie contacted the *Leadville Herald* and gave an exclusive interview, explaining that the child did not belong to the Moores but to a local decent woman who was too poor to care for her. Mollie had taken in the baby until the mother could contact relatives for assistance. She ended the interview by angrily reminding the general public of all the charities, churches, and hospitals she made donations to on a regular basis. Most interestingly, Ella's mother never reclaimed her child, and Mollie adopted her. She was called Ella Moore, despite Mollie's earlier claim that the Moores were not the child's parents. As soon as she reached school age, little Ella was sent off to St. Scholastica's Institute in Highland, Illinois. Her guardian was listed as one Robert Buck.

Mollie May died in 1887, and her funeral was one of the largest processions to ever take place in Leadville. The services took place in Mollie's brothel at 129 West 5th Street before a $3,000 hearse and eight carriages accompanied the body to Leadville's Evergreen Cemetery. Her obituary, circulated as far away as Pueblo, stated, "[S]he was a woman who, with all her bad qualities, was much given to charity and was always willing to help the poor and unfortunate."[13]

Mollie had worked as a prostitute for fifteen years. Her estate, which included investments in cattle ranches out east, was valued at $25,000, with $8,000 in diamonds. The administrator of her estate, J. H. Monheimer, sold her personal property for $1,500. Her house was purchased by Anna Ferguson for $3,600. The papers speculated the money would go to six-year-old Ella Moore, but little else is known about the child. In 1901 the *Leadville*

Fig. 22. Lil Lovell made the circuits in Nebraska, Creede, Cripple Creek, Leadville, and Denver. This original portrait of her hangs at the Old Homestead Museum in Cripple Creek.

(Courtesy Old Homestead Museum.)

Herald published an article about twenty-year-old Lillian Moore, adopted daughter of Mollie May, who attempted suicide in Leadville. Doctors saved her life and she was last seen on a train headed to Denver.

By 1895, Salida madam Laura Evens recalled, there were about five hundred sporting girls in Leadville. The following year the city successfully ran its prostitutes out of town, at least for a little while. Laura Evens was among those who packed her bags and left town. Of course, prostitution in Leadville began to grow again almost as soon as the last girl was gone. A later madam of Leadville was Winnie Purdy, who was said to be among the local bank's largest depositors. Winnie eventually sold her lavish house, including the furniture, to Lillis Lovell. Lil, whose real name was Emma Lillis Quigley, hailed from Nebraska and was formerly a well-known opera singer who for reasons unknown took up prostitution as a profession. Throughout her career Lil allegedly worked as a prostitute in Creede, where she earned the nickname Creede Lil before migrating to Leadville during the late 1880s. She also allegedly worked at the Old Homestead in Cripple Creek. In Leadville Lil's house was at 118 West 5th Street. Later she purchased another house that was said to be adorned with Oriental decor, velvet carpets, and beautiful tapestries.

In about 1901, at the age of thirty-six, Lil moved to Denver and married a banker. In 1907 she was proprietress of Verona Baldwin's old place, the Tenderloin Resort at 2020 Market Street. In March she died of pneumonia. In her will Lil left her estate to her siblings, her attorney, and her husband, Clarence J. Trimble. Four brothers, a sister, and an assortment of nieces and nephews received $1 apiece, illustrating the hard lines drawn between a prostitute and her family. Another brother received 320 acres in Nebraska, and another sister received $3,500.

It was said that one of Lil's sisters, Lois, worked with her in Denver. (The only sister Lil listed in her will as living in Denver, but to whom she left only $1, was identified as Mary Nirene Quigley Wilder.) Lois ultimately fell in love with a Denver businessman. Knowing that her seedy reputation could ruin his budding career, Lois spurned her beau's proposals of marriage. Various sources state that Lois, brokenhearted over her lost love, committed suicide by poison or a bullet. Tragically, the lover returned for one more try, and upon learning of Lois's death, blew his brains out at her grave.

One other enigmatic woman of Leadville was Grace Berkey, or Grace Egner. When she appeared in Alma, it was as the wife of Johann Louis Hoffman, whom Grace married in 1914. The couple lived on a ranch near town. There were others of the Hoffman clan living nearby, but Grace's in-laws barely knew what she looked like. Whenever family members visited, Grace would sprint from the house, running into the woods and hiding until they left. Whenever she went to Alma, she wore a brown veil over her face. Grace died in 1927, the truth about her paranoia unknown. Only a few items, including some very fancy clothing, a photographic card illustrating several girls in risqué clothing, perfume bottles, and a cookbook with some cryptic notes regarding sex, gave any indication as to her mysterious past life.

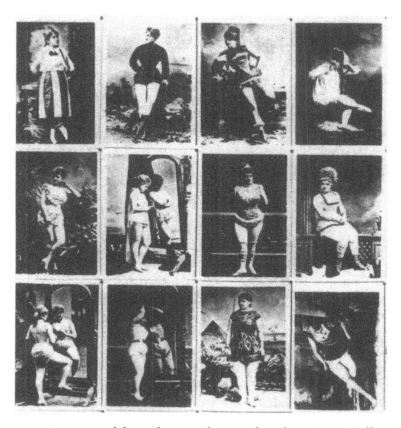

Fig. 23. Some scandalous photographs were found in Grace Hoffman's belongings when she passed away in 1927. Cards like this were actually no bigger than a baseball card to be carried in one's wallet.

(Courtesy Erik Swanson.)

Prostitution in Leadville was officially closed down in 1915. However, it is known that prostitutes continued in the business through at least the 1930s.

In 1879 yet another town appeared on the western slope: Crested Butte. Most of the town's saloons were located along Elk Avenue and 2nd Street. Miners coming home from work at the Big Mine had to pass through the district. The Slogar Bar, Croation Hall, the Kikel, the Elk, the Spritzer, and the Bucket of Blood were all popular saloons in town. Nearby, the Forest Queen Brothel was run by a prostitute known as "One-Eye" Ruby. Even today the place is allegedly haunted by a prostitute who jumped out the window into Coal Creek and killed herself. In the late 1920s there were still seventeen saloons in Crested Butte. Near Crested Butte was the town of Irwin, where a grand ball in the 1870s was attended by prostitutes Durango Nell and Timberline Kate. In 1879 Irwin's main street was a mile long and featured twenty-three saloons and approximately nineteen brothels.

In the central part of the state, Georgetown was also holding its own during the 1870s. Belle London was one of many early women who operated a parlor house there. Short, with curly brown hair, she was known to run around with a gambler named Chalk Wheeler. In 1879 a local newspaper complained that Georgetown had twelve saloons and parlor houses, but not one school. Indeed, Brownell Street had no fewer than five expensive parlor houses at one time, as well as the usual assortment of smaller brothels, taverns, and gambling halls. Two of Georgetown's more notorious madams were Mollie Dean and Mattie Estes. Like so many before her, Mollie met her death at the hands of a jealous lover after being seen with another man. By then Georgetown was as used to violence as any other western town. Shortly after a miner was shot to death in her brothel, madam Jennie Aiken was killed when her brothel burned to the ground. The newspaper hardly batted an eye. Despite the presence of shady ladies, Georgetown was still upholding its ordinances prohibiting "women, lewd or otherwise," from entering bars as late as 1908.

The next town to make prostitution history was Salida. Located in central Colorado, Salida was founded in about 1880 when the city was named by ex-Colorado Governor A. C. Hunt's wife. The name is Spanish for "gateway," and many a prostitute looked at Salida as just that. The earliest mention of prostitution in the newspapers is reference to Lizzie Landon in the 1880s. In Garfield, an outlying town near Salida, Lu Morrison took six grains of morphine on January 15, 1881. One Van Werden was summoned and pumped her out, and she presumably lived. Lu's appearance in local newspapers was followed by many other racy stories about Salida and the vicinity, including an 1883 shoot-out at Arbour's Variety and Dance Hall, during which outlaw Frank Reed killed marshal Baxter Stingley.

Salida immediately jumped on the antiprostitution bandwagon and began imposing ordinances and their accompanying fines. But it proved to be rather difficult to get the girls of Salida to comply. Salida's newspaper, the *Mountain Mail,* reported in November of 1893 that Police Magistrate Hollenbeck told the city council, "I have collected nothing from the lewd houses for the months of September, October, and November. They refused to pay and said they could not pay on account of hard times."[14]

Whether the red-light ladies were granted any leniency is unknown. But Salida seems to have been an exception to the general rule with regard to accepting prostitution within the city limits. In fact, it seems as though Salida was an exceptional place where a prostitute could actually be regarded as somewhat respectable—or at least no worse than anyone else. When Mrs. E. F. Atkinson died of inflamed bowels in 1894, the death records shamelessly listed her as a married prostitute. Long-term prostitutes like Laura Evens remained as faithful to the city as the city was to them. In fact, Laura established herself as a very prominent madam, a position she enjoyed for over five decades. Perhaps it had something to do with her decent upbringing and a good education. In her old age, Laura recalled, "I was pretty young when I first became a sporting woman, and loved to sing and dance and get drunk and have a good time. I had a lovely contralto voice. God knows it cost my father plenty of money."[15]

Little is known about Laura Evens's upbringing aside from the speculative. Allegedly from the South, she was married by the time she was only seventeen years old. As one might guess, married life and a possible child were not what Laura wanted. Leaving her husband, Laura arrived in St. Louis with a new name and a new career. She next appeared on Market Street in Denver where, she later recalled, strippers were paid $5 per show. She also gave Mattie Silks and Jennie Rogers a run for their money. It was said Laura once referred to Mattie's establishment as "the Old Ladies Roost." Ultimately, however, Laura departed Denver in the wake of the 1894 "Strangler's Row" murders along Market Street. Laura first went to Park City, near Fairplay, before migrating to Leadville, where she remained throughout 1895. In 1896, after Leadville authorities set about chasing the lewd women out of town, Laura departed with a suitcase of champagne— a parting gift from the saloon keepers of Leadville. Laura remembered sharing the champagne with the train crew on the way to her next destination:

Salida. There she used the remaining five bottles to bribe local officers into letting her set up shop. One of Laura's competitors in 1902 was known simply as Big Jess.

In about 1904 Laura built a brand-new set of cribs at 130 West Front Street (now Sackett Street), which quickly evolved into the main part of Salida's red-light district. The 1907 city directory lists Laura as residing on Lower F Street and notes she could be reached at the Saddle Rock Restaurant by telephone. The address at 130 West Front was still in business, too, as evidenced by a Miss Hazel Dean residing in Apartment 1 during 1907 and 1908. There was another brothel at 125 West Front occupied by one Bertha Madden, and yet a fourth one at 117 West Front. The cribs, which were small but ample apartments with joining walls, were numbered one through six. Surrounding brothels included the Mascot at 129 West Front Street. About twelve prostitutes were plying their trade in the district in total.

Over the years Laura Evens amassed a comfortable fortune. "I used to be mean, too," she once said. "I never let a customer get away while he

Fig. 24. Laura Evens's crib housing on West Front Street still sported its original look in 1996. By 2001 the building had received a stucco makeover. The cribs now serve as apartments.

(From the author's collection.)

still had a penny in his pocket. That would have been against our religion."[16] Eventually, Laura hired Lillian Powers to manage her cribs at 126–130 Front Street under the name of Fay Weston, and the cribs became known as Weston Terrace. The number of prostitutes working in Salida numbered roughly thirty-eight women in 1909. Among them was Ruby Franklin, who was working at the brothel at 129 West Front Street.

After Lillian Powers set out to gain her own fortune in Florence in about 1911, Laura Evens reclaimed management over her girls. Working for her at 117 West Front were her cook, Mrs. Jennie Wright, and prostitutes Cora Galloway, Rose Miller, Alice Wellingsworth, Nettie Larson, Virginia Toy, and Lena Moore. Interestingly enough, Lena Moore was a black prostitute from Colorado City. In 1902 she was working there for Hattie Milligan at 623 South Sixth Street, where she may also have been known as Selina Moore. In 1909 Selina was arrested for selling liquor without a license. Sometime after that, she moved to Leadville before settling in Salida. The March 21, 1911 issue of the *Salida Mail* notes that Lena had died the previous Friday. She was buried at Fairview Cemetery in Salida. Lena had set out from Colorado City and ended up in Salida; shortly after her death, prostitute Mary Stone, also black, set out from Salida and wound up in Cripple Creek. So did a mulatto named Edna Thomas.

In 1913 Laura Evens purchased a building in the 100 block of West Front Street. For unknown reasons, she had only two employees: Cora Galloway and Eva Mayes. Indeed, the number of girls in Salida was slowly shrinking. In 1913 there were only fifteen prostitutes in town. One of them was a gal named Dick Valentine who committed suicide with pills. Dick refused to give her real name or the names of relatives as she lay dying. Nobody knew who she really was, even though she had been in Salida since 1909.

Laura Evens took advantage of the low prostitution population to secure more power in Salida. In 1915 she bought more property in the 100 block of Front Street from Alma Osborn. The deed of trust was paid by Lillian Powers, however, illustrating a continuing partnership between the two women. After buying yet another lot in the 100 block in 1920, Laura was eventually forced to sell some of her other property. Courthouse documents are riddled with transactions bearing Laura Evens's name through the 1920s, and local rumor states she nearly lost her properties on several occasions.

The 1922–23 directory lists Laura at 129 West Front Street, where she was to remain for the rest of her life. There were about fourteen prostitutes in Salida that year. Within another five years, the only prostitutes said

Fig. 25. When this photo was taken in 1948, Laura Evens's bedroom
was filled with dolls, bearskins, fancy linens, and all the comforts
of home. The girl on the bed is identified as Anne Patterson.

(Courtesy Colorado Historical Society.)

to be left in Salida were Margaret Weber at 117 West Front Street and Laura
Evens. The 1936–37 directory lists Laura as a widow, indicating the sudden demise of an apparent ceremonial husband. Her house was officially
closed down in 1942, forcing her to post a sign on the front door reading,
"No girls." She did continue renting rooms to railroad men, however, playing poker with them and often taking their money in the game. Laura herself passed away in 1953, at the approximate age of seventy-five. People who

knew Laura Evens claim that up until just a few years before her death, Laura continued to maintain her home as a brothel. Historians Fred and Jo Mazzulla were lucky to interview Laura before she died. Classy to the end, hers was a flowered, ornate, lavender-colored coffin.

Back on the western side of the state, the town authorities of Ouray counterbalanced the easygoing authorities at Salida. During the 1880s and 1890s Ouray's red-light district was on 2nd Street, mostly between 7th and 8th avenues. The red-light houses included the Temple of Music, the Bon Ton, the Bird Cage, the Monte Carlo, the Clipper, the Morning Star, and the Club. About a hundred girls worked in Ouray. There were also dance halls; a dance and drink cost 25¢. A drink for the girl cost 15¢ more. The girls were paid a percentage of what they sold. There were roughly thirty-five saloons.

In 1881 the Grand Pacific was constructed on Main Street. It was a two-story affair with liquor and gambling downstairs and rooms upstairs. The Grand Pacific had the distinction of being the site of the first recorded shooting in Ouray. Shortly afterward complaints began about dance hall girls and prostitutes appearing in decent society, using vulgar language and making a nuisance. Before long the *Ouray Times* published a petition against the Grand Pacific, with unsatisfactory results.

Ouray was a most interesting town when it came to prostitution, because most of the bawdy houses were ruled by a large number of families who also owned saloons, gambling dens, and dance halls. Probably the best-known family business in town was run by the Vanoli clan, which managed operations in Ouray as well as the nearby towns of Red Mountain and Telluride. John Vanoli first built property in Ouray's red-light district in 1884. The Vanolis owned the Gold Belt Theater, which had a large stage for variety shows as well as small adjoining rooms for private parties.

Like almost every other Colorado town, Ouray had its own ordinance against prostitution, with fines varying from $10–$100. In 1886 the population was fifteen hundred. Most of the residents were Italians; many others were Irish and Swedes. By then the Vanolis owned a brothel called the "220," and a barrage of disgraceful incidents began. The first of these was reported in February, when a drunken prostitute was seen "reeling along the sidewalk, scattering school children—on their way from dinner to school—right and left, in her wild flight." At last the girl fell and "wallowed all over the sidewalk" until someone helped her up.[17]

The following year Vincent Gates, "the Dago fiddler" at the 220, shot his prostitute girlfriend at the brothel of Carrie Lennel. Another prostitute was shot at the 220 a short time later. She lived, but the man who shot her blew his brains out while being pursued by police. Then, in March of 1888, John Vanoli himself was arrested for fatally shooting a customer to prevent him from striking another man. Whether Vanoli did any time is unknown. What is known is that in 1891 he purchased yet another saloon and brothel from Baptiste and Minnie Fey at the nearby boom camp of Red Mountain. The brothel came complete with a red plush couch and four beds.

Shortly afterward John Vanoli was arrested once more. This time he was charged with selling liquor without a license, but his biggest crime was the shooting of another customer at the Gold Belt. In anticipation of serving jail time, Vanoli transferred his property to his brother Domenick. Vanoli was cleared of the charges and took a trip to California in 1895. There he shot himself to death on December 26 after learning he was terminally ill.

Prostitution remained a viable industry in Ouray as late as 1908. Throughout the 1920s complaints were still being filed with the newspaper about bootlegging, gambling, and prostitution. Eventually the prostitutes of Ouray faded into obscurity, save for a few memorialized in the cemetery. One of them is known only as Charlotte:

> Here lies Charlotte
> She was a harlot
> For 15 years she preserved her virginity
> A damn good record for this vicinity.[18]

Farther north, the small rough-and-ready town of Tin Cup served miners from all over the region. Between 1880 and 1890 Tin Cup featured a booming little red-light district on the south end of Grand Avenue. Old-timers recalled that the girls did not come outside much during the day except to get the occasional bucket of water from a nearby ditch. Later, as Tin Cup's mining era played out, those prostitutes who stayed moved to an alley behind Washington Avenue. The new location earned them the nickname "Alley Girls."[19] In 1900 the decent women of the town succeeded in running the remaining girls out of town.

Unlike in Tin Cup, prostitutes experienced more freedom in the western slope town of Gunnison. One of the best-known law officers there in 1884 was Cyrus "Doc" Shores, who not only maintained law and order among the red-light districts but was also friends with Denver prostitute Molly Foley. The 1880s were a prime time for prostitutes in Gunnison, who entertained right along Main Street near Tomichi Avenue. The entertainments in town included the Red Light Dance Hall and Fat Jack's Amusement Palace, plus no fewer than three two-story houses of ill repute. In 1882 two men named Walsh and Yard fought it out over a dance hall girl named Viola. Walsh was killed, and Yard's trial ended in a hung jury before he was acquitted.

During the early 1880s, Salida had little competition. The only other nearby red-light district of note was at Arbourville, located on the way to the mining town of Monarch. Arbourville boasted the only brothel in the area, making it a real attraction to miners. One newspaper speculated that the reason Arbourville failed to progress was because the town's social life revolved around its single sporting house.

In 1886, however, Salida began experiencing a little competition from the nearby town of Buena Vista. Buena Vista's ladies of the evening included Lizzie Marshall, who advertised in the *Traveler's Night Guide of Colorado*. But the town's most famous prostitute was probably Elizabeth "Liz" Spurgen. Born in 1857 and better known as Cockeyed Liz, she was said to have begun her career in Denver back in 1870. According to Liz, she had been married at age thirteen to a man old enough to be her father, who forced her into prostitution. "I used to run away, but he would always find me and bring me back. He would beat me so badly, that I finally gave up."[20] In fact, Liz once attributed her "cockeyed" look to a particularly bad beating. In 1886 Liz purchased a brothel in Buena Vista called the Palace Manor, nicknamed the "Palace of Joy." She stayed in business until 1897, when she married Alphonse "Foozy" Enderlin and retired. Foozy expanded the former Palace of Joy to make an apartment for rental income, and the couple lived there many years. In 1968 the building was known as Edwards Apartments.

By 1890 the western slope was well into its mining era. Even small towns, such as the railroad town of Ridgway, sported healthy red-light districts. Ridgway's streets were christened with names of both men and women. Allegedly, the female names were derived from the town's red-light ladies. Most locals debunk this myth, however, and the only sign of prostitution in Ridgway today is a former house of ill repute on a side street off the main drag. Even so, Ridgway featured a number of saloons. One of them had a pet mountain lion tied up in the back; once a week the owner let the creature loose for a "lion hunt" that did not involve bullets.

The nightlife in the nearby blazing boomtown of Telluride was as rambunctious as in any other mining camp in the state. Among other bars, the Senate Saloon at 125 South Spruce Street was used by prostitutes to solicit customers for their cribs around the corner on Pacific Avenue, also known as Popcorn Alley. Nearby, the Silver Bell Saloon and Dance Hall, built in 1890, housed a brothel upstairs. Prostitution flourished so well in Telluride that brothel owners from other towns, including John Vanoli of Ouray, came to town and invested in their own dance halls.

The local police, however, did their best to curb prostitution. Doc Shores recalled visiting marshal Jim Clark in Telluride. The two were patrolling "the Row," considered the slum of Telluride brothels. A heavy blonde woman stepped from her crib wearing only a wrapper and accompanied by an older pug dog. The woman made some facetious remark to Clark that her dog was so old, she wished Clark would just shoot him. Clark shot the dog on the spot and calmly walked on. As Clark and Shores left the hysterical woman screaming on the sidewalk, Clark's only comment was, "Damn them, I will not fool with them."[21]

In comparison to Telluride's rowdy nightlife, Aspen was much more subdued. In August 1884 a $5 "tax" was imposed on prostitutes. When prostitute Fanny Chambers died that fall, her funeral was noted by local papers as elaborate and bearing an expensive coffin. Only four women identified themselves as prostitutes in 1885, but the district was surely larger than that. That year there was only one dance hall but fifteen brothels located within two blocks on Durant Avenue. And, there were also an amazing number of saloons: forty. Lizzie Gordon was one of the few who plied her trade in Aspen. In 1897, prostitute Mary Murphy was fined $5 for getting drunk and disrobing in public. Mary could not pay her fine, even though police helpfully sought out some people she said owed her money. Ultimately Mary worked out her fine in jail and upon her release expressed sincere regret for her indecent act.

As part of a relatively crime-free town, Aspen's red-light district was discreet and largely ignored—at least until the Colorado Midland Railroad built its station on Deane Avenue, one block south of Durant. Disembarking passengers, many of them prominent and wealthy, had to pass through the district to access the town. The prostitutes of Durant were politely asked to move to a different locale, which they willingly did. Aspen's red-light district isn't even detectable in the 1900 census. Today Durant Avenue faces Aspen's ski slopes and is lined with luxury hotels and fancy restaurants.

Chapter Six

Southern Belles and Ladies of the Plains

✠

The average man would rather behold her nakedness than Ulysses Grant in his full dress uniform.
            —Mark Twain, on a high-class working girl

The vast Colorado plains saw some of the earliest prostitution in Colorado. The Santa Fe and other trails provided the only access from the east as early as the 1840s. The majority of women in the region back then were native Mexicans, Spanish, and Native Americans, many of whom plied their trades with men coming west. Women who drifted between places like Bent's Fort and outlying camps were labeled "camp followers."[1] Other women migrated, many in the safe company of a man, from such distant places as New Mexico.

One of the very earliest accounts of prostitution in the state was documented at the settlement of Greenhorn, located twenty-five miles south of Pueblo. There, in 1841, fur-trapper John Brown fought a duel with an Indian called "Seesome" over a Mexican flirt known as Nicolasa. During her flighty reign, Nicolasa was said to have been the cause of two other duels as well. It was said that Brown won, but Nicolasa was nowhere to be found when the ex-trapper set up a trading post at Greenhorn in about 1845. In her stead was Luisa Sandoval, alleged ex-wife of that scout and tall-tale teller, Jim Beckwourth.

According to Beckwourth's autobiography, he married a woman he called Louise Sandeville at Taos in 1842. Shortly afterward the couple departed for Colorado. Explorer John C. Fremont reported seeing Luisa at a camp along the Platte River a short time later. In 1843 Beckwourth left Luisa and a daughter named Matilda at Pueblo. When he returned in 1846,

Luisa had married John Brown and the two had settled at Greenhorn. Beckwourth later claimed that Brown had tricked Luisa into marrying him by showing her a forged letter, allegedly from Beckwourth, telling her their marriage was over. He also said that Luisa tried to come back to him, and that he refused her. The truth, if there is any to this story, is lost to history.

The Browns lived at Greenhorn until about 1849, when they closed shop and moved to California. In San Bernardino John Brown became very prominent in business affairs, and the couple raised ten children. It is highly unlikely the couple ever revealed Luisa's previous marriage to Beckwourth. It is also possible that Luisa never denied Beckwourth's statements in his autobiography because she was once a fallen woman. Her notorious reputation, fortunately for her, was overshadowed by that of the flirtatious Nicolasa, who was known to frequent Greenhorn, Fort Lancaster, Hardscrabble, and Pueblo.

In 1869 the town of Old Kit Carson in Cheyenne County consisted of tents, dugouts, and rough wood structures, many of them occupied by prostitutes, gamblers, and con men. When the Kansas Pacific Railroad moved its rails west and away from Old Kit Carson, the tents and ramshackle buildings were accordingly moved to the new town. In time the town evolved from its rough beginnings to become a fairly respectable railroad town.

Pueblo, meanwhile, had developed its own reputation not only with Mexican and Indian prostitutes but also white women. Long before Pueblo became an official city, Fort Pueblo was a military base whose beginnings date well over 150 years ago. The population at the fort no doubt included a few Mexican and Indian prostitutes up to and after 1860, when the city was officially founded. In a short time Pueblo grew from a rural fort in Colorado's vast mountain prairies to a bona fide community with settlers from all races and backgrounds.

Pueblo's earliest brothels in the new era were not confined to one red-light district; there were several. One district was located by the Arkansas River near what is now central Pueblo. Another was near Santa Fe Avenue and Front Street (now 1st Street). During the 1870s prices ranged from 25¢ to $1 for crib girls, $1–$10 for brothel women, and $5–$50 for parlor house visits. Most girls averaged four to ten tricks per day. Some of the more notorious bordellos in Pueblo included the Stranger's Home on the east side of Santa Fe near 2nd Street. Operated by Tom Suttles, it was the scene of numerous suicides and fights, including the 1872 death of prostitute Kitty Austin. Another bordello was the Hotel de Omaha, where thirty-three-year-old Esther Baldwin, born in Canada and also known as Sarah Fox, reigned as madam. Other popular resorts were the Cricket Variety Theater on 2nd Street and the Theater Comique.

On October 30, 1872, the *Pueblo Chieftain* expressed no surprise at the stabbing of a prostitute near the Arkansas River. By then prostitutes were numerous in downtown Pueblo as well as in the incorporated town of South Pueblo. They were nearly impossible to pin down since they moved around so much, but city authorities did their best to maintain some sort of control. In 1874 Esther Baldwin moved to 3rd and Court streets and opened the European Dance Hall. The new place featured a quadrille band, wine, beer, liquor, and good cigars. Another woman, Mrs. Gropp, ran Mrs. Gropp's Railroad House opposite the South Pueblo depot. Mrs. Gropp managed to stay one step ahead of police by moving to 4th Street (now Victoria Avenue), opposite from the Grand Central Hotel.

Despite a few fines that had already been imposed on prostitutes, Pueblo did not pass its first ordinances against prostitution and gambling until January of 1875. The laws included prohibition of brothels, forbidding women to work at or patronize bars, forbidding dance houses in saloons, and prohibiting anyone under the age of twelve from habitually visiting saloons. On January 13 the *Pueblo Chieftain* reported that one drunken customer was beaten with a board by an actress after he insulted her. "After pounding him to her heart's content, she leaped back upon the stage, and the play went on swimmingly."[2] Later that month twelve prostitutes were fined $5 each plus costs. In April another eight prostitutes were fined $10 each. In December the elusive Mrs. Gropp moved into the Denver & Rio Grande Hotel on 5th Street (now Union Avenue). The following March Esther Baldwin's European Dance Hall burned. Undaunted, Esther rebuilt and in time her place was described as the best around.

Other changes came in subsequent years. In 1877 the Theater Comique closed and reopened as the Red-Light Saloon. Prostitution seemed to be everywhere, including a brothel and dance hall owned by one S. A. Smith that operated out of a cabin beside the bridge across the Arkansas River. In September Smith was fined $20 plus costs for selling liquor without a license. He couldn't pay and went to jail.

Esther Baldwin died in 1877 or 1878 at the age of thirty-nine. In her place came Marie Lockhardt, who announced she held a promissory note on the Hotel de Omaha for $400. At seventy Marie was well past her prime as a working girl. Just what Marie's relationship to Esther Baldwin was and whether she won her case is unknown. By 1880 she was living at

636 15th Street with her seventeen-year-old grandson, Allen Graham. Marie died in October of 1881 at the age of seventy-two. She is buried in the same family plot as Esther Baldwin in Pueblo's Pioneer Cemetery.

Throughout the 1880s a number of other prostitutes made the newspapers for the fines they were paying. They included madams Nellie Moon, Lizzie Dunkard, and Jennie King. Employees of the three women included Sis Emerson, Nellie Kelly, May Rose, Olive Smith, Lulu Barbar, Willie Arnold, Alice McCormich, Nellie Adams, and Rose Campbell. Other prostitutes of Pueblo included Belle O'Neil, Mattie White (alias Mattie Fields), Clara Wilson (alias Clara Trott), Belle Bunnelson, and Lydia White. The girls and their coworkers were finding gainful employment in such notorious resorts as Tammany Hall, the Bagnio, and the Bucket of Blood, which was located in the 100 block of South Union Avenue. Over the years the Bucket of Blood was alternately known as the Bella Union and the Central.

Pueblo Prostitutes in 1885[3]

Name	Age	Birthplace
Josie Austin	16	New York
Annie Bower	28	Louisiana
Edith Burns	21	Indiana
Rosa DeSoto	35	Mexico
Mae Dudley	27	Massachusetts
Lulu Flynn	28	Virginia
Cora Hicks	20	Massachusetts
B. Holmes	17	Missouri
Attie Lee	22	Indiana
Alice McConnant	21	Indiana
Sydney Noble	40	Connecticut
Maud River	20	Texas
Isabel Robinson	16	Missouri
Allison Ruby	21	Indiana
Alice Sayer	19	Ohio
Belle Sherwood	25	Ohio
Jennie Smith	26	Indiana
Madge Thomas	26	Colorado
Ida Warren	17	Wales
Louisa Williams	20	Minnesota

By 1886 Pueblo's official red-light district was located on 1st Street between Santa Fe and what is now Albany Avenue. The following year the Pueblo City Council passed stricter ordinances against prostitution. The fine went up to a $10 minimum for owning a brothel, with a $100 maximum fine. Interestingly, the fine for "keeping" a brothel varied between $5 and $300. In 1889 the ordinances against prostitution changed yet again. Keeping a house of ill fame cost $6–$300. Soliciting on a public street or from a door or window of a house was fined the same. Engaging in prostitution as a business was $6–$100. Employing women in a saloon brought $5–$100. Keeping a dance house was $10–$100.

Fines Paid by Madams in 1895[4]

Name	Date	Fines
Emma Brace, Nellie White	April	$69
Em Brace	May	$48
Em Brace, Nellie White	June	$71
Em Brace, Nellie White	July	$69
Em Brace, Nellie White	August	$67
Em Brace, Nellie White	September	$75
Em Brace, Nellie White	October	$65
Em Brace, Nellie White	November	$62
Em Brace, Nellie White	December	$50

Pueblo's ladies of the evening appeared to have no problem paying the law to keep out of their hair. Throughout 1896 women who paid fines included madams Em Brace and Nell White as well as prostitutes Mable Miller, Stella Fisher, Nellie Marcus, Minnie Cumming, Jennie Holmes, and May Rivers. On occasion Em Brace paid fines for her prostitutes, including Lillian Clark, Myrtle King, and Pearl Young. Authorities struggled to close the bordellos in central Pueblo, but newcomers such as Etta "Spuds" Murphy of Leadville were undaunted.

The 1900 census shows only five brothels in the red-light district, with five prostitutes per site on the average. One of the brothels was known as the Senate Bar. The largest brothel had ten residents: eight girls, a cook, and a musician. Altogether that year there were thirty-six prostitutes in Pueblo, averaging twenty-eight years of age. The oldest was sixty-one, the youngest eighteen years old. There were eight children among them. Most were single, but two were married. Fifteen were foreign born.[5]

The next major town south of Pueblo was Trinidad. So popular were the girls of that Santa Fe Trail town that they inspired poems like the following:

The Ballad of Gertie's Jit

Life was good at Gertie's!
There were women, cards, wine and song
And a man was a man at Gertie's!
And as such could do no wrong

He couldn't make money at Gertie's Jit.
Only a tin horn would've thot of it
But he could forgit it, tho it cost his pay
The miserable hole where he worked all day

Sure the gambling games were fixed for the house
Like the molls who'd hold you tight
While a tenor sang in a nasal twang
Of home at the kid's last fight.[6]

Because Trinidad was located right along the Santa Fe Trail, its illicit nightlife is likely to have begun a lot earlier than that in most Colorado towns. Permanent settlement at Trinidad began in about 1861. Some of the earliest notes on prostitution include the 1874 murder of a former Las Animas prostitute named Moll Howard. Moll's killer, a man named Spinner, admitted to killing the woman with a rock after she attacked him with a butcher knife. He said she owed him $1. In an act of true frontier justice, a visiting party of prostitutes from Las Animas formed a mob and hanged Spinner by the Purgatoire River.

Moll Howard was likely a traveling prostitute, and her end came long before the first red-light district in Trinidad was formed very near the Santa Fe Trail behind Commercial Street. Trinidad's first houses of prostitution were on Mill and Plum streets, which included many different types of parlor houses. The upper echelon had dance floors, Saturday-night musical trios, and weeknight piano players. The Grand, at Santa Fe and Main Street, even had a swimming pool and Turkish baths!

The caste system of brothels in Trinidad also included "bar girls," girls who worked above the taverns along Main Street. Bar girls could also function in certain restaurants that had curtained booths, where waitresses could ply their trade on the side. But no matter their status, the girls of Trinidad caught the eye of many an admirer. A Romanesque building constructed in 1888 at 115 East Main Street came complete, unbeknownst to the owner, with a bust of a local madam in the front facade. Allegedly, the architect was in love with her.

If Trinidad had ordinances outlawing prostitution, the city does not appear to have enforced such rules until about 1891. They included allowing law officers to inspect brothels at any time, and the girls were put through the usual monthly health exam, for which they received a health card to display. Some of the working girls in town included L. Eperson, sisters Jane and Belle Sherer, and Maud Scott. Maud may have had a daughter named Maria Scott, a prostitute later listed as having been born in Trinidad. Maria later left Trinidad and worked in Colorado City before migrating to Cripple Creek in 1911.

By 1895 Trinidad's red-light district was described as located on the west end of town near an area known as Carbon Arroyo. A bridge, named for the Bridge of Sighs in Venice, spanned the arroyo, allowing customers easy access to the district. Bridges above the alleys in back of Trinidad's taverns also allowed customers access to the red-light ladies from an adjoining hillside.

The best-known prostitute in Trinidad at the turn of the century was Mae Phelps, who in 1900 was at 228 Santa Fe Avenue with ten employees. There were only an additional ten prostitutes noted by the census that year. Their average age was twenty-nine, with the oldest being fifty-seven and the youngest nineteen. Thirteen children of the working girls were also listed. Eight women were married and seven were single.[7]

But there were many more girls than the census takers cared to list. By 1900 there were said to be upward of 500 soiled doves around Trinidad, as compared to 150–200 residents, who could service the Santa Fe Trail and the railroads coming through town. The reason for the high number may have been because, allegedly, there were no brothels in nearby company-owned coal camps. That meant men from places like Berwind, Ludlow, Morley, Jensen, and Starkville had no choice but to come to Trinidad for female entertainment. Whether this is true is up for speculation; by then, it was a known fact to mine owners that their miners were happier if surrounded by the prospect of alcohol and prostitution. Also, the girls of Trinidad would have been foolish not to pay visits to company towns, especially around payday.

Unlike most of her counterparts in Trinidad, Mae Phelps dressed very regally and conducted herself with the utmost grace at all times. She had her portrait taken several times throughout her career by photographer O. E. Aultman, who made a name for himself photographing much of early Colorado while surveying roads. Mae also made it clear that she wasn't afraid of public officials, especially those speaking out of both sides of their mouths. Once, during a court appearance, attorney Jamie McKeough asked Mae if she "operated a public place on the Santa Fe Trail." Mae replied, "You ought to know, you've been there often enough."[8]

Fig. 25. Mae Phelps, with her matronly appearance, was an astute businesswoman. She enjoyed having her portrait taken often at Aultman's Studio in Trinidad.

(Aultman Collection, courtesy Colorado Historical Society.)

Indeed, most of the girls in Trinidad exhibited little fear of the law. On warm summer nights, the fire department was occasionally called upon to "rescue" girls from the second floors of their brothels, a feat that required putting ladders up to the windows and watching the girls descend from above. The catch? They weren't wearing underwear! Both the madams and their inmates appear to have been the most benevolent of women, however. Before the Madams' Rest Home was established in 1927, most madams sent their ill or injured girls to recuperate at the homes of various ranchers for a few weeks. One of the ranchers, a Mr. Thompson, was once quite embarrassed by a friend who mistook his new bride for a prostitute on the rest.

The Sanborn Fire Insurance maps of 1901 show that no fewer than seven brothels existed in Trinidad. There were probably many more in the form of tents and camps on the outskirts of town. Even so, many citizens seemed more willing than usual to mix with prostitutes. When the West Theater was built at 432 West Main Street in 1908, respectable folks attended shows despite the theater's close proximity to the red-light district.

Trinidad Madams in 1910[9]

Name	Age	Marital status	Number of children	Number of employees
Margarita Carillo	24	Married	0	3
Edith Crosland	40	Widow	4	5
Sarah Cunningham	58	—	9	—
Antonia Gonzales	36	Married 9 years	0	5
Mae Phelps	45	Widow	0	6
Ida Pickler	—	—	—	—
Laura Smith	34	Single	—	—
Lillian Smith	31	Single	0	4
Mattie Swain	37	Widow	1	4

Throughout the early 1900s, prostitutes appear to have led a fairly peaceful existence in Trinidad. In 1910 Mae Phelps was employing six girls and cooperated with other local madams to form a Madams' Association. Their achievements included constructing a special trolley system that led to the red-light district. The system was built by agreement with the city trolley line and ran along Newall Avenue to Main Street. By then there were forty-nine shady ladies in Trinidad. Most interestingly, census records show their combined number of children was seventeen— much more than any other district in Colorado. Thirty-one of the women were single, twelve were married, four were widowed, and two divorced. The district was comprised of a total of eight brothels, two two-resident cribs, and one single crib. All of the women were listed as knowing how to read.

In fact, the census takers of the day may have exaggerated or faked some of their notes. Taking the census in a red-light district was embarrassing, to say the least, and it is not surprising that some census takers interviewed the houses of ill fame as quickly as possible. Even so, the 1910 census for Trinidad does show some interesting statistics. Madam Edith Crosland was a widow twice married. Madam Sarah Cunningham had a black cook from Kentucky and three girls working for her. Madam Ida Pickler had two piano players and a bartender. Margarita Carillo had a three-year-old Italian boy living at her brothel. Margarita's employees were all from New Mexico, and the census notes she had a husband working in a mine.[10]

By 1912 the number of Trinidad bordellos had grown to twenty-two, with their transient numbers fluctuating on a constant basis. Tulsa native Lilly Lewis was just one of many girls who left Trinidad in 1912 to ply her trade elsewhere. In Lilly's case, the traveling gal next appeared in Cripple Creek. Again, the city official documenting her presence may have been a bit nervous; Lilly was described as "¼ white, ¼ Negro and ½ white."[11]

In about 1875 the Denver & Rio Grande Railroad extended its rails into El Moro, about four miles down the Purgatoire River from Trinidad. The company town quickly became an ever-growing mix of businesses, hotels, and restaurants. Four bars flourished, and George Close kept a dance hall around the corner from the New State Hotel with its fancy saloon. As competition built between El Moro and Trinidad, a number of shady ladies migrated to the new railroad town from Trinidad and Pueblo. One of them was Jennie Lawrence of Pueblo, a dance hall girl working for George Close. A disgruntled and drunken Indian, Navajo Frank, expressed his displeasure with Close by firing a random shot into the dance hall from outside one evening. The bullet pierced Jennie's heart before passing through the coat sleeve of her dance partner, mildly wounding the fiddler and lodging in a wall.

Farther east, even some of the lesser-known trails had towns with sporting houses. Trail City was one of these, laid out in 1884 along a popular cattle trail on the Kansas border in Prowers County. Trail City quickly became popular among outlaws and prostitutes, since one could enter the front door of a business in Colorado and exit from the back door literally within a few feet of the Kansas state line. Soon, most of the thirty or more buildings consisted primarily of saloons, gambling houses, and brothels. Horse racing was a popular sport, and often the ruffians of Trail City expanded their antics to include the quieter towns of Coolidge, Kansas, and the Colorado city of Lamar. On its wildest nights, horse races conducted from

Trail City to Coolidge and back consisted of drunken cowboys with nude prostitutes riding on the backs of their horses.

From 1885 through 1887 Joe "the Bird" Sparrow's saloon at Trail City catered to cattlemen on the failing National Cattle Trail. Sparrow also ran a brothel, a rented large-frame room that was partitioned off for his working girls. Sparrow made the papers in 1887 when he shot I. P. "Print" Olive to death at the Haynes Saloon. Apparently Sparrow owed Olive money and shot him rather than repay the debt. Witnesses claimed that even as the wounded Olive lay on the floor, Sparrow stood over him and administered a final fatal shot to the head.

A local hack driver, Murph Ward, was known to transport Trail City's naughty girls to Coolidge and back as a way to drum up extra business for his taxi service. Some sources state there were really never more than two brothels at Trail City, and their girls were of the traveling variety. Emma Brace of Pueblo, Debbie Green, May the Innocent, Mattie Prince, and Sadie Burr were just a few soiled doves who flew through the town during its short existence.

Trail City easily rivaled the Baca County cow town of Boston as among the wildest in Colorado. Though short-lived, Boston also sported a wild nightlife that has been lost to most historians. In 1888 the town had several saloons and over a thousand residents. Soon rustlers, outlaws, and a good number of prostitutes constituted the transient population. Mysterious murders and other shootings took place often. Eventually, due to lack of a railroad and competition from neighboring, more upstanding towns, Boston's wild and wooly residents moved on, and the place was becoming a ghost town by 1892. Many of them may have migrated to Petersburg, located much farther north in Arapahoe County roughly eight miles south of Denver.

Though founded as just another suburban farming community, Petersburg took on its wild reputation when Pap Wyman remodeled the Petersburg Inn into a saloon and restaurant. Soon there were no fewer than six roadhouses at Petersburg, complete with gambling houses, prizefights, and prostitution. The Petersburg Inn in particular had constant scrapes with the law through 1912. After 1916 Petersburg made some feeble attempts to keep its illegal gambling, bootlegging, and prostitution alive before succumbing to prohibition altogether. If nothing else, places on the Colorado plains like Trail City, Boston, and Petersburg may have served as excellent refuge for retired prostitutes if the towns had survived. Blanche Alexander, who worked in Cripple Creek at the turn of the century, died at the age of ninety-nine in the eastern Colorado town of Brush.

Prostitution in the southern half of Colorado flourished as much as in any other part of the state. In an area where the chief industry was mining, men could outnumber women as much as twenty to one. Often miners and prospectors would migrate from faraway places and settle in a town or camp until they could afford to send for their families. The process could take months or even years, during which lonely men yearned for the sight of a woman—any woman. Thus red-light districts and brothels were highly acceptable among male-dominated communities, including company towns. Later, as the cities across the state grew, railroad travel improved, and women became a more common sight, the social need for such distasteful places began to dwindle.

By then, however, most red-light districts were set firmly in place. Most districts were located within a block of the main drag, paralleling and backing up to respectable business houses. The names may have changed over time, but the game was always the same. A house of ill repute was a house of ill repute, and few decent citizens dared to try and integrate the neighborhood as part of the process of closing it down. Pleasure resorts that were closed down often remained so for a very short time before being reopened under another name or by another owner or occupant. So ingrained were red-light districts in their designated neighborhoods that some failed to lose their reputation as a bad part of town for several decades after prostitution ended.

While they were alive and kicking, however, almost all red-light neighborhoods contributed heavily to the city fund. Fines and fees were heavily enforced on prostitutes on a weekly or monthly basis. Some girls paid rents twice as high as legitimate businesses simply because of their industry. Liquor, which most distributors knew would be sold at exorbitant prices, was more expensive if it was delivered to the row. Doctors, pharmacists, cosmetics dealers, laundries, women's clothing shops, and seamstresses could get away with charging the soiled doves a little more for their services and wares. Even the newsboys could report receiving as much as $1 tip for deliveries or at Christmas. No doubt about it: houses of prostitution were good for business.

Most of the red-light districts in Colorado came about more or less the same way. After all, the "world's oldest profession" had already had plenty of time to practice. Each town, however, seemed to have its own individual quirks and characters. Altitudes, climates, local industries, and ethnic origins had much to do with the making and shaping of any camp, town, or city, as well as the prostitution districts therein. In the southern part of the state, a good number of coal-mining camps were company towns, run by large organizations that housed, fed, and employed their men. Wisely, most company towns also included a small red-light district or at least contracted with the ladies from larger cities to make scheduled visits.

Not all of southern Colorado's mining towns were company run. Florence, founded in 1873 between Canon City and Pueblo, flourished in coal mining, cattle, oil, and agriculture. Lillian Powers was Florence's most famous madam. She arrived after serving Laura Evens in Salida for several years and set up her own place south of the railroad tracks. It was said that Lillian had been a schoolteacher in Wisconsin before coming west. She was educated and looked younger than she was. She had formerly been a laundress, and her boss fondly dubbed her "the Laundry Queen." But such work was dull to Lillian, and before long she had made her way to South Dakota, where she heard about the money prostitutes were making in Denver.

Lillian actually had her start in Denver right around the turn of the century, when she ran a house called the Cupolo. But she didn't like the way prostitutes were being treated or the low wages they received. In about 1907 Lillian moved first to Victor, for four years, and then to Cripple Creek, where she ruled over her own crib. Lillian preferred running a crib to working in a confining parlor house. It was said she kept her place neat with clean linens and towels, frilly curtains, and other comforts. Lil's landlady was a French woman known around town as Leo the Lion, whose real name was Leola Ahrens. Leo drank a lot and threw violent temper tantrums. In her early days in Cripple Creek, Leo had run a sporting house and invested her profits in the cribs. When Lillian worked for her, Leo had lost the house and was a working madam in her own cribs.

Because Lil's place was so neat and clean, and because she was always willing to lend a sympathetic ear, she made friends with many of her regulars, with the result that she had an excellent income within just one short month. It was said that some of Lil's customers came to visit her for her friendship rather than sex. Unlike some of the other cribs girls, Lil also served beer as part of her favors. Leo ultimately got jealous over losing her customers to Lil. One day, in a drunken rage, Leo began pounding on Lillian's door, gun in hand. "You double-crossing bitch, you get out, and I mean get out!" she screamed. "You get out of this crib and out of town. Or I'll kill you!"[12]

Lil fled out the back door to the telephone office and called madam Laura Evens in Salida, asking for a job. Then she hired a local boy to help her pack, a process that took all night. For some reason Lil took the earliest train to Colorado Springs first, before going on to Salida. At Laura Evens's, another young woman answered the door and reported to Laura the new girl looked "dirty and old." Laura rented a crib to Lil anyway. The following day, after a good bath, Lil dressed up and paid Laura a visit, giving her rent in advance. The two became good friends, and Lillian eventually managed the cribs for Laura in return for a percentage of the profits.

In about 1911, shortly after going to work for Laura, Lillian moved to Florence near Canon City and opened her own place. At least one of the girls from Salida followed her and may have gone to work for her. Laura Evens came to visit her there, and Lil made occasional visits to Salida as well. "Lil's Place" in Florence afforded many amenities, including two or three girls, a beer garden with a dance floor, and a high wall around the backyard for privacy. She spent $30,000 on her house, which featured a ballroom with a player piano. It was also said she had a huge collection of fine-cut glass and diamonds, including a diamond cross that was once given to Mattie Silks by prostitute Lizzie Preston. Lil slept downstairs and her boarders upstairs. Roy Pray, who was born in Victor in 1910 and grew up in Florence, recalled visiting Lil's house while he was in college during the 1930s. One of the girls kept sitting on the lap of Roy's friend. Unable to stand it any longer, the shy and embarrassed boy finally admonished the girl with a "There now, tut tut!"[13]

From time to time over the years, Lil was shut down. Eventually she hired a couple to cook and maintain the house. By the 1940s Lil could afford ten girls and was no longer a working madam, but she was eventually closed down for good and simply retired, passing away at a local nursing home in 1960. After Lillian's death Colorado author Caroline Bancroft attempted to contact Arthur Mink, a friend of Lil for some thirty years. In a letter to Ms. Bancroft, Mink confirmed a promise he had made to Lil not to reveal anything about her past.[14] Such was the attitude for many years regarding the privacy of prostitutes.

It is said that Florence's rival town, Canon City, had no red-light district. Part of the reason may have been that Canon City is home to the Colorado State Penitentiary. Just outside the city limits, however, a suburb of Canon City called Prospect Heights offered what Canon City could not. At Prospect Heights, bars were open day and night. The town's only mercantile, a giant building with several floors, also served as a hotel, bar, and brothel. Bells were installed in the upstairs bedrooms so they could be rung from the downstairs bar. A tiny jail on the main drag held those who got too rowdy or drunk. During the early 1900s actor Tom Mix often landed himself in the jail at Prospect Heights while filming silent westerns in Canon City.

In addition, prostitutes could be accessed at a handful of other dance halls outside the city limits. The tiny village of Guffey, located about thirty miles northwest of Canon City, today sports two bars and restaurants, a few antique stores, and some real estate offices—but no gas station. These days, the town is unique in that for the last few decades its mayors have come in the four-footed variety—with a cat or dog reigning supreme. In its time, however, Guffey was very much part of an active mining district and was said to have had a few cribs.

The even more southerly town of Creede surpassed Canon City and several other towns in the prostitution industry. As early as 1879, Creede boasted five saloons, three dance halls, one variety theater, and a number of brothels. Creede Lily was one well-known prostitute of Creede whose death coincided with the murder of Jessie James's killer, Bob Ford. The illustrious gambler, who gained notoriety for killing outlaw Jesse James in 1882, was only nineteen years old when he took his place in history. After being pardoned for killing his infamous cousin, Bob Ford roamed the country. Eventually he landed in Colorado City, where in 1889 he was said to be dealing faro at the Crystal Palace. He also worked for Laura Bell McDaniel and for the Nickel Plate Saloon.

During one of his many sudden departures from town, Bob Ford tried his luck in Creede. When he opened his Exchange Saloon in 1891, he was already employing a prostitute named Dot. Still, Ford made frequent trips back to Colorado City, where he was arrested for gambling in December of 1891. When he decided to seek greener pastures in Cripple Creek, he was turned away at the city limits by sheriff Hi Wilson.

What happened next is an interesting footnote in history. On February 3, 1892, the *Colorado City Iris* announced that Ford had gone to try his luck in Creede once more. Success came easier there, and Ford soon found himself officiating prizefights and even running a dance hall and brothel out of a tent. Ironically enough, a rumor briefly circulated that Ford had been killed in Creede shortly after he departed Colorado City. That fateful rumor would soon ring truer than anyone realized. In June Ford was back at his dance hall tent in Creede. Edward or Edmund "Red" Kelley (who has been alternately identified as Ed O'Kelley and Ed O. Kelley) was waiting for him. A former deputy sheriff from Pueblo, Kelley was one of hundreds who didn't like Ford. On June 8, according to most accounts, Kelley walked into Ford's, said, "Hello, Bob!" and fired off a double-barreled, sawed-off shotgun a mere five feet from Ford's throat. It was said that one of Ford's girls chewed out Red Kelley for not giving any warning before killing Ford. Even more folks congratulated Kelley on ridding Creede and the rest of the world of that "dirty little coward who shot Mr. Howard."

Ford's funeral procession included Hugh Thomason, a reporter for the *Creede Daily Chronicle* who spoke over the grave of prostitute Creede Lily, who was found dead in her tent of unknown causes within a day or two of Ford's killing. Her real name and origins will probably never be known, but locals described her as beautiful and refined. It was not Lily's habit to drink or mix with drunks, but she was good at faro and had a lot of money from her winnings.

Lily's funeral was greatly overshadowed by Ford's. Some one hundred miners, gamblers, and dance hall women followed his funeral procession to a spot outside the cemetery that was designated for prostitutes and other undesirables. A collection had also been taken for Creede Lily's funeral, and she must have been buried nearby. There was no minister attending the services, so Thomason spoke: "Dear God, we are sending you the soul of Creede Lily. Thou knowest the burdens she had to bear. Be merciful."[15] The memory of Lily was forgotten, or at least lost, in Ford's wake. The festivities there included whiskey and Champagne, imbibed by a large number of soiled doves and local townspeople. Allegedly, the wake turned into a drunken debauch that lasted several days.

Other prostitute graves in Creede included Silver Plume Kate, Georgetown Jenny, Leadville Lucy, Slanting Annie, and Lulu Slain, who took her own life with morphine. Lulu's housemate, known as the Mormon Queen, attempted suicide at the same time as Lulu but was saved. Likewise Rose Vastine, also known as Timberline, was revived by doctors after an intended overdose. Any of these girls may have worked at Zang's Hotel, built in 1892 by Denver beermeister Philip Zang. The hotel had four rooms upstairs, plus a stone and brick building with five more cribs in the back.

Toward the central part of the state, the tiny town of Bonanza mined lead, zinc, silver, and gold. Early in Bonanza's history as a mining camp, miner Charles Brown wrote to his wife back east, "Thus far I have seen no prostitutes in Bonanza, but I understand there will be some soon as they are looking for them every day."[16] Brown was correct that the painted ladies would soon converge on Bonanza. Pioneer Anne Ellis, who traveled the gold camps of Colorado as a child and later as an adult, wrote in her memoirs of breaking the rules as a young girl and visiting a brothel: "And this is what I remember: first, a strong sweet smell, several pretty girls with lots of lace on their clothes . . . one is sitting on the floor in a mess of pillows, two men, dressed and seemingly in their right minds, are sitting there laughing. They give me candy, and I leave after having a very pleasant time."[17]

Helen, an employee of Laura Evens's Salida brothel, had a very different picture of the way things were in the underworld of Bonanza. "I have fucked from coast to coast," she said, "and never yet have seen such illiterate women, as there are here in Bonanza."[18]

South of Bonanza, just above the New Mexico border, Durango also had its share of prostitution. Early on, Durango's red-light district soon grew out of hand as city officials recognized the value of assessing fines versus closing the bordellos down. Like most of Colorado's towns, the city simply enacted a monthly fine and enjoyed the profits. Authorities did voice their disapproval, however, when the mountain town of Silverton managed to rid itself of a group of gamblers and prostitutes, and the group ambled over to Durango to set up shop once more. Another bone of contention was the magnificent Strater Hotel, built in 1887 by twenty-year-old Harry Strater. For many years, the Strater maintained a class of elegance that was rare among such hotels of the West. Within a few years, however, Strater leased his hotel to H. L. Rice, and the two soon had a falling out over "differences in policy."[19] Their problems may have been that Rice expanded the Strater's basement saloon and gambling hall to include prostitution.

John Arrington of New Mexico recalled that during his boyhood, Madam Bessie Rivers operated a bar, dance hall, and brothel in the Strater with as many as forty women. Rivers's services included a big safe to keep her customers' valuables for them. Indeed, Bessie was honest and decent, and even upstanding citizens often stopped into her place for no more than a drink. When Arrington was spied by Bessie on his one-time visit, she immediately sent him away for ice cream and arranged for him to be taken back to his uncle's cow camp and put to bed. Author Joanne West Dodds claimed that the brothel was located on the fourth floor of the Strater and was known as "Monkey Hall."[20] Outside of Durango were other towns such as Ignacio, where the Fabian Hotel served as a dance hall and house of ill repute one and a half miles west of town. In nearby La Plata was a brothel known as the Convent or Jessie's Convent after the madam who ran it.

Chapter Seven

The Shady Ladies of Colorado City

※

Don't you think she's awful,
Slightly on the mash?
See how close her lips are
to that young man's mustache.

O heavens! He has kissed her.
Her parents are away.
But if they saw her actions
What do you think they'd say?
            —Sung by Viola Clifton
at the Palace Theater in Denver, circa 1879

Very early on, Colorado City—that rough and notorious transient town west of Colorado Springs—was a virtual den of sin, although a good number of churchgoing, hardworking citizens lived there. The class of most residents seldom rose above the blue-collar variety. Gold-processing mills, the Colorado Midland Railroad, and a number of labor industries made Colorado City unattractive to white-collar, wealthier people. And Colorado City had long been a transient supply town with liquor, gambling, and prostitution present right out of the gate. Thus respectable, working-class folks who lived, worked, and raised families in "Old Town" were largely overshadowed by the saloons, dance halls, and brothels brimming along the south side of Colorado Avenue.

Newspapers were rife with tales of the wicked goings-on in the redlight district. In some cases, certain issues and disputes could be discussed for months. Colorado Springs's *Gazette Telegraph*, the *Colorado City Iris,* the *Colorado City Independent,* and the *Colorado City Argus* all took turns publishing news of what was happening among prostitutes and their beer-slinging counterparts. The *Gazette* and the *Iris* in particular tended to side with organizations like the Women's Christian Temperance Union and the ax-wielding, bar-smashing Carry Nation. The *Independent* and the *Argus* were more inclined to remain nonpartisan, taking one side or the other as the editor saw fit.

Among Colorado's red-light districts, Colorado City appears to have been average in size, location, and population. Also, the district's battles with the law were similar to those fought in other cities. But the women of Colorado City are much easier to trace, perhaps because their industry was more socially acceptable in a working-class, blue-collar town. Because it is easier to access their pasts, the women of Colorado City bear closer examination.

Laura Bell McDaniel

In 1888 Colorado City was nearly thirty years old and still growing, with a population of fifteen hundred. In contrast to nearby Colorado Springs, where liquor was illegal, Colorado City sported sixteen saloons. Several prostitutes plied their trade along Colorado Avenue. The best known of these was Laura Bell McDaniel.

Laura Bell was born on November 27, 1861 in Missouri. Both her father, James W. Horton, and her mother, Anna Eliza Horton, were born in Kentucky, James in 1828 and Eliza (as she was known) in 1839. The 1860 federal census shows that James and Eliza were farming in Buffalo Lick, Missouri, with a one-year-old son named James who was born in Missouri. Ten years later the 1870 census notes that Eliza Horton was without her husband in Buffalo Lick. James Jr., now aged twelve, was still living at home, and there are two other additions to the household: eighteen-year-old David Hasbly, relation unknown, and Eliza's ten-year-old daughter, Laura.

Sometime between 1870 and 1880, Eliza married another farm laborer, John Warmoth. The 1880 census lists the Warmoth household as consisting of several people, including thirty-eight-year-old John, forty-year-old Eliza, and a two-year-old daughter named Merlie. The other residents were two nephews, twelve-year-old Fredrick Horton and eight-year-old Wiley Short. James Horton Jr. is identified as Warmoth's stepson. Most telling is the listing of Eliza's nineteen-year-old daughter, Laura, whose name is changed in the 1880 census to Bell. The boys, with the exception of Wiley

Short, were occupied as farm laborers. Eliza was listed as "keeping house," while Bell was noted as being "at home." Despite living in what appears to be a fairly large household with many mouths to feed, Laura Bell apparently received a good education, learning to read and write at an early age. Between her lessons, she likely assisted her mother in performing all the household duties while the men of the house were at work.

On November 1, 1880 Bell Horton married twenty-two-year-old Samuel Dale, the son of a wagon maker in nearby Brunswick, and it is fun to speculate that the two met when Samuel's father repaired a wagon for the Hortons.[1] Shortly after the marriage, Sam and Bell migrated to Colorado. It is believed that Laura Bell spent time, alone, in El Paso, Texas or Las Cruces, New Mexico upon leaving Missouri. At either place, she was said to have met Henry McCarty, alias Billy the Kid. Laura Bell also met Henry's cousin, Rhody W. "Dusty" McCarty, and the two were destined to be lifelong friends.

All that is known for sure is that Bell Dale surfaced in Salida, Colorado in about 1882. In the mid-1880s Eliza Warmoth followed her daughter to Salida. She may have been there as early as 1884, when a Mrs. Lizzie Warmoth is noted as a laundress in Salida. John Warmoth may have died by that time, since Eliza later listed herself as a widow in census records. James Horton and Wiley Short also seem to have disappeared by the time Eliza came to Colorado. At about this time, Eliza began going by her first name, Anna. Also, another daughter seems to have appeared with her, Birdie May. Birdie was born in Missouri in 1877 or 1878. There is little doubt that Birdie, who was still a toddler, accompanied her mother to Colorado.

In Salida Laura Bell was first known as Belle Dale. Salida was just two years old at the time, but the presence of several other Dales in Salida suggests that Laura Bell may have been persuaded to move there by family or in-laws. Within a year of her arrival, Laura gave birth to a daughter, Eva Pearl Dale. Sometime after that, if he was still present at all, Sam Dale seems to have disappeared. The 1885 Colorado census notes that Mrs. Dale was now going by the name Laura Bell and was living alone with her daughter in Salida. The first time Laura Bell appeared in the newspapers of Salida was during the winter of 1886–87. Her home at the time was identified as being located next to Mulvaney's store and across from the railroad; since this location was across the river and some blocks from Salida's red-light district, Laura Bell may not have been practicing prostitution just yet. She was also courting John Thomas "Tom" McDaniel, with whom she took a trip to Leadville that winter.

During the couple's absence Laura Bell's home burned to the ground. As it happened, Laura Bell was very highly insured, and arson was immediately suspected. A man named Morgan Dunn was thought to have set the fire. Dunn, a man of questionable character, was boarding at the home of Laura Bell's mother, forty-five-year-old Anna Warmouth. To Tom McDaniel the fire must have seemed like a good opportunity to get ahead—tax records reveal that McDaniel's personal property in 1886 was valued at a mere $25.

Laura Bell relocated to a new home near the heart of Salida's red-light district, within just a few feet of the Arlington Hotel, located at F Street

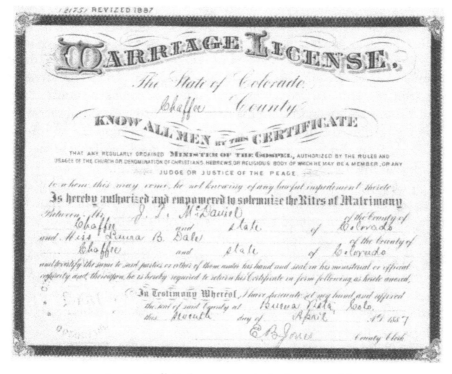

Fig. 27. Laura Bell Dale apparently had respectable intent when she married Tom McDaniel, but the union ended in acrimony. The couple's discarded marriage license surfaced years later at a Colorado City yard sale.

(From the author's collection.)

and Sackett. Despite her seemingly new association with the red-light district, Laura Bell married McDaniel on April 7, 1887 at nearby Buena Vista. Barely a month after the marriage, in May, Laura Bell received her insurance money. Just a few days later, on Friday the 13th, Laura Bell reported to Tom McDaniel that Morgan Dunn had tried to kiss her. Tom retorted, "Why didn't you kill the son of a bitch?"[2]

The couple had been planning to hop a Denver & Rio Grande train to the resort town of Red Cliff the next morning. The trip, however, was forgotten as Tom and his bride set out for Anna Warmouth's house. Dunn was eating dinner when the McDaniels came into the room. Dunn began "abusing" Tom to the point that Laura Bell suggested they just go home and asked her mother to accompany them.[3] Later that evening Tom went out for candles. He returned to find Dunn at the McDaniel house. Dunn became "abusive" again and finally challenged McDaniel, stating, "We're all [here] alone," he said, "and we might as well settle it now as any time."[4]

When Dunn placed his hand on his hip pocket, Tom McDaniel drew a gun and fired five shots. Two of the shots were fatal. Three employees at the Arlington Hotel next door heard the noise and ran to the house. They found Tom standing in front of the door. Laura Bell and her mother were clinging to him and screaming, and Anna was exclaiming, "Oh Tom! Oh Tom! Why did you do that?" McDaniel replied coldly, "He had no business in my house."[5]

Tom McDaniel was found innocent because he was acting in self-defense, but the general public had other notions. The fuss probably started when Dunn's wife in New York wrote to Judge McComas in Salida with a barrage of questions. She had been informed of the murder by Morgan's half brother, John Dunn. Apparently Mrs. Dunn was illiterate, for the letter was written by a woman named Agnes McSweeney. Mrs. Dunn, apparently unaware of her husband's questionable lifestyle in Salida, wanted to know where he was buried, the details of his death, and what his occupation had been.[6]

The *Salida Semi-weekly Mail,* meanwhile, speculated freely about the killing. It was said that Tom McDaniel was a jealous husband, and that he may have killed Dunn in order to keep him quiet about the mysterious fire that had burned Laura Bell's first home. The paper also noted that not only was Dunn unarmed, he had also recently suffered a broken arm and collarbone from a fight he'd been in with a railroad brakeman the previous winter. The paper further commented how Dunn was "buried without care or decency."[7]

Furthermore, the *Mail* asserted that the five shots McDaniel fired showed he had more of a desire to kill Dunn than protect himself. In court, the paper said, attorney J. M. Lawrence practically forced the jury to acquit McDaniel. In the wake of the accusations, one J. W. McDaniel of McFall, Missouri—probably a relative of Tom—also wrote to Judge McComas requesting details of Dunn's killing.

Possibly in an effort to clear the matter up, both Laura Bell and Tom McDaniel gave the newspaper an interview. But facts were distorted by both the newspaper and the McDaniels. For example, Tom and Laura Bell both testified that Dunn took his coat off and threw it on a bed, when in fact Dunn was wearing his coat when he died.[8] Anna Warmouth testified that Dunn had not put his hand behind him before the shots were fired, as had been previously reported.

It can be safely assumed that the McDaniels continued to receive suspicious looks from the townspeople of Salida regarding both the fire and the killing of Morgan Dunn. A short time after the trial the couple left Salida and may have in fact parted ways, for Laura Bell appears to have been alone when she surfaced in Colorado City in 1888. She listed herself on Colorado Avenue as Mrs. Bell McDaniels. Whether Eva Pearl was with her or her mother is unknown, but Laura Bell seemed to have little trouble shedding her skin as an abused housewife and starting over with a whole new attitude.

Before long Laura Bell reigned as "Queen of the Colorado City Tenderloin."[9] Her first brothel in Colorado City was at 25th and Vermijo. Laura Bell's was said to be the best bordello in town, and she hobnobbed with the rich, the famous, and the powerful. Rumors abounded about an alleged affair she had with millionaire Charles Tutt, whose riches came from Cripple Creek and the copper mines of Utah. Old-timers recalled watching Laura Bell and other ladies of the evening walking to the corner drugstore in broad daylight to buy magazines and toiletries, noting that the girls dressed and behaved like ladies. The shady ladies of Colorado City did not solicit on the streets and kept close to their district.

Laura Bell was indeed a woman of character who also did much charity work. She quickly became known as the classic "whore with a heart of gold," who helped those down on their luck, donated to charities regularly, and helped the homeless find shelter. At Christmas the newsboys who delivered her paper could always count on a silver dollar tip, and even the proper folk of Colorado City seemed to be in awe of her.

One of Laura Bell's closest friends in Colorado City was John "Prairie Dog" O'Byrne. By the time Laura Bell met him, he had already lived a full life for such a young man if the stories about him are true. Born in 1862 to immigrants from Ireland, O'Byrne was raised in Ohio and Kansas. Eventually he hired on with the railroad and worked in Texas and California before landing in Trinidad, Colorado. The colorful hack driver was also employed as a passenger brakeman on the Atchison, Topeka & Santa Fe Railroad between Colorado Springs and Denver when he decided to make Colorado Springs his home.

During Christmas in 1889, O'Byrne dressed as Santa Claus and drove his carriage up and down Tejon Street in Colorado Springs. The wagon was pulled by two tame elk that had been captured in Colorado's North Park during the spring of 1888 and auctioned at the Denver stockyards. O'Byrne purchased the pair from judge A. W. Rucker of Aspen and trained them himself. On the back of the buggy was a small cage with O'Byrne's pet prairie dog, hence his colorful nickname.

O'Byrne used his carriage to provide hack service between Colorado Springs and Colorado City. Presumably he favored passengers who were seeking entertainment and libations at Colorado City as a relief from the stodgy laws that forbade alcohol in Colorado Springs. He delighted in treating his passengers to wild rides between the two towns, covering the span of two and a half miles in just six or seven minutes. O'Byrne also enjoyed riding through Garden of the Gods and amusing tourists with stories about the city.

Although he lived a somewhat respectable life, Prairie Dog was openly friendly with the prostitute Laura Bell. The two could often be seen in Prairie Dog's carriage as he gave Laura Bell rides between Colorado City and Colorado Springs. The friendship seemed a perfect match; Laura Bell appreciated O'Byrne's respectable status as much as O'Byrne appreciated her notorious reputation.

By 1890 "Mrs. Bell McDaniels" was residing on Grand Avenue. Nearby was her mother, now married to a Civil War veteran named John Kistler. Laura Bell's sister Birdie may have been in Colorado City as well, and it was probably about this time that the two women began a series of jaunts to Denver. It was a trip they seemed to enjoy embarking on often. They even had a friend there in Prairie Dog O'Byrne, who had moved north due to a change in his job with the railroad. On Denver's downtown streets, however, the wild smell of O'Byrne's elk often caused domesticated horses to bolt.

Despite her numerous friends and successful business, life was not always grand for Laura Bell. In January of 1891 an employee of hers named

Clara attempted suicide. And there was competition in the form of Minnie Smith, the notorious gambler who bounced around places like Creede and Cripple Creek and was known to beat cheaters with a horsewhip. The hard and crass Minnie was no match for suave and sophisticated Laura Bell, however. As the owner of a brothel that featured a ballroom, costly furniture, and even livery servants, Laura Bell was clearly a cut above the rest.

One day Dusty McCarty showed up in town. Sometime after their first meeting back in 1882, Dusty was apparently blinded in a mining accident. Laura Bell immediately hired her old friend as a bartender, and it was soon known that Dusty made the best drinks along Colorado Avenue. He also knew what was happening and who was who. In his spare time Dusty enjoyed hanging out at the corner of 26th Street and Colorado Avenue, directing folks to the tunnel system connecting Colorado City's bars to the brothels. Laura Bell maintained a lasting comradery with both Dusty and Prairie Dog O'Byrne. When Prairie Dog moved to Chicago in 1892, Laura Bell accompanied him and assisted him in selling his elk. Prairie Dog later recalled happening across the same elk in Streator, Illinois, about a year after he'd sold them.

In June of 1893 Laura Bell officially requested a divorce from Tom McDaniel on grounds of failure to support. The divorce was granted October 27. Information is scant on just what Laura Bell was up to in the years immediately following her divorce. After John Kistler died in March of 1898, Anna Kistler continued living on Grand Avenue around the corner from Laura Bell's and the red-light district. The 1900 census shows one big happy family, with Anna E. Kistler at 405 Grand Avenue. Residing with her was daughter Birdie Moats, as well as Birdie's husband, Edward or Edwin; their infant son, Cecil; and an invalid boarder named Jusef Morris.

Little is known about Birdie Moats before this date. She was born in Missouri in 1878 seventeen years after her infamous sister, and had been married to Edward since about 1898. Edward told the census taker he owned his own home, a fallacy since the Moats were living with Birdie's mother. Eugene Cecil, the Moats's only son, was just six months old when the census was taken, having been born in Colorado.

Laura Bell was living just a few doors up the street at 419 Grand with two boarders, Edith Simmons and Maud S. Ivers. There were also two black servants, Sarah Watson and Margaret Scott, and two male lodgers, Patrick Delea and Jake Goldson. A child belonging to Margaret Scott, who worked as a chambermaid, may have been living there as well. Laura Bell's cook, sixty-one-year-old Sarah Watson, told the census taker she had given birth to six children, three of whom were still living. It is unlikely, however, that Sarah's grown children were living with her. As for Laura Bell, she is listed as head of household, mother of one child, and divorced. Her occupation is noted as an "unemployed landlady."[10]

Within a year Laura Bell left her mother's neighborhood and moved one block north to 609 Washington Avenue. When her house succumbed to fire (not thought to be intentional), she relocated to 615 South 6th Street, dropped the name McDaniel, and became known simply as "Laura Belle." Living with her were Edward and Marguerite Stock as well as Mae Fields. Birdie Moats was at the time living with her husband, Edwin, in the Colorado Springs suburb of Roswell. Also in 1902, Eva Pearl appears for the first time in city directories as Pearl McDaniel, a boarder at her grandmother's house.

Some sources state that Pearl was sent away to live in a convent and had no idea of her mother's occupation, but Pearl was the exception to children with prostitute mothers, who often had little chance for an education or advancement outside the home. According to interviews with those who knew her, Pearl was proud of her mother. Laura Bell's success enabled Pearl to receive a good education, and she does not appear to have been encouraged to follow in her mother's footsteps.[11] No doubt Pearl also appreciated the admiring looks her mother got as she strolled down Tejon Street in Colorado Springs in her regal and refined clothing.

Birdie Moats likewise declined to choose prostitution as a career. Birdie married twice, gave birth to two children, and resided in respectable blue-collar neighborhoods all her life. Birdie's continuing friendship with her prostitute sister is both interesting and uncommon.

In 1903 Laura Bell moved yet again, this time to 615 Washington. Her employees at this address were Helen Briggs; Maud Smith, who was a three-year veteran of the tenderloin; and Charles White, a musician whose wife, Mabel, probably worked as a domestic in the house. Pressure may have been bearing down on Laura Bell, as she made a court appearance on charges of prostitution in June.

Soon after, again perhaps due to pressure from authorities, Laura Bell moved to Cripple Creek. Her first residence was at the Waldorf House in a respectable residential neighborhood known for its boardinghouses. Later she had a brothel on Myers Avenue, and it is known she was in town long enough to rack up property taxes in the amount of $74.24.[12] The debt was never paid, however, as Laura Bell returned to Colorado City in 1905 when her mother died. At the time Birdie was living with Anna. Ed Moats had disappeared. The sisters held the funeral at Anna's home. The Reverend Duncan Lamont, who happened to be a devout crusader against the red-light district, officiated. Anna was buried beside John Kistler at Fairview Cemetery.

Laura Bell likely found consolation in the arms of her good friend Prairie Dog O'Byrne, who returned to Colorado Springs in about 1906. But the Colorado City directory also notes Laura Bell had returned to Cripple Creek. In March the *Colorado City Iris* reported that two bawdy houses had been closed by authorities and that the occupants of one house had gone to Cripple Creek. In all likelihood Laura Bell was one of them. In 1907 city directories list Laura Bell at both 611 Washington in Colorado City and 310 E. Myers Avenue in Cripple Creek. Laura Bell's dual residency may have been inspired by Birdie, who in 1907 was living in Cripple Creek. Birdie had met and married Harry Hooyer, and the two were living in a respectable neighborhood on the other side of town. On March 7, the couple gave birth to their only son, Harry Hooyer Jr.

Dusty McCarty, Laura Bell's good friend, does not appear to have accompanied her to Cripple Creek. The 1907–8 directory lists Dusty and his wife, Nellie, as renting furnished rooms on the second floor at 529 Colorado Avenue. Dusty was working as a bartender for W. W. Howd. Before long "Mrs. Laura Bell McDaniels" had rejoined her friends in Colorado City, returning to her place at 611 Washington. She was also known to list her residence as her old house at 421 Grand Avenue.

Laura Bell's frequent changes of address were more than likely due to more pressure to close the red-light district down. In January of 1909 mayor Ira Foote issued a warning that all prostitutes had ten days to get out of town. The point was emphasized by two mysterious fires that burned down most of the red-light district. The Trilby, Laura Bell's house of ill fame, was one of the casualties. But Laura Bell rallied once more, despite experiencing her third house fire in twenty years. In April her old enemy, the *Colorado City Iris,* referred to Laura Bell as "the oldest and most influential sinner of them all."[13] But such name-calling and dastardly acts barely fazed the brazen harlot, who commissioned contractor John Guretzky in May to build a better bordello. The new structure, called the Mansions, was even grander and built of brick at a cost of $10,000. To top it off, Laura Bell paid $365 in fines throughout the year.[14]

To the *Colorado City Iris*, such a brash act meant war. A May 7 editorial expressed alarm at the building of the Mansions in the "old" red-light district because "[t]his is construed to mean that the attempt will be made to restore the old red-light conditions, since it is thought hardly probable that the former owner, Laura Bell, would erect a building on the old site except for the old purposes."[15] Such statements must have been terribly insulting, especially in light of the fact that other cities, including Cripple Creek, were voting to keep their bars open, thus encouraging their illicit nightlife.

Friends of Laura Bell's were having it no easier from authorities. In January of 1910 Dusty and Nellie McCarty were proprietors of the Brunswick at 530 Colorado Avenue. It was Nellie, however, noted as keeper of the Brunswick House, who was fined $50 plus costs for selling liquor without a license. Dusty quipped to the press that there was no need for detective work, since the couple never denied selling liquor.

Likewise, Laura Bell appears to have kept a clear head when it came to dealing with authorities. In February of 1911 she boldly married Herbert N. Berg, financial editor of the *Colorado Springs Gazette Telegraph*. On the marriage application, fifty-year old Laura Bell discreetly listed her age as thirty-six. So did Berg, who also stated he had never been married before. Laura Bell listed her divorce from Thomas McDaniel back in 1893, and certified that her ex-husband was not deceased.[16]

After the marriage Laura Bell's life went on most likely in the exact fashion she planned it to. Her employees included the usual variety of women from her profession. One of them was Winnie Steele, a.k.a. Winfield Butler, who had been working in Cripple Creek. Winnie was only eighteen years old. In June of 1912 she left Cripple Creek for Colorado City, returning on July 28. Later, in October, Winnie departed to work for Laura Bell McDaniel in Colorado City. The Cripple Creek city register noted: "She has commenced to use coke."[17]

As for Eva Pearl, she had moved away from Colorado City in about 1909. She may have married or, for reasons unknown, changed her last name to Langdon. The Denver City directory for 1912 lists her as "Miss" Pearl Langdon, working for Hext Music Company while rooming at 1475 Court Place. If there was a Mr. Langdon, he did not stick around for very long, but Pearl recorded her name as Langdon when she wed Charles Robert Kitto on July 24. Witnesses to the marriage were her mother, who signed her name Laura Berg, and her aunt Birdie Hooyer.

Mamie Majors

While Laura Bell McDaniel was without a doubt the most prominent madam in Colorado City, she experienced her share of competition.

Hundreds of other soiled doves flew through the district during its thirty-year heyday. Some competed with Laura Bell to maintain the finest house in the district; others simply jumped on the bandwagon, hoping to make a little money.

Of the reigning madams in Colorado City, Mamie Majors appears to have come closest to achieving the fame and success of Laura Bell McDaniel. In Colorado City, both madams ruled over their respective kingdoms with grace and finesse. Both madams also paid their monthly fines to the city on time, subscribed to newspapers, and donated to schools, churches, and other charities. Even after employee Carrie Briscoe married Burt Wells in 1902, Mamie Majors paid for shipment of Carrie's body when she died of tuberculosis in 1906. The cost was $113.50.[18]

Although she may have arrived in Colorado City as early as 1897, Mamie does not appear in city directories until about 1901.[19] That year she roomed with several other women at 615 Washington Avenue, a brothel owned and operated by Nellie White. Nellie had apparently purchased her brothel from Mary Jones. The 1900 census lists Mary as the thirty-one-year-old madam of the house. Mary was born in Indiana, could read and write, and listed herself as a housekeeper. One of Mary's borders, Nellie Jones, may have been a sister. Nellie stated she was born in Indiana in 1868, just a year after Mary, and also listed herself as a housekeeper. A third boarder was Nellie Thomas, who said she was born 1876 in South Carolina. Nellie Thomas could also read and write and stated she had been a musician for the past two years.

Mamie Majors and Nellie White were destined to maintain a business relationship for many years, even after Mamie opened her own brothel in 1902. The bordello was at 617 South 6th Street. Her employees there were Katie Stephens and Emma West. Nellie White, whose brothel had burned in the fire of 1902, found herself again working with her former employee. The women became partners of sorts. Nellie had the brains, and Mamie had evolved into a smart, fashionable businesswoman. Mamie did her shopping in downtown Colorado Springs and was a law-abiding citizen, paying her monthly fines on time and upholding the law—the exception being her profession.

By 1903 Mamie's business was blooming. Nellie White continued working with Mamie, as did employees Blanche Freeman, Mary Stevens, and Emma West. Two musicians, James Tennison and William H. Robison, played regularly for the house. Emma Jones worked as a cook. A $50 fine in June for running a house of ill fame hardly fazed the illustrious madam.

Mamie's brothel teemed with success even after she moved to 617 Washington. Mamie had purchased the brothel from Laura White, another prominent madam.

Laura told the 1900 census taker she was born November 1860 in Missouri. Before coming to Colorado City Laura had resided in Pueblo. Somewhere along the way she had married, but her husband had died. In 1900 Laura owned her home but was forced to take out a mortgage. Her employees included two nineteen-year-olds, Killie Duffey of Kentucky and Laura Logan of Missouri. Laura's financial woes were probably what caused her to sell her brothel. When Mamie Majors took over, the place became known as both the White Elephant and the Mansions.

In fact, so successful were the brothels on Washington Avenue that by June of 1905 Colorado City authorities had had enough. Mamie, like the other madams in the district, paid fines of $25 in April and May. Her employees at 617 Washington included Nellie White; boarders Minnie Gardner, Dot Hamilton, Blanche West, and Ioma Williams; domestic Maggie Butts; and musician William Edwards. City officials, however, were no longer satisfied with the monthly "bribes" and raided the red-light district. Mamie Majors was targeted and arrested on June 22, along with Annie (Anna) Wilson and Mamie Swift. Byron Hames and Otto Fehringer came to the rescue, posting a $1,500 bond for the three women. Mamie Swift was ill and could not come to court, but charges against her and the other two women were filed by district attorney C. C. Hamlin.

Mamie's case came up on July 17 and caused quite a stir in Colorado City. The wealthy madam lost little time in hiring not one but three attorneys to handle her case. The first was Samuel Kinsley. Thin with a beakish nose, the studious Kinsley came from Cripple Creek, having served as a judge there in 1892. A founding figure in Cripple Creek history, Kinsley quickly established himself as a leading lawyer in Colorado Springs. The other two attorneys, Arthur Cornforth and William D. Lombard, were equally reputable. Cornforth and his wife, Fannie, lived in an elite neighborhood of Colorado Springs, and the attorney became a state senator in 1906. William D. Lombard was born in Nova Scotia and attended college in Canada before arriving in Colorado Springs. Lombard later also served as an attorney for Laura Bell McDaniel. No doubt Mamie had every confidence in the world when she reappeared in court with the three attorneys.

In fact, Mamie's antics seem to have been quite bold, for even while she was awaiting trial her business continued at 617 Washington. The 1905–6 directory lists Mary Crain, Stella Ingram, and Zoe Wallace, with

Lottie Donaldson employed as a domestic. Hence it could not have been much of a surprise that in spite of Mamie's plea of "not guilty" and the diligent work of her lawyers, she was found guilty. The determined madam was undaunted and used every power she had to fight the guilty charge. A motion for a new trial was filed on July 31.

Unfortunately for Mamie, the cards were stacked against her. Witnesses for the prosecution consisted of police chief George Birdsall, city detective John Rowan, police magistrate and former mayor J. D. Faulkner, and police officers Leroy Gilliland and Ed Rettinger. Also called to testify against Mamie were Anna Rook, who had worked for Mamie in 1903, and Ioma Williams. When Ioma took the stand, she stated, "I live at 617 Washington with Miss Majors. I refuse to answer to what kind of a house she kept there, as it might degrade me."[20]

Mamie's other boarders were Minnie Gardner, Dot Hamilton and Blanche West, as well as her domestic servant Maggie Butts and musician William Edwards. Apparently these people were not called to testify, but further evidence showed Mamie had averaged one court visit per month in the previous eighteen months. Although it was established that Nellie White owned the house and paid the bills there, Mamie continued to be prosecuted for her actions. On August 3 the motion for a new trial was overruled. Judge L. W. Cunningham sentenced Mamie to six months in El Paso County Jail plus court costs. Mamie appealed Cunningham's decision to the state supreme court. In September of 1906 the original judgment was upheld.

The 1906 city directory illustrates that, at least at one point, Mamie moved again, this time to 615 Washington. The occupants in that building during 1904–5 were Rose Healey, Jeanette St. Clair, and Clara Stillwell as well as black servant Margaret Scott. When Mamie moved in, however, she appears to have been the sole occupant. Still determined to clear her name, Mamie enlisted her influential friends to secure a governor's pardon. On September 20, 1906, the *Colorado City Iris* printed a copy of a letter from Colorado state governor Henry A. Buchtel. The letter was addressed to the Reverend Frank W. Hullinger of Colorado City. Buchtel's published letter was a reply to one he had received from Colorado City's WCTU, a letter he called "discourteous." The note read in part, "Senator Cornforth came with a bundle of letters from your most prominent people, asking for the pardon of Mamie Majors, but I did not pardon her at all."

Buchtel's letter goes on to include excerpts from letters written by N. B. Hames, Judge Orr, and several other prominent citizens. Each letter requested that Mamie be released from serving her upcoming jail time. Hames's letter stated in part, "Having known Miss Mamie Majors for twenty years and found her always upright and honorable in her business dealings, we would consider it a great favor if you would pardon her from the charge that is now against her."[21] Judge Orr's letter stated she had ceased business. Most interesting were letters from J. D. Faulkner and Officer Rettinger, since they had initially testified against Mamie. All of the letters made Mamie Majors appear more innocent than a June bride.

Governor Buchtel reiterated in his published letter, "Now in the face of all this, I did not pardon Mamie Majors. Please fix that in your mind. I would like to say it over and over about 10,000 times, *I did not pardon Mamie Majors.*"[22] The good governor's name was cleared in the eyes of Colorado City's do-gooders. What the *Colorado City Iris* failed to mention until a few days later was that Buchtel had reduced Mamie's sentence from six months to thirty days. The newspaper further emphasized that senator Arthur Cornforth had informed Buchtel that Mamie was not even in jail. Upon discovering this, the governor insisted she immediately be incarcerated.

After serving her thirty days in jail, Mamie returned to her wicked ways. She moved back to 615 Washington, and the 1905–6 directory lists Lola Siggars living there as well as Margaret Scott. Like many madams, Mamie experienced a high turnover. The employees listed as living with her one year tended to change by the following year. In the wake of her scandalous court case, Mamie's former employees parted ways with her. By 1907 Mamie's cook, Emma Jones, had given up her life in the red-light district and was a boarder at 114 South Conejos in Colorado Springs. William Robison was working with Robison Brothers and resided at 549 East Cimarron with his wife, May. Mary Stevens is listed in the 1907 directory as a boarder at 223 South Nevada, Colorado Springs. Ioma Williams apparently left Colorado City soon after her humiliating experience in court.

Undaunted, Mamie continued to rebuild her business. In April of 1909 the *Iris* noted that despite a short-lived reformation, Mamie had now "fitted up the old 'City Hotel'" and was back in full operation.[23] The city directory lists her at 626 Washington. By May, Mamie and her cohorts had reverted to paying their customary $25 in monthly fines. From September 1909 through February 1910, Mamie paid an average of $41 per month in fines, all for keeping a bawdy or disorderly house. In 1910 Mamie had relocated to 710 Washington, where she stayed through

1913. That year Mamie and inmates Marie Fitzgerald and Jennie Johnson were fined again. Jennie also worked as a domestic in Cripple Creek in 1900 and in Colorado City as late as 1908. Mamie remained in business through at least 1916, when Colorado City succeeded in declaring liquor unlawful within city limits. With the demise of the saloons and gambling houses, the pressure to cease business was even greater on prostitutes. Eventually Mamie gave in to the law and, like so many others, disappeared without a trace.

Nellie White

Nellie had spent some time traveling before landing in Colorado City. She first appears in Pueblo, where in 1895 she paid fines for prostitution from June to the end of the year. Additional fines were paid in Pueblo in April and again from June through November of 1896.[24] Simultaneously, a copy of the *Denver Times* in 1896 reported on a Mrs. F. C. Probasco, who borrowed $5 from Nellie White of Market Street. When Nellie demanded "security" for the loan, Mr. Probasco had his wife put up a sixteen-year-old girl who was a friend of the family. Probasco was promptly arrested, and Nellie seems to have disappeared.[25]

In 1901 "Mrs." Nellie White was running a house of prostitution at 615 Washington. In her employ were Millie Arnold, Edith Baker, Mamie Majors, Laura Smith, Zoe Wallace, Fredy Bowers, and Lou Riley (also spelled Reilly), who worked as a cook. In 1896 both Fredy Bowers and Laura Smith had paid fines for prostitution in Pueblo. Lou Riley was apparently also a veteran in the business, having run a brothel the year before on the north side of Washington, between 6th and 7th streets. Because Lou Riley was black, she probably worked as a domestic for Nellie, who was white. Lou remained as an employee of both Nellie and Mamie Majors through 1903.

In 1902 Nellie's brothel burned, and she moved in with Mamie Majors at 617 South 6th Street. The directory lists her as a roomer, although court records suggest Nellie owned the building she worked in. Nellie remained with Mamie through June of 1903, when she was taken to court for prostitution. In a rare show of mercy, the court dismissed her case. The 1903 directory also lists Nellie as the widow of E. F. White. Little more is known about her, except that she was fined $25 plus court costs in May of 1909 for running a bawdy house. From 1911 through 1913 she is listed at 615 Washington. After that, Nellie disappears from record.

Laura Gipson

Also known as Laura Gibson, another of Colorado City's madams operated a brothel at 625 Washington in 1902. Her employees included Irene Blake, who had worked at Cripple Creek's Bon Ton Dance Hall in 1900, as well as Hallie Hayhurst, and Loretta Williams. Another inmate was Carrie Briscoe. The *Gazette Telegraph* reported in July of 1902 that Briscoe married Burt Wells in Cheyenne, Wyoming. Wells worked for Keller Hack & Livery in Colorado Springs, and so was no doubt aware of his bride's profession. Furthermore, after her marriage, Carrie Briscoe appears to have continued her employment with Laura Gipson for at least another year.

In June of 1903 Laura paid a $50 fine for keeping a house of ill fame. Two years later Laura moved to 619 Washington and took over operations from madam Laura White. Working for White at the time were Mamie Colwell and Myrtle Reed, who had paid fines for prostitution in Pueblo back in 1896. Also at the house were two "colored" domestics, Celia Bassett and Ophelia Woods. When Laura Gipson moved in, Carrie Briscoe and Sybil Clayton were working there. Other employees in the house at that time were a domestic named Emily Crowdy, musician William Edwards, and cook Lizzie Newman, plus boarders Ioma Gerhart and Dottie Vaughn. Later Laura moved to 625 Washington, where her employees included Sybil Carson, Hattie Cooper, Anna McGrew, and Helen Warren. Anna Hawkins worked as the cook. In January of 1906 Laura was tried for selling liquor to minors. The *Gazette Telegraph* noted that the defense offered no testimony, and Gipson spent ninety days in jail. After serving her sentence, Gipson moved first to 617 Washington and then to 530 Colorado Avenue. The 1907 directory lists her as keeper of furnished rooms.

Sadie Stewart

Born in Kentucky in 1863, Sadie arrived in Colorado City sometime before 1900. The census that year notes that Sadie had been married fourteen years and had no children. She owned her home on the north side of Washington Avenue free and clear. Boarding with her were twenty-six-year-old Grace Bennett of Iowa, who had been married for six years and had one child still living. Grace listed herself as an unemployed seamstress. Another employee was twenty-five-year-old Hallie Fretti, born in Louisiana and working as a "laundress." All three women were listed as knowing how to read and write. A third boarder was fifty-one-year-old Gus Huffman.[26]

In 1901 Sadie's house was at 621 Washington (now 2616 West Cucharras). Previously the house had been occupied by Hattie Faetli. Hattie was reported by the 1900 census as born in 1875, literate, and occupied as a "laundress," though she had been unemployed four months. With Hattie was Noel Hazel or Nazel, a white male servant born in 1874. Among Sadie Stewart's employees was a musician, twenty-five-year-old Charles Bascom, who had previously been married for two years to a woman also named Sadie. Mrs. Bascom had filed for divorce on grounds of nonsupport in 1902.[27] Also employed was a coachman named George Moblie and a domestic, Nellie Brooks. The census lists Nellie as black, a native of Kansas, aged twenty-five, married seven years. Her one child was dead, and she could read and write.[28] Two other working-girls, Marion Clayton and Lillie McArthur, also resided at Sadie's home during 1901. The following year Hattie Cooper also came to work at Sadie's.

Fig. 28. This house was occupied by madams Hattie Faetli in 1900, Sadie Stewart from 1901 to 1905, Mamie Majors in 1905, and Anna Wilson in 1905 and 1906. Today an apartment house, it is one of the few brothels in Colorado City to remain in its original condition.

(From the author's collection.)

Sadie's employees in 1902 included Nellie Brooks and musicians Carl Griffen and Russell Dere. Also working for Stewart at that address were Lottie Collins and Hattie Cooper. By the next year Sadie had experienced a complete turnover with the exception of Russell Dere. In June of 1903 Sadie paid a $50 fine. Her girls in 1903 were Emma Byrns, Dot Comstock, Leta Edwards, Dedie McMillan, and Sadie McMillen. Dye Meadows was a domestic. Because Dedie McMillan and Sadie McMillen have such similar names, they may have been the same girl under two different aliases. The only Sadie McMillen in Colorado Springs records was granted a marriage license in January of 1903 for her marriage to Eugene Crysette.[29] In 1907 the directory lists her as a nurse residing at 830 North Weber in Colorado Springs. What became of Dedie McMillan is unknown, but Leta Edwards continued working for Sadie through 1905.

As for Sadie Stewart, she also continued working at the same address. Her employees in 1904–5 were Sadie Frank, Stella Matthews, Mildred Rowe, and a "colored" domestic named Lillie Wright. In 1905 Sadie was raided along with other madams in the district. Sadie took the raids to heart. The city directory for that year shows that she moved to Los Angeles—where she no doubt continued in her profession.

Dolly Worling

Dolly Worling's downfall was Tucker Holland, and she was his. There was no doubt about it, Tucker had it bad for Dolly. The twenty-four-year-old thought nothing of spending his time and money on the soiled dove of Colorado City's red-light district. In fact, for a good six months leading up to Tucker's death, his love for Dolly increasingly turned from mere infatuation into downright obsession. It was said Tucker was a good boy, residing in Colorado Springs and holding a steady job. But the enticement of Colorado City was his undoing. Tucker and his brother Tony were frequent visitors to the red-light district, and both boys had a fondness for Dolly's house of ill fame, the Cottage.

On the night of January 18, 1908, Tucker and Tony were out buying sandwiches for the Cottage girls when Dolly's ex-husband, Frank Shank, arrived. Frank was a foul-mouthed bartender, but his love for Dolly was undying. The couple had been trying to reconcile for some time. Dolly's love for Frank and Tucker had become precariously balanced, tilting in favor of Frank whenever the boisterous man darkened her door. When Tucker returned with the sandwiches, he discovered he'd been unceremoniously ousted from Dolly's house. Employee Nettie Crawford met him at the door. Instructions to find somewhere else to sleep were accompanied by a pile of Tucker's clothes.

Crestfallen Tucker went away, muttering to Tony, "This is the end of me."[30] The following morning, the brothers were once more received at Dolly's house. Tucker and Dolly retired to her boudoir, where Tucker sat on the bed playing with an Iver-Johnson .33 revolver. Dolly stood at the window making light of Tucker's intentions as she listened to him declare his love for her. Outside, a small boy on the sidewalk below was pointing his toy pistol at Dolly's dog. Dolly joked, "See, Tucker, he's going to shoot my poodle!"

But Tucker Holland was in no mood for jokes. "Well, here's another," he replied. A second later a shot rang out as Tucker shot himself in the head. Dolly screamed, and the other girls rushed into the room. Dolly's cook, Birdie Ward, took the gun from Tucker's dying hand and laid it on the dresser. Dolly grabbed the gun and turned it on herself, exclaiming, "If he's dead, I must die too!" Her girls succeeded in wrestling the gun away from her, and Tony summoned the police.[31]

When authorities arrived, they found Tucker bleeding profusely as he lay across Dolly's bed. The pistol was on the dresser. Birdie Ward explained that she had placed it there after Tucker shot himself, but the police refused to believe her story and arrested each occupant of the house, including customer Roy Catton. Tucker was hurried to St. Francis Hospital, where he died at 3 P.M. He never recovered sufficiently to make a statement.

An inquest included questioning of Tony Holland, Nettie Crawford, and Birdie Ward as well as prostitutes Mary Catlin and Myrtle Van Duyne. Frank Shank also was questioned but mostly spewed forth epithets for answers. Dolly was also questioned. The inquiry concluded that Tucker Holland had indeed ended his own life. Tucker was buried at Evergreen Cemetery, and his untimely death inspired the city authorities in Colorado City to close the brothels. The prostitutes of Colorado City were accordingly given ten days to leave town. Where Dolly Worley went is unknown, but her baggage certainly contained the memory of the boy who loved her—and lost.

Hattie Milligan

Hattie Milligan first appears in city directories in 1902, when she ran a brothel of black prostitutes at 623 South 6th Street. Her employees there were Lena Moore and Hannie or Nannie Thompson. In 1903 Hattie moved to 624 Washington, where she worked with Cassie Elliott. Cassie may have served as a cook and stayed with Hattie through 1904. The 1905 directory lists Hattie at 626 Washington along with Hattie Crockett, Helen Ward, and Alberta Montell. Alberta was a Denver transplant; she had worked at 1917 Market and been taken to court for not having a proper liquor license. She was still at 626 Washington in 1906, but after 1905 Hattie Milligan disappears. Cassie Elliott eventually moved to 719 South Weber, a predominantly black neighborhood in Colorado Springs. In 1907 Cassie is listed as the widow of John K. Elliott and living at that address. As for the brothel at 626 Washington, it was soon occupied once more by working girls Ruby Lewis, Alberta Montell, Camille Morris, Ethel Reynolds, and Vernice Taylor.

Eleanor Dumont, a.k.a Madam Mustache

It is said this French bombshell from Paris began her first gambling house in 1850 at Nevada City. Hers was a straight house, with no profanity or violence allowed. Eventually Eleanor began following the gold and silver booms in the West, landing in places in Montana and New Mexico and in Colorado City. Being a woman alone was no problem for Eleanor Dumont. She had several lovers, including a man named Charlie Utter, and could defend herself just fine with a horsewhip or pistol. Once, it was said, Dumont horsewhipped a fellow she caught cheating at cards in Colorado City's Hoffman House. As she grew older, Dumont sprouted the moustache of her famous nickname. How long she was in Colorado City is not clear. Later she became a madam in Eureka, Nevada. She committed suicide in Bodie, California, one of the roughest towns in the West.

Lulu Collins

Lulu was a black prostitute who appears to have arrived in Colorado City in about 1908. Born in Texas circa 1877, Lulu was described by census records as a "mulatto." Her brothel, located on Washington between 6th and 7th streets, was raided one evening in May. The police, who had been watching the house for some time, forced the front and back doors open simultaneously in an attempt to make quick arrests.

Four white men escaped from the building but a fifth man, George Todd, was arrested within and fined $25. Lulu pleaded guilty and was sent to jail to work off her $100 fine. Apparently this one incident was enough to convince Lulu Collins that her life of prostitution in Colorado City was not meant to be. She, too, disappears from city records, but she does resurface in the 1920 census, forty-three years old and working as a maid for a family in Colorado Springs.

Era Clay and the Davenports

In 1902 Era Clay worked and resided at 623 Washington with Eula and Fannie Davenport. Eula may have in fact been Eula Hames, another would-be madam who later became the daughter-in-law of saloon owner Byron Hames. Fannie was probably Eula's sister. Eula eventually moved to 626 Washington, where in 1903 she resided with Margaret Epps and Pearl Livingston. Era Clay's whereabouts are unknown after that. In 1903 Eula Davenport was fined $50 for keeping a bawdy house, after which she and Fannie disappear from city directories altogether. The Davenports may have had a third sister, Minnie, who was reportedly a laudanum addict.

Eula N. Hames

Eula was said to be a prominent madam during the 1890s despite her marriage to a well-known saloon owner's son. N. Byron Hames, operator of one of Colorado City's biggest and best-known taverns, hailed from the town of Silver Cliff in Custer County. The 1880 census shows Hames living with his wife, Viola, and a male infant. This was Gus, the Hames's only child. The success of Hames's saloon in Colorado City enabled him to give Gus a proper education. In 1898, while attending the state agricultural college at Fort Collins, Gus gave a performance at the opera house. The song was "Break the News to Mother," a tune which certainly prophesied his imminent marriage to a madam.[32]

Gus and Eula appear to have married sometime between 1902 and 1904. Eula first appears in city directories in 1903, but the couple is first listed as husband and wife in 1904. Gus Hames worked for some of the finest saloons in town—namely his father's. City directories for 1905–6 list Gus working with his father and living with Eula at 801 Colorado Avenue. By then Gus had become at least as troublesome as his prostitute wife. In 1906 Gus and saloon owner Henry Coby were accused of receiving eight stolen chickens. They were acquitted. Gus remained married to Eula through at least 1907 or 1908, when directories continue to list them at 801 Colorado, but records do not indicate whether the couple ever divorced.

Throughout 1909 Eula paid fines nearly every month ranging from $35 to $65. In April, following fires in January of 1909 that were intended to burn down the red-light district, Eula and Gus continued living on Colorado Avenue. Eula rented "furnished rooms" at 628½ Colorado, while Gus continued working for his father. A few months later Gus was busted for visiting an opium joint. In February of 1910 Eula paid another $102.50 in fines, this time for her brothel at 625 Washington. When Gus died at his father's home in 1911, there is no mention of the widow Eula in his obituary even though Gus had long resided with Eula at 625 Washington. Eula continued living there alone through 1913, and charges against her continued to be levied sporadically during 1913 and 1914. In 1915 she was arrested at the whiskey-totin' town of Ramona. She disappears from city records shortly afterward.

Alice Hill

Miss Alice M. Hill resided at 732 Washington in 1903, and it is probable she ran her own crib there. Two years later Alice moved to 827 North Corona in Colorado Springs. The 1907 city directory states Alice died on April 21 at the age of thirty-eight. While very little else is known of Alice Hill, her presence on Washington Avenue indicates several characteristics concerning the life of a prostitute. Death at a fairly young age suggests Alice may have been ill or the victim of drug or alcohol abuse. Also, Alice's age and her illness would account for her probable status as a crib girl. Alice had the misfortune to outlive her usefulness as a parlor house prostitute, only to die sooner than she should have.

Bessie Paxton

As early as 1900 Bessie Paxton ran a brothel on the north side of Washington, between 6th and 7th streets. Her address was probably that of the El Paso, which Bessie owned or managed. Fortunately for Bessie, the building carried insurance when it burned in 1909. Also in her care was the Mansions, which succumbed to the fire as well. The year 1909 was not a good one for Bessie, who also paid a series of fines beginning in May. From July through January 1910 Bessie paid an average of $58 per month for her profession. From 1910 to 1915 Bessie ran an alleged boardinghouse at 626 Washington, which was probably the Mansions. One of her employees in 1910 was "Mrs." Pearl Hopkins. Bessie disappears from the records after 1915.

Anna Wilson

Anna Wilson was in Colorado City as early as 1896, when she and prostitute Laura Gilson were convicted of contributing to juvenile delinquency after allegedly luring some children into their bordello. In 1905 Anna was living in Sadie Stewarts's old place at 621 Washington. Before long Anna was in trouble with the law. By January of 1906 she was on trial for contributing to the delinquency of minors. The court accused Anna of "selling or permitting to be sold" liquor to Ed Mulley or Mulloy, a minor, back in September. The jury of twelve listened intently as the district attorney explained how five boys under the age of eighteen purchased beer at Anna Wilson's "resort." Wilson spent ninety days in jail.[33] Anna moved out of 621 Washington and madam Mamie Majors took over. Mamie's employees were Ethel Gray, Clara Stillwell, and musician Fred Wright. Across the street was another brothel with at least one boarder, Hazel Reynolds.

As for Anna Wilson, she later operated the Three Deuces, also located on Washington between 6th and 7th streets. The Three Deuces, originally called the Two Deuces, opened in about March of 1906. It was the eighth brothel on the row, referred to by the *Colorado City Iris* as "Twin Hells." The 1907–8 directory lists Anna at 621 Washington, along with one Ethel Wilson. Whether this was the Three Deuces is unknown. The Three Deuces may have been located next door at 623 Washington, where prostitute Lottie Edwards was working in 1907. Like several other brothels, the Three Deuces met its end in the fire of 1909. After that Anna rented "furnished rooms" at 530½ Colorado Avenue for a while. But Anna Wilson was undaunted. By July, if not sooner, Anna was back in business—and paying a $55 fine for keeping a house of ill fame.

Anna Boyd

Anna Boyd is one of a few prostitutes who raised a family while she plied her trade. Born in Germany in 1857, Anna came to America in 1880 and married John Boyd in about 1882. In 1888 the couple had one child, a daughter named Nina. The Boyds appear to have moved to Colorado City in about 1890. Anna and John may have been involved in prostitution as early as 1897, when the couple rented property to Lydia E. Kinney and Belle H. Ord on Washington. In about 1899 the Boyds built or added onto a home at 734 Washington while transacting real estate deals in the nearby red-light district.

The year 1900 proved to be the most interesting and colorful for the Boyds. By 1900, forty-three-year-old Anna was working as a madam and owned her brothel at 625 Washington free and clear while maintaining the home at 734 Washington. At the same time, the 1900 Giles city directory lists Anna as residing on the "south side of Grand Avenue on the first street east of 8th Street." The 1900 census reflects that Anna had borne six children, but the only one living was eleven-year-old Nina, who was away at school. Both Anna and Nina could speak English, read, and write. Anna also had a boarder named Mary Franklin. Twenty-seven-year-old Mary told the census taker she was born in Canada and had come to the United States in 1877. She had been married for six years, and one of her two children, a four-year-old daughter named Elizabeth, was still living. Mary said her occupation was housemaid.[34]

Fig. 29. Anna Boyd conducted prostitution in this house while raising her family in another. When Anna died in 1905, her husband, John, continued operating the brothel.

(From the author's collection.)

According to the 1900 Cripple Creek District directory, John Boyd was working as a stonemason at the Trolley House in Cripple Creek. Simultaneously, the 1900 Colorado City directory lists him as a stonemason residing at 734 Washington (now 2729 West Cucharras). Meanwhile, the couple fell into financial straits, and in December Anna took out a mortgage against the house. As of 1903 it would appear that John and Anna Boyd were no longer together, since John is listed in the city directory as residing at 114½ North Pitkin. Whatever his relationship to Anna at this time, John did continue having business dealings regarding 625 Washington even after Anna's death on March 25, 1905. Interestingly, there is no record of her burial in El Paso County.

After her mother's death Nina Boyd moved into the family home at 734 Washington. In 1907 Nina listed herself in the city directory as an actress. Because of Anna Boyd's prior association with the red-light district of Colorado City, Nina may have lived a less than wholesome life in her pursuit of a career in the acting field. Next door to Nina, a woman named Florence Montgomery may have been operating her own small crib at 730 Washington or was at least employed in the red-light district (by 1910 Florence had moved to the opposite end of the district and was living at 419 Washington). In addition, a lawsuit against Nina also names one John L. Baker, who was noted as living out of state. Neither Baker nor Nina appeared in court, and Nina subsequently lost her parents' home. What became of Nina G. Boyd after that is anyone's guess. A Nina G. Baker and John Baker were listed in the Milford, Massachusetts city directory in 1911–12. A Nina G. Boyd is also listed as living in Natick, Massachusetts in 1931.[35]

As for John Boyd, there is further evidence he remained in Colorado City. Boyd remarried to a woman identified as Ella or Ellen B. in city directories. From 1908 to 1916 the couple remained at the family home on Washington and continued working in the red-light district in some capacity. In 1909 John Boyd owned the Stone Fort, a brothel or dance hall also known as the Stone Front. The Stone Fort also burned in January of 1909. The building had no insurance and was not rebuilt. At the same time John and Ella Boyd acquired 625 Washington Avenue, where Anna had worked in 1900. This address may or may not have been the location of the Stone Fort, but it appears to have stayed in business, as evidenced by the presence of prostitute Louise Montgomery in 1907. After the fires of 1909 the Boyds sold the property to William Williamson and disappeared from record a few years later.

The Boyds were not the only family to make their home on the row; the city directory for 1901 also lists miner Thomas J. Morgan and wife Clara residing on the north side of Washington between 5th and 6th streets. Also in 1901, Fred Smith lived at 420 Washington. By 1904 Smith was living with his wife, Kate, and three children—Olive, Rena, and William—at 912 Washington. The following year the family had moved to 925 Washington. Ultimately, Smith moved to Cripple Creek, where he was working for a saloon at 301 Myers Avenue in 1915.

Domestics

Certainly not all women who worked in the brothels of Colorado City were prostitutes. Mrs. Josie Anderson, for instance, was a domestic on South 5th Street and nothing more. Celia Bassett worked as a maid for about a year in the district. Any self-respecting whorehouse always kept a cook, house-keeper, or chambermaid on hand; the more servants, the more prestigious the house. A good many of the women who worked for the madams of Colorado City were black. But they are a puzzling lot. Some of the women who worked in the kitchens of the red-light district were certainly young enough to enter the profession if they had chosen to do so. Why they did not is anybody's guess. Dye Meadows is a prime example. Dye first appears in city records in 1898, when she obtained a divorce from William Meadows. Sometime after that, Dye met Jennie Robinson. In 1901 and 1902 the women, who were both black, resided together at 624 Washington. Also at the house in 1901 were Lula and William Munroe, with Lula employed as a cook. (From 1904 to 1906 the Munroes lived up the street at 718 Washington, indicating that while they probably continued to work in the red-light district, the couple was able to secure their own housing.) Either prostitution was not suitable to Dye, or perhaps she was employed by Robinson. By 1903 Dye Meadows was working as a domestic for Sadie Stewart at 621 Washington. What became of Jennie Robinson is uncertain.

Nannie Dayton is easier to identify, with her matronly name and easy-to-analyze track record. Nannie, who was also black, married one Richard Dayton in May of 1902. What happened to Richard is uncertain, but after the couple apparently parted ways, Nannie retained her husband's name and went to work on the row. In 1903 she resided at 619 Washington with Alice Kimball and Corinne Roache. Nannie then disappears for a few years. Interestingly, a woman by the same name resurfaces in the 1907 city directory as the wife of George F. Dayton, a deputy sheriff.

Other domestics eventually worked their way out of the prostitution industry. The 1905–6 directory lists Mrs. Etta S. Kemp working as a cook for Alice Griffith at 710 Washington. In 1906–7 she was residing at 516 Robinson, her place of employment unknown. The year 1909 found her back in the red-light district at 720 Washington, but by 1911 she had moved far down the street to 315 Washington.

Still other women did eventually cross the line and dabble in prostitution. Emma Wilson was one of these. The 1890 directory shows Emma residing on Washington Avenue. In 1896 she was living in hoity-toity Colorado Springs at 203 North Wahsatch. Yet the 1900 directory finds her back on Washington, working as a cook for Laura White. The 1900 census shows Emma was black, born in December of 1860 in North Carolina, single, and could not read or write. Emma continued to bounce around the district for some time. In 1901 she was at 626 Washington. Later that year she moved to 620 Washington, where she inexplicably became a madam and employed three girls by the names of Henrietta Frink, Edith Hennesy, and Mamie Dedrick. A boarder, or possibly another working girl, was B. V. Smith. Working for Emma in 1903 were Belle Dedrick and Carrie Kitchin.[36] In June of 1903 Emma paid a $50 fine for running a house of ill fame. In 1904 she still had at least two boarders, Epsie and Theodosia Lee. Boarders in 1905–6 included William Ellis, Pinky Hopkins, and a "colored" cook named Leanna Taylor. Belle Dedrick moved next door in 1905, but Emma continued to live at 620 Washington through 1906.

By 1907 Emma had moved west to 622 Washington, where she was arrested in November for keeping a disorderly house. Emma was unable to pay her $250 bond and went to jail. Upon her release Emma left town for about two years, returning in 1909. The *Colorado City Iris* noted: "Numerous Negro joints have sprung up of late. . . . Red Em evidently considers that race, color or previous condition should be no bar." Accordingly, Emma Wilson was again run out of town, never to return.

Chapter Eight

The Cripple Creek Influence

Cripple Creek was rough and ready
In the days of which I sing—
New found wealth is very heady
And a camp must have its fling.

"Good" folks thought the town was awful
Because some things it did
While maybe not exactly lawful
Were not exactly hid.

Sin and lust I ain't defendin';
But history must be fair;
And there ain't no use in pretendin'
The avenue wasn't there.

And down on Myers Avenue
When the District boomed her best
Lived ladies who would welcome you
Or any payin' guest.

And many were the golden dollars
That they'd take in of nights—
And many were the drunken hollers,
And many were the fights.

The Old Camp boasted "better classes"
But distinctions warn't too fine,
For wealthy miners had wed lasses
They first met upon the "line."

Them days the Avenue was clinkin'
With the sound of ready dough;
Then the scarlet lights kept blinkin'
With a reckless kind of glow.

And miners, often drunk or fuzzy,
Went shoppin' among the cribs
A-hopin' they might find a hussy
As would suit their royal nibs.

Sourdoughs' stomachs warn't too queasy
And though the prices were steep
The sudden wealth had come too easy
For most guys to want to keep.

The sportin' dames were well assembled,
As females were regarded then;
And not a few of them resembled
Bargains to the lonely men.

Bargains, yes, in boughten kisses
And professional good cheer—
Bargains in the things man misses
On a rough and tough frontier.

The town was good, the town was bad,
And somethin' to behold;
And in spite of all her vices had
A heart of purest gold.

So you who write historic slush
Please try to keep it true—
The great camp needs no white-wash brush
For Myers Avenue.
—Rufus Porter, a.k.a. the Hard Rock Poet

C olorado City's red-light district began to really blossom during the
early 1890s. Part of its success was due to a new town, Cripple Creek,
springing up beyond Ute Pass. Stories of the gold found there quickly
drifted back to Colorado City. Such tales were concocted and aided by
Cripple Creek's first prospector, Bob Womack, who bragged about his gold
finds in both the saloons and brothels of Colorado City. Soon many a
wagon passing through Colorado City was headed to Cripple Creek,
where riches seemed guaranteed.

Colorado City was considered among the wildest towns in the state
until Cripple Creek boomed in 1891. It was a transient and varied population that migrated to the new town, with people from all walks of life.
Folks traversing Ute Pass on the way to Cripple Creek hardly gave any
thought to the panicked officials they encountered in Woodland Park,
located about halfway between Colorado City and Cripple Creek. By
March of 1891, in anticipation of the new gold rush, Woodland Park's city
fathers enacted a string of ordinances. The new laws included prohibition
of public nudity, public drunkenness, gambling, prostitution, vagrancy,
and disturbances as well of as the abuse of animals, firing guns, reckless
driving, and unlawful assemblies.

Prospectors, real estate men, attorneys, and businessmen eagerly set up
shop in tents and log cabins. The new business owners of Cripple Creek,
eager to make a bundle off the new boom, welcomed them with open
arms. Visions of gold nuggets spilling from miners' pockets and rich millionaires displaying wads of cash enticed many a prostitute to scramble for
Cripple Creek. Blanche Burton, later of Colorado City fame, is said to
have been the first madam in the district. Blanche arrived in the summer
of 1891, just as things were starting to heat up for the oncoming gold
boom. She set up her tent in Poverty Gulch, just below the shack of her
good friend Bob Womack. Sometime after her arrival in Cripple Creek,
Blanche was duped in a mining scam.

Still, sweet success came to Blanche Burton. By 1893 she was operating a parlor house over a saloon on Bennett Avenue, one of two main business drags. One time Womack rode his horse up the front steps of her

parlor house in Cripple Creek, a feat he commonly accomplished at the local saloons as well. Whenever Bob fell ill, Blanche would send her girls to his cabin to take care of him. Another woman of note was Milda James, a kindly black prostitute who helped nurse Bob Womack when he caught pneumonia just before Christmas of 1893. Milda gave Bob a dose of kerosene every two hours, and he recovered.

By 1893 there were a dozen or more saloons on Bennett Avenue. Above them, primitive parlor houses run by Blanche Burton, Lolly Lee, Minnie Smith, Molly King, and others flourished. But the arrangement of brothels along Bennett didn't sit too well with many townsfolk. The soliciting grew so outrageous that it got to where a man couldn't go to the grocery store without being propositioned. Accordingly, Sheriff Wilson made the girls and dance halls move one block south to Myers Avenue. Wilson promised the girls no one would bother them as long as they paid their fines, donated to charities, and behaved themselves in public.

Fig. 30. Though small, this brothel at 317 Myers Avenue obviously aspired to be an elite parlor house. The house likely predates the 1896 fires. In 1911 and 1912 prostitutes Ada Fitzgerald, Bessie Hyser, and Rose Duprey worked at this address.

(Courtesy Cripple Creek District Museum.)

Fig. 31. Two ladies of the evening engage in poker with their customers. Playing cards was just one of the many amusements offered inside Cripple Creek brothels.

(Courtesy Pikes Peak Library District.)

Once the girls settled on Myers, Wilson remained true to his word, at least for a little while. The influx of prostitutes was ever growing. There were rumored to be eleven parlor houses, twenty-six one-girl cribs, and four dance halls in town. Lola Livingston was one of many women enticed to move to Cripple Creek from Denver. One time an associate of mining millionaire Spencer Penrose was sent to collect a bill—possibly rent—of $45 from Lola. Forty minutes later, the red-faced associate returned without the money, with the explanation that he and Lola had decided he should take the debt out in trade.[1]

By the end of 1893 several brothels and dance halls were in full swing along Myers Avenue. They included the Bon Ton, the Casino, the Great View, the Red Light, and the Topic. Women who were openly plying their trade included Jessie Armstrong, Mary Davis, Georgia Hayden, Nellie Marcus, Mary Marshall, Kitty Maxie, Bell Ricker, Anna and Emma Smith, Lou Thompson, and Marie Williams. By the time Blanche Burton retired to Colorado City in 1894, her counterparts were doing just fine. Customers were being serviced in anything from tents to shacks to the upper floors of saloons to freestanding brothels.

The freedom was short-lived, however, as more and more houses took advantage of Hi Wilson's promise. In 1894 M. Vogie and Pearl Webster were arrested for prostitution. Both pleaded "not guilty" and were released without fine. Martha Petersen was not so lucky. In August Martha paid $75 for a violation at her saloon. In October she paid another $173. By then, the authorities were surely starting to lose control over the wild red-light district.

The nearby infant city of Victor already sported five saloons: the Arcade, the Kentucky Sample Room, Miller & Babcock, Strong & Sullivan, and the Victor Saloon. And the number of other watering holes was growing daily. Evidence of Victor's illicit nightlife was also blatantly present during mining labor strikes that took place in the Cripple Creek District during the years 1893 and 1894. During the strikes, a Mrs. Haillie Miller was employed by mine owners to bed striking miners and obtain information from them. Unfortunately, Haillie was often far more interested in the whiskey before her than listening to an unhappy miner rave about his job.[2]

Still, Haillie unknowingly served as a prototype for hundreds of prostitutes who flocked to Victor within the next two years. One of the most popular dance halls was Rose Gordon's, where a shady lady and gang moll known as Hook and Ladder Kate committed suicide. In her day Hook and Ladder ran with the Jack Smith gang after arriving from Denver. Kate's lover was George Pabst. Allegedly she once masterminded the holdup of a Wells-Fargo wagon outside of town for $16,000. She also frequented the cabin of Victor mining magnates and best friends Jimmy Burns and Jimmy Doyle. Once, when Burns tried to make Hook and Ladder leave the cabin, she turned him over her knee and spanked him while his friend Doyle laughed.[3]

Within a year of Victor's incorporation in 1895, even more saloons had appeared on the southern portions of 3rd and 4th streets and other parts of the city. Unlike in Cripple Creek and other large cities, however, the red-light houses in Victor were as scattered as their prostitutes. Although most towns, blue collar or otherwise, objected to the offending sight of soiled doves gracing their streets, Victor, with its large male population, appears to have been an exception. Brothels seemed welcome to coexist with other businesses throughout the town. Most of them were located above dance halls and bars. A thicker gathering of prostitutes lived near Victor Avenue between First and Second streets.

With prostitutes peppered throughout the downtown area, however, it is little wonder that eventually certain Victor residents took offense to the illegal goings-on. Similar sentiments were echoed in Cripple Creek, since not all residents of Myers Avenue were inmates of prostitution. In 1894, for instance, a Mrs. E. A. Bowen rented furnished rooms at 322 Myers. In the year before Mrs. Bowen began taking in boarders, the directory listed her as an employee of A. F. McDonald. By 1896, however, Mrs. Bowen had removed herself from the red-light district and resided at 338 El Paso Street. The 1900 directory lists her as a laundress at 112 East Eaton. Considering the number of legitimate jobs and respectable addresses Mrs. Bowen claimed within this seven-year span, it is unlikely she was ever employed as a prostitute. It is also unlikely Mrs. Bowen had a difficult time cleaning her tarnished reputation after mistakenly living on Myers Avenue. It wasn't long before Bowen and others like her didn't want to be associated with Myers Avenue, even though a good number of them lived on it. To alleviate

Fig. 32. This photograph of shady ladies could have been taken anywhere in the Cripple Creek District but most likely came from Cripple Creek or Victor. Note the theater poster in the background on the right.

(Courtesy Cripple Creek District Museum.)

further embarrassment, the name of Myers Avenue from the middle of 3rd Street and west to the city limits was renamed Masonic Avenue.

Folks living in nearby Poverty Gulch suffered the same problem. The Gulch, located just on the other side of the railroad trestle at the very south end of Myers, was populated with common poor folk. A good many of them simply couldn't afford to live elsewhere, but their numbers also included alcoholics, drug addicts, outlaws and, of course, prostitutes. By 1895 several black prostitutes were living in Poverty Gulch. They included Amanda Green, whose flavorful character earned her a spot in Cripple Creek history. Mandy, as she was known, apparently made a habit out of drinking at Jorden's Saloon and fighting. The hefty woman was also inclined to pull a knife on whoever displeased her, especially when she had overimbibed. Mandy countered her aggressive behavior by writing music. She was remembered as being quite intelligent and a great composer of "Negro" songs.

According to former Cripple Creek police officer Edward Carberry, Amanda was the rightful author of the song "There'll Be a Hot Time in the Old Town Tonight" in 1895. Carberry stated in an 1898 newspaper interview that actor Ernest Hogan obtained the original words and music from Mandy and later claimed the song as his own. Carberry also recalled throwing Mandy in jail on several occasions. One trip to jail was the result of a knife fight between Mandy and her sometime lover, "a yellow coon" named Tripp. A dancer who arrived in Cripple Creek with a theater group, Tripp stirred Amanda's ire when he visited the home of another woman. During another excursion to the "gray bar hotel," Mandy kept sitting in the snow and refusing to budge. After several snowbound wrestling matches, Carberry finally succeeded in getting Mandy to jail, only to have her put up yet another fight.[4]

Amanda Green's antics were typical of Cripple Creek, which fairly brimmed with crime from petty theft to riotous brawls, from suicide to murder. Scams of all sorts were also common. Many prostitutes were paid in gold dust for their services. Those who didn't know better could be duped, especially in the early days, if the "gold" was actually iron pyrite. Ultimately a kindly assayer showed the girls how to tell the difference between "fool's gold" and the real thing.

Between 1895 and 1897 many of the property owners along the red-light district on Myers Avenue were men. Some of the better known were saloon owner E. H. Asmussen, Colorado City founder Anthony Bott, city physician W. J. Chambers, and coroner Oscar Lampman. Female property owners included prostitutes Louise Bohm, Marie Brown, Jennie

Buck, Maggie Coyle, Julia Glenn, Isabelle Martin, Eva Prince, Lucy W. Drexel, Phebe W. Carrington, Mary E. Cross, Clara Simmons, and Mrs. W. H. Strom. Among the more prominent property owners were none other than millionaires Spencer Penrose and Charles Tutt. In fact, the business partners owned several lots along Myers, including Lola Livingston's house of ill repute and the Topic Theater. Some, such as the editor of the *Cripple Creek Morning Journal*, didn't care who owned the Topic. Declaring the business a "variety den and skin dive," the editor stated the dance hall should "be removed with the rest of the filth."[5] That was in 1895, when Tutt and Penrose also had a racetrack and casino stationed at the district town of Gillett. In fact, both men were quite the risqué bachelors in their day. One scandal in particular circulated around the district and beyond about Spencer Penrose: that of his questionable relationship with Sally Halthusen.

Love was not in the cards for Sarah Elizabeth Halthusen, better known in Cripple Creek as Sally. Hers was a striking figure; she was a towering amazon with dark eyes and an ample bosom. She was also an accomplished equestrian with a knack for breaking difficult horses. But for some reason Sally's talents and admirable features failed to attract men. It was even rumored that the one time she had been engaged, to a gentleman in Denver in 1892, she had been paid $10,000 by her fiancé's father to call off the engagement. In 1894 Sally moved from Colorado Springs to Florissant, where her father had raised sheep and grown grain since 1888. A true pioneer, Herman Halthusen even had a lane named after him in the early days. Today his red barn, known locally as the Bee Barn, remains situated near the Hornbek Homestead and across from the Florissant Fossil Beds National Monument on Teller County Road 1.

In Sally's eyes her father's proceeds were not the quickest way to fulfill her dream of a huge horse farm. Ultimately, she moved her beloved horses to a place on Bennett Avenue in Cripple Creek and began scouting for a rich husband. Soon it was no secret that Sally was courting Spencer Penrose, whose wealth came from investments in Cripple Creek and the copper mines of Utah. The two first met in Colorado Springs. Neighbors were aghast to see Sally riding her favorite white horse right up to Penrose's shack in Cripple Creek. And she declined to use a sidesaddle! Perhaps such brazen tactics turned Penrose off. Others said Spencer's brother talked some sense into him, expounding on the dangers of a marriage between an eastern blue blood and a western horse trainer. In any event, the affair allegedly ended nearly as abruptly as it had started.

Penrose and his riches merely whetted Sally's appetite for a millionaire husband. For a time she continued cruising the streets of Cripple Creek on her magnificent white horse, looking for love but finding none. Sally's last act of record in Cripple Creek was in 1895, when she lent her white horse to promoter Joe Wolfe for a parade down Bennett Avenue, advertising the world-famous bullfight in the district town of Gillett.

If Sally's love was not requited by the males of her own species, however, it was at least returned by her horses. When her trusty white steed died, Sally had him buried with dignity in Cripple Creek's Mt. Pisgah Cemetery. Even today, the horse is the only known four-footed creature at Mt. Pisgah to have such an honor.

In 1895 Sally returned to Colorado Springs. Eventually she did get married, to hotel owner Thomas Gough Jr., and continued her favorite occupation of breaking horses. Still, rumors abounded about Sally's brief fling with Penrose. One day, after overhearing a chambermaid talking about the affair, Sally beat the woman with a horsewhip and was arrested for assault. Her fine was $10 and costs, but the additional mark on her reputation secured her place in the lower middle class. Despite cruel references to her as a budding prostitute, however, Sally retained her dignity as well as her secrets. It is said her fine was allegedly paid by none other than her old beau Spencer Penrose, but the truth will never be known.

Such scandalous incidents involving wealthy men became fewer and farther between as Cripple Creek's millionaires sought to protect their class status. Eventually many of the male property owners sold out, especially those who had made a fortune in the mines. Penrose, Tutt, millionaire Winfield Scott Stratton, and their friends were forced by their wealth to quit making appearances on Myers Avenue in order to save their reputations from the media and their upstanding associates. But making gobs of money failed to stop these men from their love of working girls. Accordingly, call girls made discreet visits to their homes instead.

Still, embarrassing incidents were known to rear their ugly heads now and then. One call girl, Candace Root, sued Stratton in 1895 for $200,000 with the charge of breach of promise to marry. Root claimed Stratton lured her to his bed and also that she was pregnant. The case was dismissed.

Such stories certainly made for interesting reading in the local papers and beyond. Even so, Cripple Creek continued to boom, with a population growing far beyond that of Colorado City. The two towns remained linked in many ways, however. Colorado City was often the last supply stop on the way to Cripple Creek, where prospectors laid in supplies while avidly listening to tales of the gold boom. Over time several mills, mainly the Golden Cycle, processed ore shipped by wagon and later by train from Cripple Creek. Many millionaires of Cripple Creek eventually built their lavish mansions along Wood Avenue in Colorado Springs.

As of 1896, some 350 soiled doves were plying their trade in Cripple Creek. While much of the red-light district was confined to the 300 block of Myers, more than a few soiled doves did manage to spread their wings on either side of it. The red-light district basically extended north along Myers from Second Street, past Third and Fourth, and into the 500 block. To the south, Warren Avenue also provided lodging for more than a few working girls. Both 2nd and 3rd streets between Bennett and Warren harbored working girls as well.

In Poverty Gulch alone, at least three dance halls and several parlor houses and cribs flourished. The latter bore no address, just the name of the working girls painted on the door. Here, poorer crib girls such as Nigger Mollie and Mattie Harper resided among miners and other blue-collar workers. Scarface Liz and Liverlip, their names indicative of some abuse they had suffered in the past, migrated from Leadville to set up shop in Poverty Gulch as well. In 1896 two gangsters from Altman, Jim Gray and Joe Welch, were arrested with Liverlip and another woman called Fighting Mag near Leadville. A community of black prostitutes grew in Poverty Gulch as well. Two saloons were located at the mouth of the gulch: the Last Chance Saloon and Mahogany Hall. At the Mahogany, rules appear to have been the exception. There were few restrictions and one could view the real "cancan" being performed there, wherein women kicked up their legs, revealing their underpants.

It is interesting to note that the first of two devastating fires in 1896 began in the red-light district. The tale of Jennie LaRue has gained as much notoriety in Colorado as that of Mrs. O'Leary's cow in the great Chicago fire. It all began on a windy spring day—April 25, 1896—in Cripple Creek. A lone figure made his way down Third Street and onto Myers Avenue, turning in at the Central Dance Hall and heading up to the second floor. Upstairs was Jennie LaRue, ironing near a gasoline stove. Some sources say the two argued when the angry visitor accused Jennie of stealing his money; others say Jennie was upset because the man had missed a date with her. However it happened, the couple began to argue, then to physically fight. In the mayhem the stove overturned, quickly igniting the floor with spreading gasoline flames.

The fire was devastating. About 3,600 people were left homeless as the fire burned over a million dollars in buildings and belongings. And at the root of it all was the hapless dance hall girl Jennie LaRue. For a brief time hers was a household name. Newspapers as far away as Denver did not hesitate to spew forth Jennie's name, but most accounts left out the name of her fightin' man. Over the years, various periodicals have narrowed the suspects down to three. One is an unnamed bartender from the Topic Theater. Another is Mr. Jones, who ran the lunch counter at the Central. But the third suspect is most likely our man. He's that fellow with the funny name, Otto Floto.

Otto Clement Floto was born in Cincinnati circa 1863. After attending a Jesuit school in Dayton, he did some sportswriting in Chicago before drifting west. The 1896 Cripple Creek city directory lists Floto as the manager of the Cripple Creek Bill Posting Company. The twenty-two-year-old actually had many occupations, if each report about him is to be believed. Several sources say he was a bartender. Marshal Sprague states Floto managed the Butte Opera House, and his obituary touts him as a friend and advisor to world-famous boxer Jack Dempsey during the latter's youth in Victor.

As for Jennie LaRue, city directories fail to acknowledge her presence in Cripple Creek at all. Yet in Cripple Creek she definitely was on the day of that fire. Perhaps the most significant clue to Jennie LaRue's mystery man lies in a marriage certificate filed at the El Paso County courthouse. Dated October 20 1896, the document reveals the marriage of Otto C. Floto to one Jennie Ried. If the lovely Ms. LaRue was true to her profession and sported an alias, Ried could have been her legal surname. Within months of their marriage, Otto and Jennie left town. If they were seen together again, it was no doubt in a city far away where they might have explained their hasty departure from Cripple Creek with classic Victorian flair: "We had a most unfortunate incident in Cripple Creek. Completely out of our control, you understand." Incidentally, neither Jennie nor her mysterious companion appears to have been held lawfully responsible for the fire.

It was Floto who next surfaced, in Carson City, Nevada, in February of 1897. At a boxing match between Gentleman Jim Corbett and Ruby Bob Fitzsimmons, Floto met Harry Tammen, publisher of the *Denver Post*. Tammen wanted to use Otto's delightful surname for a performing circus act the *Post* owned and hired Floto to report sports. "Floto admitted when he took the job that he couldn't write," Tammen later recalled, "and the truth of the matter is I hired him because he had the most beautiful name in the world. It fascinated me."[6]

Shortly after Floto's Dog & Pony Show was organized, Otto and Jennie parted ways. Jennie disappeared. Floto continued writing for the *Post*, becoming one of the most prominent sportswriters of his time. In 1897 Floto caught the eye of writer Gene Fowler, who reported on an incident he witnessed between Floto and his longtime friend, lawman Bat Masterson. The two had parted ways after Floto allegedly duped Masterson in a business deal. In 1899 the two chanced to bump into each other in Denver. "Did they indulge in fancy steps, neat left hooks, graceful fiddling?" wrote Fowler. "Nay. They advanced like any two charcoal burners of the Black Forest, and began *kicking each other in the groin!*" Ultimately Masterson won, chasing Floto off. "He is the best runner I ever saw," Masterson later said.[7]

By 1905 the Floto Dog & Pony Show had blossomed into the Sells-Floto Circus. While traveling with the circus, Floto met and married bareback rider Kitty Kruger. The two were married in Denver in 1906 and remained together throughout Floto's life. Four years later Floto made sporting editor at the *Post*. If Jennie still lived at that time, she may have been Miss Jennie A. Reed, who resided at 1648 St. Paul in Denver.

In later years Floto's associates would remember him as somewhat of a vain ladies' man who insisted on using a youthful photo of himself to illustrate his column. Floto's passion for pretty girls was no secret around the office. A coworker recalled the time Floto was held up by business. The young lady who had appeared around quitting time grew impatient waiting for the writing Romeo and left. In fact, Floto's charisma is questionable; he reportedly weighed 250 pounds at the time of his run-in with Masterson. Gene Fowler, however, remembered Floto fondly as "lovable, generous and loyal."[8]

When Otto Floto died of epilepsy at sixty-six, the *Denver Post* ran his extensive obituary on the front page. It was a fitting reward for thirty-two years of service for that newspaper. He left behind no children, only Kitty and his brother William. But a handful of notable sports figures sent condolences. Among them was Jack Dempsey, whose boxing career actually began in the Cripple Creek District. In its own way, the obituary was a last salute to Otto Floto's Cripple Creek beginnings and his link to one of Cripple Creek's two infamous fires.

Just why the media in general neglected to mention Floto's name will never be known. The papers lost no time in telling how Jennie LaRue's mistake resulted in the destruction of most of Cripple Creek's red-light district. Among those buildings to burn were six one-girl cribs on Myers: J. D.

Bauman's, Ella Holden's "the Library," Kittie's, Lottie's, Mother Jones's, and Pearl Sevan's "Old Faithful." Other losses included the houses of Florence St. John and Victoria Stuart as well as the Topic, owned by Charles Tutt and Spencer Penrose. Whether the millionaires rebuilt is unknown, but other brothel owners certainly did. Within hours of the first fire, Kitty Townley had twenty laborers building one-girl cribs for her. Kitty's efforts were in vain; a second fire just four days later destroyed what Jennie LaRue's error had not, as well as the entire commercial district on Bennett Avenue.

If city authorities thought this second fire would be the red-light ladies' undoing, they were wrong. The brothels sprang right back up, many on the same sites that had burned. As late as June, prostitutes such as Nina Wetteruth were challenging their rights to improve their properties. Nina wanted to raise her house to meet the street level on Myers Avenue. Whether she was allowed to complete her mission is unknown; city council minutes only note the fact that Nina's was a house of prostitution; the council instructed the sheriff to carry on as usual. Even today the elite Old Homestead Parlor House just up the block remains well below the street grade, an indication that Nina probably did not get her wish.

Despite being a mere dance hall girl, Jennie LaRue was thrown into the same category as the other fallen women of Myers Avenue. Neither the media nor the authorities paid much attention to the abuse and neglect these girls suffered. In 1897, tired of being lumped in with their prostituting counterparts, the saloon girls of Cripple Creek formed the Dance Hall Girls' Protective Association. In a letter to the mayor and city council, the women made their mission clear: "We the undersigned petition the committee on ordinances to repeal the law in which the theatrical profession and dance hall girls are compelled to pay a monthly fine of $6 for the privilege of earning our living. We do not wish to be classed with the demi-monde. We beg you will give this your kind attention and immediate consideration."[9] Accordingly, the city council changed the ordinance and the fines were dropped. It was said the union even went on strike at one time, with success.

Not all the girls of Myers were ruled by unfair overlords. Some were lucky enough to work in parlor houses for madams who exhibited kindness and concern for their welfare. The girl who secured parlor house employment was fortunate indeed, as such a job guaranteed a cleaner and healthier working environment and better wages. From miners to millionaires, the men of Cripple Creek and beyond came to Myers Avenue for a good time. The variety of entertainment could accommodate any budget, but only those with fat wallets could gain access to the plush quarters of a fancy parlor house. Of the parlor houses on Myers, the Old Homestead rated five stars.

In just under a year, the Old Homestead racked up a reputation that is still talked about over a century later. The property was first purchased from Bob Womack's family by a Mr. E. T. Wells, but it is not known if Wells had anything to do with the brothel that allegedly opened on the site in 1891. The brothel's first owner of note was Mrs. Isabelle Martin, better known as Pearl DeVere. Allegedly a native of Evansville, Indiana, Pearl's first foray into the underworld began when she married an unnamed gambler. It was said that Pearl's husband blew his brains out after breaking the bank at Paris's Monte Carlo Casino. Later, she allegedly married one Ed Martin sometime before, or upon reaching, Denver. The two appear to have parted ways before Pearl set out for Cripple Creek.[10]

Why Pearl came to Cripple Creek is unknown. She is thought to have arrived in about 1893 with her new nom de plume, but courthouse records do not record Pearl DeVere officially purchasing the Old Homestead from saloon owner James Hanley until 1896 or 1897. She may have taken her new pseudonym from a Madam Vida DeVere, clairvoyant, who was locating mines with her crystal ball out of the Cabinet Saloon in 1894. Little else is known about Pearl in those early years. She married Charles B. Flynn, who had a small mill in the district, in about 1895. (There is no record of this marriage in Colorado.) When the Old Homestead burned in 1896 along with much of the red-light district, Flynn's sawmill was also ruined. He went south to Monterey, Mexico, where he took a job smelting iron and steel.

Pearl was undaunted, however. In November the city directory notes her as operating at 327 Myers Avenue, which was later changed to 353, the site the Old Homestead currently occupies. It was said that even in those early days, Pearl employed a cook, housekeeper, two chambermaids, two butlers, and a musician. An advertisement in the undated *Traveler's Night Guide of Colorado* lists Pearl DeVere's at 329 Myers Avenue, along with an appropriate slogan:

> *"The Curfew will not Ring Tonight"*
> *But our lunch bell rings at 10:30 every*
> *evening. All are cordially invited.*
> *Ten attractive entertainers attired in*
> *white will wait upon you at*
> *Pearl DeVere's, 329 Myers Avenue.*[11]

In December of 1896 Pearl borrowed two notes totaling $3,100 from an investor, Orinda J. Straile, to build an even better parlor house. Straile was a widow who in 1890 was residing at 38 East 26th Street in New York City. Pearl's married name, Isabelle Martin, is written on a pair of sliding doors shipped to the Old Homestead during its construction. It was said the illustrious madam even went to France and studied the bordellos there to design the new building. Every modern appliance, including electric lights, running water, a bathroom, and a telephone, was installed to assure maximum comfort for both residents and visitors. Wallpaper was imported from Europe. Brass fixtures on the inside doors were imported from London.

Pearl's taste for fine furnishings is evident in the way she furnished the house throughout. Three parlors, a ballroom, a wine room, and the dining room were located downstairs. The fancy furnishings included several

Fig. 33. The Old Homestead's music room, as seen from the parlor. The braided rope hanging in the foreground was called a portiere, a decorative must for any fancy home.

(From the author's collection.)

upholstered settees and chairs, moquette carpets, several rugs, rocking chairs, and solid oak tables. A Kimball upright piano was located in the ballroom, and the oak dining-room table seated eight. Several sets of sheets, pillowcases, and towels were on hand, and all of the windows featured cloth or lace curtains. Even a Racine fire extinguisher was on hand in the dining room.

Upstairs, five bedrooms awaited the girls and their visitors. Each was fitted with a different chamber set made of various woods as well as two pillows, a bedspread, a quilt, two wool blankets, and two sets of sheets. Each room had its own toilet set, chamber pot, two washbowls, and heating stove. Each woman had at least one corset bag, a cloth poke made for storing rolled-up corsets. Most girls sported curls and waves in their hair, made with curling irons heated in the chimneys of their oil lamps. Belladonna leaves were kept in each bedroom. Placing the dampened leaves on the eyes made the irises big and glassy, creating that "bedroom" look. The leaves could also be made into a tea and served as a stimulant for clients.

Pearl had her own suite downstairs, where her bottom-floor bedroom was decorated with even more finesse. Among the furnishings were an oak bedstead, four pillows instead of two, a writing desk, sofa, table, two rocking chairs, a wardrobe, and a $25 moquette carpet. There was also a larger heating stove and a standing clock. The toiletries in this room included an oak commode. Here, Pearl could conduct business, do her books, relax, and receive guests.[12]

With the Old Homestead exquisitely decorated and ready for action once more, Madam DeVere staged a grand reopening with a lavish variety of entertainment never before seen in Cripple Creek. Pearl's employees were beautiful and gifted women, many of whom later became madams themselves. Pearl took extra good care of her girls. A bill from Drs. Chambers and Kanavel in the Palace block on Bennett Avenue reveals regular calls, including night visits and office consultations. During the month of September 1896, for instance, Pearl was billed for daily office visits from the 14th through the 20th. During a six-month period, she was charged no fewer than seven "night calls" at $5 each—an indication that while talented, classy, and educated, Pearl's girls were known to overindulge in drugs or alcohol. Pearl also consulted with Dr. J. H. Hereford on occasion, racking up a bill with him throughout the last half of December 1896.[13]

The girls of the Homestead were expected to turn five tricks per night at $50 each. Pearl and subsequent madams took a 60/40 split, paying the girls $20 to $100 per night. In comparison, regular parlor house girls could only hope to earn their $5 tricks plus a cut from drink sales and perhaps a tip from the musicians. At least half their earnings went to their madams, plus $5 to $6 per week for room and board. Women who committed indecencies could not expect to work at the Old Homestead, but those who conducted themselves properly were fairly spoiled in the profession. Most inmates of the Old Homestead were in their late teens or early twenties. A well-trained staff served two nourishing meals per day, usually consisting of a lot of red meat, vegetables, and milk. Because the profession required somewhat strenuous work, it was important to maintain a healthy diet. An ill prostitute was an unprofitable prostitute.

Today the Old Homestead is a museum, and its furnishings reflect the way Pearl would have kept the house. Among the period furnishings in the museum today is a gambling table from Johnny Nolon's saloon, which in its time was one of the biggest casinos in town. A serving table in the dining room had a mirror installed underneath, so the girls could be assured no petticoats protruded from under skirts. Other interesting features of the Old Homestead include a corset chair. The girls would straddle this chair and hang onto its back for dear life as another girl cinched them into their tight, waist-slimming corsets.

One of Pearl's first employees in Cripple Creek was allegedly Laura Evens, who later made her fame in Salida as a prominent madam. Lola Livingston also worked for Pearl before moving to the Mikado, where she reigned as madam in 1900. Nell McClusky was another employee of Pearl DeVere. While Nell is never listed in Cripple Creek city directories, it is said she opened her own place down the street sometime later. Nell was alternately known to go by the name of Molly or possibly Annie. Among her possessions in 1905 was a long and ornately handled knife, filed and sharpened to make one deadly weapon. A Mrs. Annie McCloskey died in September of 1912 at the St. Nicholas Hospital, destitute.

Pearl may have entertained clients herself. Being of higher stature than her employees, however, Pearl picked her own customers rather than the customers picking her. Being a working madam also came in handy for those times when certain delicate "business transactions" with the law or other prominent citizens were deemed necessary. Pearl's profits reflected a budget to ward off stiff city ordinances regarding prostitution. Despite such strict ordinances, Pearl was by all accounts content with her occupation. It was said she was fond of renting a spirited mare named

She-Devil from Welty's Livery Stable in Cripple Creek and riding the horse around town. She also enjoyed riding around town in a carriage with red wheels, pulled by a team of black steeds. Whenever she hired a new employee, the new girl most likely accompanied Pearl on her rides to advertise the new arrival.

The refined entertainment offered by Pearl DeVere was expensive—and available only to the privileged few. Most clients to the Old Homestead were millionaires from Cripple Creek, Colorado Springs, and Denver, and they had to satisfy prerequisites. Only men of prestige could patronize the parlor house, and their reservation had to come with a $50 deposit. This was followed by a waiting period, during which the prospective customer's credit was checked. If Pearl was satisfied with the man's financial background, she arranged an appointment with him. The Old Homestead charged $50 per "trick," or $250 for all night. The fee was paid in advance in order to avoid any misunderstandings later. Compared with most parlor houses, where girls earned $5 per trick or $15 to $30 for an all-night stay, the Homestead was pricey indeed.

At the Homestead, the services also included dinner, a wine room, and a variety of entertainment including poker, singing acts, and dancing. Only the finest food was offered, and both the Silver State Liquor Company and Asmussen & Erickson delivered the best in liquor to Pearl's every week. Three parlors were provided for entertaining clients. Card games were a service men had to pay for, even if that was the only reason for their visit. In another parlor, guests might be entertained by singing and dancing. There was an additional fee for joining the girls for a meal in the dining room. One of the most unique aspects of the Old Homestead was the viewing room, which featured an upstairs closet with a glass door. Customers could choose their partner for the evening after watching the available girls as they paraded nude through the closet. Today, the closet and house remain one of the most well-preserved examples of their kind in America.

Pearl's employees during 1896 included Wellie Boudine, Ella Dickenson, Ida Grey, Flora Hasting, Mable White, Mayme Wellington, Lola Livingston, a black cook named America "Mary" Samuels, and twenty-five-year-old Inda Allen, housekeeper. Born in New York of English descent, Inda was literate and ruled over Pearl's girls with an iron fist. Their stay at the Old Homestead made each of these naughty ladies known forever to history. Unfortunately, Pearl DeVere's fame in Cripple Creek came in another form. A mere six months or so after her grand opening, the infamous madam met her end at the Old Homestead.

Legend states a rich admirer from Denver sent Pearl an $800 dress from Paris before attending one of her famous Saturday night soirees on June 4, 1897. The two allegedly argued over whether the gent should leave his wife. Pearl lost. If an account by the *Denver Republican* of what happened next is accurate, Pearl apparently wasn't too terribly shaken by the confrontation with her paramour. After literally partying the night away, Pearl retired around 7 A.M. with one of her girls, identified by another newspaper as Maude Stone. Pearl decided to take some morphine to help her sleep. At about 11 A.M., Maude awoke to the sound of Pearl breathing heavily. Dr. Hereford, a prominent physician of Cripple Creek, was called. But even the good doctor could do nothing, and Pearl passed away at 3:30 on the afternoon of June 5.

Upon removing Pearl's body, a deputy sheriff "took possession of the house, had all the girls move out and placed a guard over the valuables."[14] In reporting her death, the *Cripple Creek Times* concluded: "There is no evidence that the act was intentional."[15] Despite a few outstanding debts, life had seemed cheery and full of promise for the divine Ms. DeVere.[16]

Pearl's husband, Charles Flynn, was notified of Pearl's death in Monterey, Mexico, but apparently saw no need to return to Colorado. Flynn's apathy was countered by Pearl's mother and sister in her home state of Indiana, who thought she was working as a successful hatmaker or perhaps as the designer of "DeVere Gowns." Pearl's brother-in-law, Mr. J. L. Weil, telegraphed to have the body embalmed and sent to her old home in Evansville. For reasons unknown, however, her sister next appeared on the scene and subsequently learned Pearl's true occupation. Shocked and disheartened, she ordered police to burn Pearl's possessions and left town. The sheriff, however, had already secured the Old Homestead and everything in it save for the girls, who were ordered to pack their trunks and leave. Pearl's probate record indicates the girls were allowed to take nothing more than their most personal possessions, leaving the furniture, coverlets, and even their toiletries behind.

Oscar Lampman's records for Pearl's funeral on June 8 reflect a cost of $210.25, including what was no doubt an ornate casket for $115.[17] Legend states that the girls of the Homestead tried to come up with the money. As they considered whether to auction Pearl's $800 dress, the mysterious man from Denver allegedly sent $1,000, along with a request that Pearl be buried in the dress (record of this benevolent act has yet to be found). Even today, Pearl's is the most well-remembered funeral in Cripple Creek history. Much of the town of Cripple Creek turned out

Fig. 34. This portrait is said to be of Pearl, right,
with her sister in more innocent days.

(Courtesy Old Homestead Parlor House.)

to salute this generous and admired lady, whose donations to the poor and help for the sick were not soon forgotten. Leading the procession was a twenty-piece band from the Elks Lodge and four mounted policemen. Admirers turned out in force, as did the painted ladies of Myers Avenue, and it was said flowers were sent from as far away as Denver. What a sight it must have been when the silent throng turned off Myers and onto Bennett Avenue, marching toward Mt. Pisgah Cemetery. Pearl was the only prostitute in Cripple Creek to receive a plot among the town's respected citizens. Only a wooden tombstone, however, was carved and placed at the grave.[18]

It is interesting that in just under a year, Pearl DeVere and her Old Homestead made history that is still talked about today.

The Girl Who Could Never Go Home

This is the tale of a different house—
"The Homestead" was its name
Which brought a famous mining town
A different kind of fame.

And those who lived at the Homestead?
Well, they were different too.
For they were the girls who couldn't go home,
The way most girls can do.

They just stayed on at the Homestead,
And each in her special way,
Played at the game of living
And flung her life away.

They say that the gayest of them all
Was a girl called Pearl DeVere,
Who had masked her shame with a trumped-up name
And a gaudy, bright veneer.

It is said Pearl had a special friend
They never tell his name—
Although the Homestead knew him well
This too, was part of the game.

He showered Pearl with costly gifts
Trinkets for her room.
Taffeta gowns, and high kid shoes,
And a hat with an ostrich plume.

And then to make her happy,
He planned a special ball,
For all the girls at the Homestead,
And he said, "Come one, come all."

Now parties at the Homestead
Weren't socially correct—
No gilt-edged invitations,
Sent out to the elect.

But there were flowers from the South,
Music from Denver Town.
Fancy food with foreign names,
And for Pearl, a handsome gown,
Sent all the way from Paris
Made of pink chiffon,
And Pearl put it on.

She laughed and danced the whole night through,
(at least, that's what they tell),
And seemed as gay and light of heart,
As a reigning social belle.

Then all at once they missed her;
Her friend said "Where's my Pearl?"
And he climbed the famous Homestead stairs,
Looking for his girl.

You know the rest of the story,
How he just "couldn't understand."
Why he found her, dead,
On her fancy bed,
The poison still in her hand.

> *On a summer's day they dug a grave,*
> *In the windswept, rocky loam*
> *And there she sleeps in her Paris gown,*
> *The girl who couldn't go home.*[19]

Further evidence that Pearl did not intend to take her own life is that she didn't leave a will. A few days after the funeral Charles E. Howard, a real estate broker who had assisted Pearl in borrowing the money from Orinda Straile to build the Homestead, put up a $2,000 bond and was made administrator of Pearl's estate. Despite the large amount, Howard stated in his initial letter to the court that Pearl's total estate, including her palace of pleasure, furnishings, and jewelry, was estimated only at about $1,000.[20] Just what Howard's interest was in Pearl is unknown, but in September he was joined by P. E. C. Burke, original owner of the famed C.O.D. Mine in the Cripple Creek District. Another $1,000 bond was put up against the estate as appraisers were called in.

In the end Pearl's property at her death included the Old Homestead, valued at $3,000, as well as property in the nearby town of Gillett worth $2,500. Pearl had also purchased two thousand shares of stock in the Victor Gold Mining, Drainage, Transportation and Tunnel Site Company, and another thousand shares in the Ela Helean Gold Mining Company [*sic*], with a total value of $5. Pearl's household furnishings, jewelry, and clothing at the Homestead were valued at $1,838.85—a total of over $7,000 in real and personal property.[21]

At a hearing in December, Orinda Straile was awarded the house in lieu of payment of her $3,100 loan. With the house came most of the household furnishings, right down to the glassware and crockery. Next came Pearl's other creditors, like the Selig Brothers' Parisian Cloak & Suit Parlor, the Knight-Campbell Music Company, and two liquor houses, laying claims to debts she owed at her death. Among the claimants was one Emma J. Gill, who said that Pearl had borrowed $183 and given Emma a diamond ring with two diamonds and a diamond stud for collateral. Apparently, Emma lost no time in selling the diamond stud off less than a week after Pearl's death. She received $105. Upon being advised that such an action was illegal, Emma was forced to take the stud back and return the money. She was duly paid the amount owed by the estate.

Charles Howard disposed of the rest of Pearl's estate at a public auction on January 8, 1897. Articles sold consisted of her jewelry and the items of her wardrobe. Although it was a public auction advertised in local newspapers, only five local businessmen ended up making a purchase: Oscar Lampman, J. F. Hadley, H. A. Clapp, J. G. Raine, and the Cohn Brothers cleaned up.

Pearl DeVere's Final Estate

Item	Purchaser	Appraised value	Sale price
Jewelry			
6 gold souvenir spoons	Lampman	$6	$3.10
1 diamond-set watch	Raine	$30	$19
1 imitation turquoise/ diamond-set breast pin with matching earrings	Cohns	$25	$15.50
1 diamond-set butterfly breast pin	Cohns	$75	$65
1 diamond-set wishbone stick pin	Hadley	$4	$2
1 5-small diamond stick pin	Clapp	$10	$17.75
1 small pearl-set lady's watch chain	Cohns	$4	$3.50
1 2-stone diamond ring	Hadley	$150	$90
1 5-opal diamond-set ring	Raine	$35	$17.75
1 3-ruby diamond-set ring	Lampman	$25	$34
1 5-stone diamond and sapphire ring	Hadley	$25	$27.50
1 loose opal	Raine	$1	$1.50
Wearing apparel			
1 sealskin coat	Raine	$100	$50.50
1 Persian silk dress	Raine	$25	$14.10
1 blue Eaton suit	Raine	$10	$5
1 blue silk tea gown	Raine	$4	$2
1 crepon wrapper	Raine	$4	$2
1 blue serge dress, silk-lined waist	Raine	$4	$2
1 black silk striped skirt	Raine	$2	$1
1 white silk tea gown	Raine	$2	$1

1 bathrobe	Raine	$1	$1.50
1 red silk underskirt	Raine	$1	$.50
1 striped silk waist	Raine	$1	$.50
2 cotton flannel shirts	Raine	$.50	$.25
2 linen nightshirts	Raine	$.50	$.25
1 black moire skirt	Raine	$.50	$.25
1 calico wrapper	Raine	$.25	$.15
1 black belt & silver buckle	Raine	$.50	$.25
1 red striped silk wrapper	Raine	$2.50	$1.25
TOTAL		**$548.75**	**$379.10**

In the end, Howard collected the money from the estate sale and compromised on collecting $199.50 from over $1,000 in loans from Pearl to Charles Flynn. The cash was used to pay off Pearl's remaining bills, and the estate was finally settled in January 1899. On July 1, 1899, Orinda J. Straile consulted with a Mr. O. A. Rowe to sell the Old Homestead to twenty-three-year-old Hazel Vernon. The final price, filed in April of 1900, was a whopping $5,000. Part of the new madam's job was to find new employees, as most of Pearl's girls had moved on after her death. Nell McClusky opened her own place, and Lola Livingston migrated down the street to the Mikado, where she was madam in 1900. After a brief career at the Mikado, Lola disappears from city directories. She may have migrated to Colorado City and changed her name to Pearl, or she may have moved to San Francisco in about 1904. For Hazel, the Old Homestead was a golden opportunity to pick up where Pearl left off, and the girls of the row knew it, too. Hazel had only four other parlor houses in the 300 block of Myers Avenue to compete with in 1900: the Royal Inn, the Mikado, Nell McClusky's and, allegedly, Laura Bell McDaniel's. Indeed, Hazel appears to have run the house with finesse despite her young age and the fact that at least some of her girls were older than she.

Hazel Vernon's Girls throughout 1900[22]

Name	Age	Birthplace	Notes
Dora Grant	—	—	—
Gladys Gray	20	Colorado	Could read and write
Edith Green	30	Missouri	Could read and write
Lillian Hill	26	Missouri	Could read and write
Edna Meade	—	—	—

Elieen or Arline Newell	26	Colorado	—
Lou Russell	—	—	—
Gladys Wilson	Possibly 15	Possibly Missouri	—
Inda Allen, housekeeper	—	—	—
Mary Samuels, cook[23]	—	—	—

Hazel's employees in 1902 included Inda Allen and Mary Samuels, as well as Charles Miller, butler; Anna Pierce, chambermaid; Clyde Rogers, musician; and James Troutman, porter. The city directory did not list any working girls, but Hazel worked as the madam of the Old Homestead until later that year when she retired to California to care for her mother. Later she died of pneumonia or syphilis. Hazel's daughter, also named Hazel, lived out her life in Montana, presumably unmarried. Hazel did not sell the Homestead until 1905. This time, the house passed into the hands of one Phil DeWilde. Under his ownership, Inda Allen next became madam of the Homestead until about 1907. Her girls included Effie Holman, Belle

Fig. 35. By 1900 Myers Avenue was back on top with saloons, dance halls, gaming houses, brothels, and cribs. This photo shows the avenue looking west from 4th Street.

(Courtesy Cripple Creek District Museum.)

Sherman, Edna Sommers, Clara Wellington, and Millie Laverty. Mary Samuels remained as the cook, and one Peter A. Samuels was employed as a musician. There is little doubt that Inda, who had been at the Homestead since 1896, continued operations in the manner she was accustomed to.

After Inda's final departure, tracing the madams and owners of the Old Homestead becomes more difficult. Girls who worked there during 1911 included Miss Pauline Russell, proprietor; twenty-two-year-old Alice Bond of California; Marill Danley of Denver and formerly from the Mikado; twenty-eight-year-old Georgia Hilton of Iowa; Dollie Holmes from Denver; Dora Miller; Lillian Newburg; Maud Rogers (who had artificial teeth); Bert Taylor, a Nashville beauty from El Paso who started her first night of work on Christmas Eve; and Mildred Sholls, also known as Mildred Schools. The city register notes that Mildred was born in Brooklyn, moved from Denver in 1911 at the age of twenty, and went to Glenwood Springs later that year. In addition, a twenty-five-year-old Negro named Cherrie Butler was employed at the house. Cherrie, lately of Kinsley, North Dakota, most probably worked as both a domestic and prostitute during her career in Cripple Creek. Earlier in 1911 she was noted as working at 441½ Myers Avenue.

The following year saw the presence of Marill Danley, Dollie Holmes, Dycie Jones, Margie Jones with her bleached brown hair from the Mikado, Sadie Lewis of Denver, Lillian Morris, Doris Reynolds, Frankie Williams, Gladys Young, and Pauline Russell, as well as the return of Mildred Sholls. Cherrie Butler still worked there, and the new madam was Miss Pauline Perkins, a.k.a. Jessie Poslerfiel. Alice Bond, Georgia Hilton, and Sadie Lewis had departed from Cripple Creek altogether. By 1913, only Pauline Russell, Mildred Sholls, and Dycie Jones appear in the city directory as residents of the Old Homestead.

During the Old Homestead's reign, it could be said that Myers Avenue was actually proud of its naughty reputation. Competition from smaller neighboring towns was hardly a problem. *Leslie's Weekly Illustrated* noted at the turn of the century that the district town of Altman featured "tin horn gamblers and faded soiled doves."[24] Gillette, located four miles from Cripple Creek, sported a racetrack and casino gambling but only three dance halls. Another district town, Anaconda, was said to have dance halls but no brothels to speak of. A suburb of Anaconda, the town of Barry, sported minimal red-light entertainment. A native of Barry, Leslie Doyle Spell, recalled when his family lived there and a brothel quietly opened one door down from his home. One of the soiled doves had a little boy who always played alone in his backyard. One day Spell's brother invited the boy over. The child replied, "No, my mother is a whore and says I am to stay home." Another time in Barry, a cowboy was sleeping off a drunk at the home of his favorite call girl. While her visitor slept, the girl donned his overalls and rode his horse down Main Street, shocking all onlookers.[25]

Cripple Creek did, however, get a run for its money from the nearby town of Victor. Although most of the money made in the Cripple Creek District came from mines surrounding Victor, the wealthy cared little for the "working man's town." Most millionaires migrated to or made regular visits to Cripple Creek, while the less wealthy miners of Victor stayed close to their work. By 1896 the 300 block of Victor Avenue fairly seethed with taverns such as the Bank Exchange Saloon, Barrett, DeMandel & Holt, the Blue Grass, Burns & Gibbons, the Combination, Dexter's, Greenwood's, Kelly's, the Monarch, and the Texas House Saloon. Turning south at 3rd Street, one could encounter the taverns of Henry Bahne, James Ducey, Joseph Fawcett, Nelson Johnson, Jerome Lewis, George Rodgers, Charles Seitz, Victor Weisburg, William Munroe's dance hall, and the "big boys" of the block, such as the Union Theater and the Turf Club. In both places the libations were accompanied by entertainment and prostitution. In 1912, twenty-six-year-old Dorthy [sic] Ward was entertaining men in her upstairs apartment at 128 South 3rd.[26]

More bars were located in and around the elite Victor Hotel. There was even a local Bartenders Union No. 8, which met each Sunday evening. The bars of Victor saw much action by both local and national performers. Lottie and Polly Oatley, two nationally popular stage performers, made their appearance in Victor in 1896. At one time the sisters danced and sang at the Regina Saloon in Dawson, Alaska. They had a small dog named Tiny, who sang along in a soprano voice.

Presumably the shady ladies of Victor ran amok at least as much as their cocktail-selling counterparts. But while Victor reveled in entertainment and debauchery, prostitutes working there and in Cripple Creek were experiencing increasing pressure from authorities. In November of 1897 two notable fallen women were arrested. One was Cripple Creek prostitute Ella Holden, who was arrested when she could not pay her monthly fine. The other was Maggie Hicks, who had two houses called the 444 and the 222 in Victor. On November 18 Maggie was arrested and extradited to Denver on an indictment from the federal grand jury on the grounds that she had been selling liquor from both houses with only one liquor license.

Still, the houses of prostitution and dance halls persevered in Cripple Creek. In 1898 one of the more notable houses was the Red Light Dance Hall, located down the street from the Bon Ton. The Red Light was the largest dance hall in Cripple Creek, employing upward of twenty-five girls. The dance floor was fenced, with a gate in the center. The men paid a quarter a dance, which included a small glass of beer. They also received a red check, which was given to the female dance partner of choice. Across from the Red Light was a saloon known as Bill's Place. Other dance halls flourished as well. At Crapper Jack's, the girls made 12½¢ per dance, 60¢ per bottle of beer they sold, and $2.50 per bottle of wine they sold. They also made tips. Most dance halls offered similar deals to their customers and employees, sometimes exchanging the glass of beer for a shot of liquor.

By 1899 a generous handful of saloons, brothels, and gaming halls fairly covered Cripple Creek's Myers Avenue as well as Victor's main streets. By then Victor's red-light ladies had settled down some and were regulated much like those in Cripple Creek, paying monthly fines and suffering numerous arrests. Also like Cripple Creek, Victor's red-light ladies suffered injury to their already tarnished reputations when a fire began at either Jennie Thompson's, Lilly Reid's, or in a shack behind Rosa May's 999 Dance Hall in August. The 999 was located in front of Paradise Alley between 3rd and 4th streets. Much of Victor was destroyed in the fire, but as in Cripple Creek, the city in general took the opportunity to build a newer and finer city.

After the fire some of the players in Victor's nightlife changed, but the game remained the same. One of the first saloons to open was the Mint, constructed on the site of the Victor Hotel. More saloons followed, including the Star of the West, the Belmont, the Roxbury Rye, and Arthur's Place. The new Fortune Club also rose from the rubble. Kegs of beer were delivered via doors at sidewalk level on the side of the building, and a handful of prostitutes operated in the rooms upstairs. The Fortune Club was only rivaled in size by the Monarch across the street. At the Monarch much larger second-story rooms accommodated both private gambling and prostitution.

In Cripple Creek, the Old Homestead reckoned with competition in the form of the Mikado, located just one door down. Competition was tough for a while between the Mikado and the Old Homestead. Early on, however, in about 1893, the madams of each house agreed to build an overhead walkway that appears on maps to connect the two buildings. Thus competition between the two ended in a healthy compromise. By 1900, three hundred women of the underworld were still plying their trade in Cripple Creek as the city peaked in population and mining production.

Several parlor houses prospered on Myers Avenue in 1900. They included the Old Homestead, the Mikado, the House of All Nations, the Gold Belt, the Boston, the Chicken Ranch, the Topic, and the Place. Crapper Jack's and the Red Light were both located at Myers Avenue and Fourth Street. Cripple Creek city directories between 1900 and 1910 show that women of various blue-collar professions also lived in the 300 and 400 blocks of Myers. Because it was common for prostitutes to list themselves under a variety of pseudo-professions, the true number of working girls on Myers Avenue will never be known.

In addition to the brothels there were also a whopping seventy-three saloons in town, including the Opera Club, Combination, Miner's Exchange, and the Last Chance. Variety theaters advertised their bands and burlesque shows by having the band and the showgirls parade up and down the street before the show. Some of the shows could get wild, and bar fights were extremely common. In 1900, for instance, bartender Bob Haviland was nearly killed while breaking up a fight at the Abbey Saloon. Prostitute Lizzie Moore, age eighteen, noted in the 1900 census as black and married, was arrested for running an opium den at her place at 512 Myers Avenue. Newspapers also noted that Lucille Moore, an employee of the Mikado, attempted suicide with carbolic acid.

Such antics were taking more and more precedence in the daily newspapers. Inevitably, temperance unions began forming in Cripple Creek shortly after the turn of the century. As early as 1900 the *Cripple Creek Times* reported that many merchants and even larger saloon owners in Cripple Creek wanted gambling stopped. Accordingly, nickel slots were outlawed. Poker tables and roulette wheels were prohibited on the first floor of all establishments and had to be moved upstairs. Cripple Creek's soiled doves were forced by these actions to retreat to the upper floors as well.

In Victor the number of people—and saloons—continued to grow as the city stepped into the twentieth century. New bars included the Bank Exchange at 306 Victor Avenue and the Senate next door. The Branch and Diamond saloons and the Red Light Dance Hall also opened on Victor Avenue. Third Street saloons included the Union Brewing Co. and Van Sickle's. Over on 4th Street, Bunte's Saloon, the Silver Bar, and the Sideboard flourished. The most popular 4th Street tavern was probably the Gem, which featured bar, restaurant, pretty girls, and rooms to rent. Other saloons around town were the Silver State, Jack Vining's, and Mrs.

Fig. 36. A box reputed to belong to black prostitute Lizzie Moore contained a stock certificate in her name, a dollar silver certificate, a knife, and a small derringer (not shown).

(Courtesy David Tritz, from the author's collection.)

Stoddard's on South 7th. Victor's wild side continued, showing itself regularly into the new century.

More arrests were being made in Cripple Creek. In 1901 miner B. McDowell, a resident of Poverty Gulch, charged that a woman of Myers Avenue had robbed him of $60. That same year Nell Worley of 365 Myers was arrested after taking a shot at a man attempting to break down her front door. Worley was arrested not for shooting at the man but because a stray bullet struck an opera house musician in the arm as he walked home from work. The severe inhumanity in both Victor and Cripple Creek was so common that it almost seemed dull and run-of-the-mill. When a man named James S. F. Roberts was shot at the Dawson Club, patrons jokingly urged the man to have a drink at the bar as he lay dying on the floor. The arrest of Ethel Brown for carving up a man's face with a razor made the papers, but only as a passing note. And when black prostitute Cora Wheeler swore out a complaint against Joe Huser for hitting her in the face with a hatchet, the papers neglected to utter a word of sympathy.

The newspapers were equally stoic in the reporting of burns suffered by a woman known as Hannah the Jap, who lived with her husband in an apartment above 426 Myers Avenue. One day, Hannah was washing a silk wrapper in gasoline near a lighted stove and it exploded. Hannah was severely burned, saved from death only by a black woman who rushed in and tore her flaming clothes off. A dog lying under the bed was burned alive. The newspaper seemed to focus only on the amusing comment by Hannah's confused and frightened husband that the pan must have been struck by lightning.

Many prostitutes who suffered injuries were taken to the St. Nicholas Hospital, also known as Sisters' Hospital. While the good Sisters of Mercy did not exercise prejudice among the ill and injured, the newspapers rarely followed up on patients' conditions. Prostitutes who died were usually buried by their sisters of the underworld in the Potter's Field of Mt. Pisgah Cemetery and quickly forgotten. One source identifies the prostitutes' burial spot as an area that is now covered by aspen trees. A 1994 inventory of Mt. Pisgah Cemetery revealed there were twice as many graves as originally thought, and at least some of these may have been the red-light women of Cripple Creek.

Throughout 1902 Myers Avenue continued to be the subject of many a news item. In spite of efforts to close the houses of ill repute, the law was of little avail in a boomtown whose population exceeded twenty thousand people. In addition to spanning Myers Avenue, the red-light district had also spread to parts of South 3rd Street, as evidenced by the presence of prostitute Rae Crawford on that street in 1902. Several miners, carpenters, waiters, and the like inhabited the 500 block of Myers, and so the girls were never in short supply of customers.

The red-light district in the 500 block continued to retain its ethnic flavor. The variety of nationalities represented in the collage of Poverty Gulch included French, Japanese, Chinese, American, Mexican, and Indian. The Parisian, a brothel consisting exclusively of French ladies, sat around the corner from Myers on Fifth Street. One of the girls there was Marie French or French Marie, who served wine to her customers. She was best known for her brazenly nasty come-ons. Other girls included Miss May Lane.

Grace Carlyle was another notorious prostitute. Grace, described as an "angel faced platinum blonde," started out working at Pearl Sevan's Old

Faithful on Myers Avenue.[27] Later, Grace earned clout by being the favorite call girl of mobster Grant Crumley. It is said the temperamental harlot was fond of performing stripteases on top of Grant's bar at the Newport Saloon, located in the bottom floor of the elite Gold Mining Exchange Building. Once, when Grace attempted suicide with laudanum, she tried to beat up the doctor summoned to her aid.

In April of 1901 the *Cripple Creek Morning Times* reported on Edward J. Sexton, a fire insurance agent from Denver who had a suite at the National Hotel. Three months earlier the married Sexton had become quite intimate with Grace Carlyle, who was at the time proprietress of a brothel known as the Four Hundred. Almost immediately the feisty Grace spelled trouble for Sexton, who already had a drinking problem. In February the twosome made the papers after Sexton shot up the Tivoli Bar. The couple had also become mixed up in some sort of lawsuit. On an early April morning Sexton left Grace and returned to his suite, where he attempted suicide by shooting himself in the chest. As Sexton lay dying in the hospital, the newspaper spent considerable verbiage on the man's wild habits. It is not known if he recovered, nor is it known what Grace had to say about the incident.

Authorities throughout the district worked harder than ever to crack down, and the bad boys and girls of Cripple Creek tried to behave themselves. July of 1902 netted only a few arrests: seven for drunkenness, one for drunk and pimping, two for being drunk and disturbing the peace, and three for disorderly conduct. Victor's Bank Exchange Saloon closed up, reopening as the National Café. Alcohol was not on the menu. But the shooting of mining millionaire Sam Strong by Grant Crumley in August of 1902 was the final straw for authorities. Gambling was outlawed altogether, but the party-hearty gamblers of Cripple Creek quickly devised a new way to escape the law by way of membership clubs. Those who failed to gain access to private clubs continued to participate in illicit gambling in the back rooms of Cripple Creek and other towns.

By 1903 membership clubs had gained much popularity. Within their private walls gamblers and prostitutes could cavort as they liked. Even so, world traveler and author Lowell Thomas, who grew up in Victor, guessed there were still about three hundred prostitutes on Myers Avenue in 1904. As a boy Thomas delivered newspapers in Victor, and his route included several brothels. Thomas described the ladies "who came to their doors in their wrappers, and sometimes less, and appeared relieved to find only the newsboy. They often chatted with me and I answered respectfully, as I had been taught to do, and this seemed to please them inordinately. . . . after learning about what went on behind those shuttered windows I remained respectful to the girls, and they were always nice to me. When I finally got my burro I promptly led it over and showed it to them. They seemed proud, too."[28]

In May of 1905 Teller County commissioners decided that a tougher crusade against gambling must begin immediately. Girls like Hazel Ward and Clara Winters were paying no attention whatsoever to the laws already in place, and Miss Julia Richardson, madam of the Mikado, was being far too brazen. A ban was once more placed on gambling and dance halls in Teller County. The news was disheartening not only to the saloon owners and prostitutes of Cripple Creek but also to their customers, friends, and even relatives. In other parts of Cripple Creek, many citizens were remotely or directly connected to the soiled section of town. One of these was Birdie May Hooyer, the sister of madam Laura Bell McDaniel. Birdie's family included her second husband, Harry, and his brother, Royal. Like Harry, Royal began as a miner in the Cripple Creek District and later sold insurance. Despite the reputation of Laura Bell, Royal's good standing in the community changed very little. From 1951 to 1959 Royal attended annual Cripple Creek Pioneer Reunions while living in Denver. He died in 1963, with no one the wiser about his past link with the underworld.

Efforts by authorities finally appeared to be doing the trick. During September of 1906 there were only four arrests in Cripple Creek: three for being drunk and causing disturbance and one for being just "plain drunk."[29] No arrests were made for prostitution, but at least one visitor noted the continued presence of prostitutes. Jesse Hanks, a tourist from Iowa, was staying with his miner buddy, Al Seals. On a trip to Cripple Creek for groceries, the men "saw four good-looking women who had ridden on horseback from Victor. They stopped their horses outside a saloon and asked for curb service, which they got about three times and drank enough to make them dizzy. During their stop, an acquaintance rolled cigarettes for them."[30]

It is probable that the decline in arrests coincided with that of the district's population. District mines were playing out, and some residents were moving on to greener pastures. Even so, authorities continued with their battle against prostitution. Fay Abbott was one of many girls still plying her trade in Cripple Creek in 1907. That same year, prostitute Goldfield Lil was killed in a fight at Victor's Senate Bar, and police never hesitated to arrest Dave and Neoma Hodge after a stray shot from Neoma's pistol hit Dave in the head. Carrie Warden of 341 Myers was another troublemaker, and Lizzie Stevenson was arrested for being "in a beastly state of intoxication." Lizzie was fined $1 and costs; when she could not pay, she was remanded to jail.[31]

Chapter Nine

Traveling Gals

Twas a frightened young girl
Who got off the train,
And took a good look around
No friends to greet,
No relatives to meet,
No place for her to be bound.

The pretty young thing
Stepped up to a man,
The only one in the light
And shyly asked,
Looking slightly abashed,
Where she might stay for the night.

The stranger took pity
And told her about
A hotel, just up the street
That a friend of his ran
Then he took her frail hand,
And gave it a pat, so sweet

The man thought a lot
Of the strange little girl
And figured she must be alright
'Till he took a chance
And went to a dance,
All on a Saturday night

The fellow walked in
To a dance hall he liked
Where a man played a nice guitar
But it was nearly his end
To see his new friend
Dancing across the bar!

The man crossed the floor
And tapped the young girl
On the shoulder, calm as could be.
The lass turned around
And gave him a frown
As he said, "Why didn't you tell me?"

"Charlie, or Bob, whatever your name,"
Said the gal,
"Would you like to be mine?
I'll dance with you,
I'll have a drink too,
But it will cost you a dime."

The stranger still goes
To the dance hall he likes,
But the girl he knew has left.
She caught the next train
Going across the plains
And left no forward address.

—Sadie A. Phillips

An integral aspect of any prostitute's career was to move on every few weeks, months, or years. Moving on was simply a necessity of the business. While certain madams such as Laura Bell McDaniel, Laura Evens, and Mattie Silks tempted fate and the law by establishing themselves in the same city for decades, common prostitutes had no such luxury. Many women moved around the West continually, sometimes traveling hundreds or thousands of miles between one place of residence and the next. Some, such as Cripple Creek prostitute Lillian Morris, came from as far away as California. Others, like Lillian's coworker Lizzie Chambers, were natives of Colorado.

Fig. 37. Mattie Silks often traveled to her ranch at the eastern plains town of Wray and was proud of her prize racehorses. A much older Mattie is pictured here with one of her girls, or perhaps it is Cort Thomson's elusive granddaughter.

(Courtesy Denver Public Library.)

The sporting women of Cripple Creek, Colorado City, Salida, Pueblo, Trinidad, and Leadville were known to travel between these respective towns frequently. The presence of prostitutes along Ute Pass, between Colorado City and Cripple Creek, escalated dramatically in 1892 with the gold boom at Cripple Creek. Traffic along the pass increased to three times what it had been. Colorado City's ladies of the night hastened to find their riches along with everyone else. Soon girls were traipsing between Colorado City and Cripple Creek in a kind of prostitute exchange program.

There were any number of reasons for a girl to pack her trunk and move along. For one thing, the prostitute who stayed in one place too long risked being labeled an "old-timer." Although many girls gained regular customers at their establishment, they could never underestimate human nature's desire for excitement and change. Many men were inclined to bounce around from girl to girl, with the prospect of "fresh meat" in town bringing a new sparkle to their eyes. The exception may have been customers who fell in love with the girls or desired to establish long-lasting friendships.

Some girls, of course, just couldn't seem to keep themselves out of trouble and were required to move along in order to stay one step ahead of the law. In January of 1897 the *Cripple Creek Morning Times* reported on police officer Alex Arnett, who went to "quell a row" in a "Negro" dance hall. He found a man named Burly beating prostitute May Rivers, "whose throat was cut last summer at the same time Frank Davis was murdered." May apparently survived the attack, which happened sometime after her arrival from Pueblo. There is little doubt that May's departure from Pueblo may have been caused by a similar incident. When Arnett saw her she was wielding a knife at Burly. In the ensuing fracas Arnett shot Burly in the foot. Another officer appeared; Burly was bandaged and sent to his cabin, while May was thrown in jail for the night. Incidentally, Officer Arnett began drinking immediately after the fracas and was so obnoxious that he himself was jailed and fined $10. Two other women, Millie Zorena and Ella Burton, were also fined. The next day Arnett was fired. As for May Rivers, "the bad coon" was unaccountably sentenced to sixty days in the Colorado Springs Jail.[1]

Another reason to keep on the move was to avoid becoming known to the law. Becoming a familiar sight to authorities on the streets of any town almost always spelled trouble. The more often a woman was arrested for "running a bawdy house," the harder police made it for her. In many cases, prostitutes could suddenly find themselves run out of town if they appeared in court enough times. In addition, fallen women who found camaraderie with each other often ended up telling more about themselves than they meant to. It was all too easy, even in the days before drivers' licenses and state identification, for someone who knew a girl to run into someone else who knew her, too. Word could travel fast in the wrong situation, revealing the whereabouts and occupation of a girl when she least desired it. Such was the case with Ella Wellington of Denver, whose friends from her former respectable married life in Nebraska unexpectedly appeared on the doorstep of her brothel and drove her to suicide.

Ex-lovers could prove just as destructive in the life of a prostitute. More times than not, romantic relationships with men ended due to abuse or greed. Witness Fanny Hall, a performing actress who doubled as a prostitute. In 1900 the *Weekly Cripple Creek Times* noted that Fanny was also a "habitue of the dance halls" who worked under the alias of Mrs. Billy Woods. Fanny had recently departed Cripple Creek, hoping to elude one Thomas Corby, who had already followed her from Denver. Corby chased the unfortunate woman to Seattle and even Dawson City, Alaska, where Fanny was rooming with another prostitute from Cripple Creek named Flora Hastings. Corby finally caught up with Fanny in San Francisco, where he promptly shot her. "He shot me! I'm dying, get a doctor," Fanny shouted, and died a short time later.[2]

Despite the high incidence of domestic violence, many women opted to travel with a male companion if possible. In May of 1912 Nita Barrington arrived in Cripple Creek from San Francisco and went to work at 435 East Myers Avenue. In June Nita left town alone but returned. In August the city register noted that Nita traveled to Walsenburg with a man named Al Bean. Whether Nita and Al's travel plan worked out is unknown; what is known for sure is that Nita returned to Cripple Creek again in November and found work at 429 East Myers.

Of course, landing in a new town meant surveying the scene, finding a place to work, and getting as many customers as possible. It wasn't always easy. Some prostitutes, such as Belle Barnes and May Jones, lasted less than a day in Cripple Creek, even though they had traveled all the way from Leadville and Denver, respectively. A 1913 arrival, Ruth Allen, returned to Denver after just four days. Mamie Cavilier arrived in Cripple Creek in 1911 but stayed for only two weeks before moving on. Grace Brown, who was working at 310 Myers Avenue, left just a little over a month later for Denver. Prostitute Nellie Craddock arrived in town the same day as Mamie and Grace. Nellie worked at 369½ Myers. She stayed a little longer, remaining until October, when she departed for Denver. Another new arrival was Alice Dorman, who worked at 459 Myers. Alice lasted six months before moving on.

Traveling hundreds of miles was not unusual for a working girl. A woman could follow the boomtowns as they popped up and make a tidy fortune as the new girl in town. Many would ply their trade along the way, earning the money and goods necessary to make the trip. Evidence of prostitutes moving around comes from the October 15, 1881 *Ouray Times*: "The floating population of Ouray just now seems to be in prostitutes. Last week there were a number went over the range and this week there has been a new lot come in."[3]

How brave these women were to undertake such a long and precarious journey! In 1884 Molly Foley traveled all the way from Gunnison

Fig. 38. Photographs such as this one of an unidentified prostitute were fun to distribute and served as a form of advertising. Unfortunately, such photos could often lead to a girl being located when she least desired it.

(From the author's collection.)

to Denver alone—a dangerous undertaking in those early times, when Indians and ruffians were still plentiful and lawmen were not. Being a working girl on the move could be lonely, frightening, and uncertain. Whenever possible, prostitutes tried to travel in pairs or groups to better protect themselves. An example is Ethel and Ruth Ayers, who were most likely sisters or at least posing as siblings. Both women arrived in Cripple Creek within two days of each other from Leadville in 1912. Both were born in Bolga, South Dakota. The two worked just two doors away from each other, presumably in upstairs cribs. In August Ruth left for Telluride. What became of Ethel, who was also known as Ethel Hughes, is unknown. Others, such as Lizzie Vinson, alias Jennie Tracey, seemed to prefer traveling alone. Twenty-seven-year-old Lizzie was born in St. Louis, Missouri. She had traveled to Pueblo and Salida before arriving in Cripple Creek in 1912.

Some women, unable to escape from the clutches of prostitution, simply outlived their usefulness no matter which town they settled in. Others were more fortunate. Pioneer Anne Ellis recalled encountering a traveling prostitute camped near the town of Bonanza. "We went over to investigate, and found a coarse, red-faced woman, her straw colored hair hanging in her eyes. She was one who had fallen so low that she drove from one camp to another, plying her trade in these tents." Refreshingly, this story has a happy ending. The woman later married an Englishman named Spencer. The two moved into "one of the best houses in town." A visit to her revealed "diamonds, very red plush furniture, and her very pale blue and bright pink tea gowns; also a parrot and a cage of parakeets."[4]

Prostitutes also were known to make business trips from their larger places of employment to surrounding camps and cities. "Helen" was one of the fast women in Bonanza who served as a "branch" employee of Laura Evens's house in Salida. At one time Helen had married a saloon keeper and tried to be respectable. She was prevented from doing so by the cultured ladies of the town, who shunned her and tried to keep her from attending social events. Eventually Helen left her husband and went back to drinking and prostitution. That was when she became Laura's "branch" employee, using the town's only telephone to coordinate girls coming from Salida to entertain at parties.[5]

Cripple Creek prostitute Eva Williams may have followed in Helen's footsteps. Born in California, Eva spent some time in Denver before appearing in Cripple Creek in 1911. In April of 1912 she was working at 433 Myers, but left. She returned in September, only to depart a month later for Leadville. Eva remained in Leadville, or parts in between, until March, when she returned to Cripple Creek once more. And there was Cora Blye of Bloomington, Nebraska, who divided her time between Cripple Creek and Denver. Between January 30 and March 12 of 1913, Cora traveled between the two cities no fewer than four times.

Many traveling girls billed themselves as actresses, and their jobs required them to accompany a show circuit from town to town. More than a few actresses doubled as prostitutes on the trail—and even when they had reached their destinations—for extra income. It was easy enough for a gal to perform burlesque in a theater, gather her tips from the stage, and then meet with her many admirers afterward, one at a time. Thus it was not permissible in decent society to socialize with actresses, nor with their male counterparts. Folks whose female relatives did work as actresses were often plied with the question, "Is she legitimate?"[6] This caused a stigma against legitimate entertainers that held through the 1950s.

Sometimes women took carefully measured steps to disappear entirely from records. When twenty-six-year-old Pathy Keller left town after working for six months in Cripple Creek, authorities could not say where she went. While on the road, Pathy most likely changed not only her name but perhaps even her looks. In the mode of the profession, she may have also discarded telltale clothing or other belongings to mask her identity even more. The same went for prostitutes Claret Grant, Vivian Edwards, Marion Kent, Dallie Sitell, and Poly Erving.

When Vola Keeling arrived in Cripple Creek from Fort Smith, Arkansas, her alias of Vola Gillette was duly recorded in the city register. On October 15, 1912, after just two weeks in town, Vola departed for Denver but apparently came back, since she is noted as leaving for Denver again in December. She returned on January 30, 1913, then left again for Victor in March. The last note on her reports her return from Victor in April. Where she surfaced next is anyone's guess. Literally thousands of women like Vola learned how to disappear forever in the eyes of city officials, documents, and even their families.

Women who immigrated to America from foreign countries consti-tuted yet another form of traveling gals. It is true that hundreds of women migrated from such faraway places as England, Ireland, and France, and many did so of their own volition. A gentleman friend or even a brothel owner in America paid the passage for some, with the understanding that the girls would work off the debt when they arrived. Many girls did just that, gained their freedom, and pursued their own lives.

The most put-upon immigrants, however, were the Chinese. Often, these girls were as young as ten or eleven years of age when they were sold to Americans or "Tongs" (the Chinese word for "pimps"), who brought them to the United States with the understanding that they could live their lives freely in the new country. In most cases the girls' families received only a few pennies or dollars but were led to believe their daughters were being sent to a better life. Many were under the impression that the girls were mail-order or "picture brides" who would marry upon their arrival to an American or Chinese man.

In reality, these girls were sold into virtual slavery. Once in America there was no way to return home, and the majority of Chinese girls were forced into prostitution in order to work off the cost of their passage. Ignorant of the English language, they were forced to sign contracts, written in English, promising to prostitute their bodies until their debt was paid to their "benefactor." Per the contract, a sick day, menstrual cycle, or pregnancy meant additional time would be tacked on. To these unfortunate, illiterate girls, there was no end in sight and no one to save them. Even if they did marry, their husbands usually ended up pimping them to the Tongs anyway.[7]

In Denver Tongs ruled over their own Chinese mafia, controlling the opium dens, whose services included prostitution. The girls were divided into classes by looks and talent, much like their white counterparts. Chinese brothel girls dressed well and painted their faces. The brothels provided a clean working environment plus a better opportunity to marry or be purchased for exclusive use by a client. Despite being considered quite valuable, however, most Chinese prostitutes were mistreated, neglected, abused, infected with venereal disease, and addicted to opium and other drugs. Lower crib girls were kept literal prisoners, operating behind barred windows and doors in tiny rooms with no more than a bed. Those who tried to escape were beaten, branded, and sometimes chained to their beds. In these squalid conditions, a girl could be expected to last no more than five or six years before succumbing to disease or illness.

Naturally, Colorado society in general objected to such inhumane treatment—once it became known what was going on. In San Francisco Donaldina Cameron had been working since 1895 to free Chinese slaves by actively staging raids alongside police. Her mission provided medical aid, education opportunities, and jobs, and many of her rescued girls even married. But it was many years before news of Donaldina's crusades reached Denver. Then, in 1910, Congress passed the Mann Act, which forbade, under heavy penalties, the transportation of women from one state to another for immoral purposes. It was well over a decade, however, before Colorado's Chinese prostitutes ultimately freed themselves from the hopeless clutches of enslaved prostitution.

Chapter Ten

Cracking Down

❧

There is so much bad in the best of us
And so much good in the worst of us
That it hardly behooves any of us
To talk about the rest of us.
　　　　　—John Brantingham,
　　　　　sometime before 1903

An early prostitute at California Gulch, even before it was known as Leadville, was a small woman "with flashing black eyes and a brilliant smile" named Red Stockings.[1] So called because of the red ribbons in her hair and the red stockings on her legs, Red Stockings was said to be cultured and refined. She said she was the daughter of a Boston merchant. Among her consorts were a French nobleman and a New York gambler. In late 1861 Red Stockings threw one last soiree for her best customers and explained she was taking $100,000 she had saved and going respectable. She reportedly moved to Nevada, married, had children, and did just that.

Likewise, Boulder prostitute Nellie Rivers appeared to be giving up the profession when she sold her furnishings in 1883. Three bedroom suites, two parlor sets, carpets, stoves, china, oil paintings, and kitchenwares were part of the inventory, indicating Nellie probably intended to retire. The stories of Red Stockings and Nellie Rivers must have seemed like fairy tales to most prostitutes. But out of the thousands and thousands of women who sold their bodies to make a living, only a minute percentage ever really achieved their goals. Anne Butler summed up the career of a prostitute: "Many prostitutes, confronted with the jaded realities and grim expectations of their lives, sank rapidly into all forms of dissipation. Alcoholism and drug addiction went hand in hand."[2]

Suicide was alarmingly common. One such case was Fay Anderson, a Salida prostitute who killed herself by drinking an ounce of carbolic acid. She died in agony. She was a graduate of a seminary in Kansas, well educated, and "of rather superior talents."[3] Ettie Barker, once a favorite actress at the Theater Comique in Pueblo, committed suicide by morphine in Denver in 1877. In 1900 Blanche Garland, employee of the Bon Ton Dance Hall in Cripple Creek, committed suicide with two ounces of chloroform after a quarrel with her lover. Nellie Rolfe was found dead in her room at 377 Myers in 1903. Dead long enough for rigor mortis to set in, the woman was crouching on the floor against her bed with her head resting on her arm. The newspaper guessed Nellie had overdosed on morphine. Three bottles of the stuff and two hypodermic needles were on her dresser.

Sometimes officials debated whether deaths were suicides or not. Most prostitutes used drugs and alcohol freely, both of which were easy to procure. Overdoses happened quite often. In 1872 Kitty Austin died at the Stranger's House in Pueblo. The *Colorado Weekly Chieftain* reported: "On making an appearance, the doctor found his patient, a girl of considerable personal attractions . . . in a comatose state, and apparently beyond all medical aid." It was never ascertained whether Kitty died of an accidental or intentional overdose, and gossip-hungry newspapers berated authorities for failing to perform an autopsy.[4] Other news reports let the reader decide. On August 16, 1878, a *Pueblo Chieftain* article was short and to the point: "Mamie, a girl at Esther Baldwin's, died from laudanum. She came here about four years ago from St. Louis. She was separated from her husband, Terry. Friends spared no expense to give her an appropriate burial in a handsome coffin."[5]

Death by suicide was in fact so common among prostitutes in the West that it was sometimes hardly newsworthy. "It does not make any difference how many of them die," wrote pioneer George Elder from Leadville, "there seems to be a perfect scramble to fill their places."[6]

Murder was also a common cause of death. In 1894 an eighteen-year-old prostitute named Trixie Lee, a Boulder transplant from Pueblo who worked at Madam Kingsley's, was murdered by Maud Hawks. The incident occurred after Mrs. Hawks and her mother had a fight with Mr. Hawks, during which the man became abusive. Mrs. Hawks's brother ordered the couple out of the house, whereupon the Hawkses took up lodging at the Boulder House. The next day Hawks went on a drinking spree and ended up at Madam Kingsley's. After procuring a carriage, Hawks and Trixie purposely drove past the Boulder House, where Mrs. Hawks sat out in front. It was said that Trixie shouted an insult at Mrs. Hawks as the carriage drove by.

Angry, Mrs. Hawks obtained a pistol and threatened to kill Trixie. Mr. and Mrs. Mel Warren, proprietors of the Boulder House, had a long talk with Mrs. Hawks to no avail. Later that evening Mrs. Hawks was taking a walk with her mother when she spied her husband once again, this time walking with Trixie and another prostitute, Jennie or Jessie Newhouse, plus three other men. One of the men pulled Mr. Hawks into the bushes, but Mrs. Hawks and her mother approached the girl. Maud shot her, and the flashes from the gunshots were seen by the editor of the *Boulder Daily Camera* from the newspaper building nearby. Maud and her mother, Mary, were both charged with manslaughter but found not guilty. "[T]he life of a scarlet woman weighs nothing in the balance against the avenging right of a woman wronged," observed the *Daily Camera*.[7]

If suicide, murder, or drug abuse did not befall a working girl, she could always succumb to disease or illness. In the days before penicillin, even the mildest of colds could turn deadly in the drafty whorehouses of a mining camp. Witness Julia Elliott of Cripple Creek, who contracted pneumonia and died at the County Hospital in 1911. In 1914 another unfortunate, Conie Russell, succumbed to apoplexy. In Leadville an aged dance hall girl named Mabel Johnson simply collapsed during a performance. The other girls carried her back to her wretched shack in Tiger Alley, set up a deathwatch, collected money for the burial, and thanked the Lord for putting Mabel to rest at last. Despite any and all precautions, many girls also contracted syphilis, gonorrhea, or some other venereal disease from their customers and ultimately died from the malady. Making a career out of prostitution could easily mean coming to a bad end. The authorities knew it, and with the Women's Christian Temperance Union and every church in town on their heels, the police set about closing down the red-light districts in Colorado with a vengeance.

For years, nearly every city in Colorado passed ordinances including laws against prostitution, gambling, and saloons. But with their coffers filled with money from fines and arrests, it was logical to isolate and control such places rather than close them down. When the town of Nederland outlawed saloons, residents simply imbibed from their liquor cabinets at home. Thus the city had to put up with drunks wandering through town anyway, without benefit of fines or money from liquor licenses.

Fort Collins, in fact, repealed its ordinances against saloons in 1875. The saloon owners and bawdy girls lost no time in taking advantage of the act. Soon ordinary businesses were flanked by gambling dens and taverns. By 1881 the law was upholding its authority as best as it could. When four "Negro" girls from a nearby dance hall drove up in their fancy carriage, complete with a white driver, the sheriff followed them inside the tavern they had entered with orders to move on. By 1883 Fort Collins was up to thirteen saloons, three drugstores, five brothels, and several gaming houses, all of which sold liquor. Most of these places were located along College Avenue, Jefferson, and Lincoln. In desperation, city authorities finally upped the price of their liquor licenses from $300 to $1,000. The plan worked. Fort Collins was soon back down to just six saloons, while many of the town's shady ladies moved on to greener pastures.

In 1895 Pueblo mayor A. T. King passed an ordinance creating the Pueblo Saloon District. No bars were allowed outside the district, which sat pretty much in the middle of Pueblo. At the time Pueblo's red-light district was located along 1st Street between Santa Fe and Albany Avenue. Cribs on the north side of the street measured approximately 180 square feet. On the south side they were roomier, with about 240 square feet. Many were owned by women who rented them to prostitutes. These were allegedly the best brothels in town and came complete with private entrances in the back.

As the turn of the century loomed on the horizon, however, officials were realizing that, city coffers or not, prostitution and all its accompanying evils had to go. A plan of reform included closing down the dance halls in Cripple Creek in May of 1900, starting with the Imperial on Myers Avenue. Several musicians and proprietors were arrested, all of whom carried on their business until literally pulled away by officers. Curiously, none of the girls in the establishment were arrested. Word of the arrests traveled quickly. By the time officers reached the Bon Ton and a "Negro" dance hall run by Tom Blue, both houses were closed—at least for that evening.

In August of 1901 yet another attempt was made to close down gambling in Cripple Creek. As of 7 P.M. on August 23, all gambling was to cease. By 9 P.M., a few law-breakers at the Antlers and Johnny Nolon's were discovered gambling in the upstairs rooms of their establishments and dispersed. But authorities weren't through just yet. In March of 1903 the mayor and his subordinates next converged on the dance halls and cribs of Myers Avenue. Business owners were duly notified that their inmates had but a few days to vacate before arrests and prosecutions would proceed. No doubt about it, the pressure was on in Cripple Creek, and a number of former saloon men like Crapper Jack, Grant Crumley, and Johnny Nolon left Cripple Creek for more lenient towns in Nevada. Likewise, Pueblo was also continuing in its mission to clean up Union Avenue by vacating the notorious brothels along the now-defunct Bessemer Street. In Crestone decent residents took matters into their own hands and destroyed a local saloon to protest the hiring of bar girls.

Only Creede proved to be the exception. A 1906 ordinance closed saloons on Sunday, but the new law didn't last long. After the local newspaper successfully argued that many miners had no warmer quarters to go to in the freezing winter evenings, authorities repealed the ordinance. The dance halls, brothels, and bars went back to their business, including opening on Sundays. Similarly, the town of Idaho Springs declined to prohibit women from entering billiards halls and saloons in its early days—for a little while, anyway. In other parts of Colorado, many working girls continued to be accepted to an extent. A newcomer to Telluride remembered watching a gigantic funeral procession through town. Later the woman learned the funeral was not for a prominent citizen, but for the town's leading madam.

Fig. 39. Telluride's red-light district along Pacific Avenue flourished well into the twentieth century. Today the three houses on the left are private homes.

(From the author's collection.)

The authorities were not so lenient in Cripple Creek and Colorado City. Cripple Creek's underworld was still scurrying to operate under stringent ordinances when the papers announced, in September of 1906, that the ax-wielding prohibitionist Carrie Nation was in town. The devout crusader was by then known across America for her tirades, including smashing windows and chopping up saloons with her trusty hatchet. From her lofty suite at the Collins Hotel, Ms. Nation actually complimented the city on its good social conditions and the presence of so few saloons, despite nationwide rumors that Cripple Creek was a wild city of debauchery and vice.

After lecturing to a crowd of nearly three hundred at the Odd Fellow's Hall, Carrie announced her intention to stay a few days longer, promising to be on hand at the local saloons to dispense motherly advice. Not surprisingly, people who later remembered her visit recalled seeing Carrie smash a few windows. She also gave out miniature hatchet pins, some set with gems in the blade. For many years the story also circulated that she tried to enter Johnny Nolon's saloon on Bennett Avenue. In varying versions of the tale, she either smashed up a nude painting or was denied admittance, was arrested and bailed out by Nolon himself, and/or was given a train ticket out of town with instructions never to return.

Tales of Carrie Nation's visit no doubt circulated to Colorado City, where in 1906 police magistrate James D. Faulkner enforced several new ordinances in Colorado City. Bars were to close at midnight and on Sundays. Use of side doors at saloons was prohibited. All billiard halls, poolrooms, and bowling alleys were commanded to close from midnight to 6 A.M. Colorado City waited eagerly for someone to break the law. They didn't have to wait long. Almost immediately, authorities pounced on Jacob Schmidt for permitting women in his bar at 612 West Colorado Avenue, now 2611 West Colorado. Schmidt argued he had a sign up barring "prostitutes or fast women" from entering, even though it was known that several shady ladies operated from small rooms above the bar. Schmidt was dismissed with a reprimand, but other arrests followed. In February there were a series of busts resulting in jail time, fines, and warnings.

The police were egged on by local newspapers. The *Colorado City Iris* reported on seven brothels where liquor was sold without a city license. "The prostitutes' presence is similar to Kansas—the proprietor and inmates appear once a month in court and are fined," the *Iris* revealed.[8] A monthly "fine" of $600 was suggested. Other newsworthy items included questioning city council for failing to close bawdy houses on Sundays. Chief of police Birdsall was clearing out male "habitues" of the disorderly houses and was issuing warnings to some of the soiled doves both "on the row and at other places," with the *Iris* watching his every move.[9] In fact, the *Iris* made sure to include a commentary on the goings-on in the red-light district in nearly every issue during this time. The February 9 issue, for instance, complained about liquor licenses being granted to bawdy houses and reported on an underage boy, whose mother had died a year earlier, who "spent the night on the row" at a cost of $20. The money was returned to the boy's father, but the article expressed much concern that the incident had been allowed to happen at all. An article in the February 23 issue warned that obscene business cards were being distributed; several hundred such cards had recently seen scattered between 6th and 7th streets, where they were picked up by schoolchildren. "There is no better means of poisoning the minds of young folks than vulgar reading," the newspaper warned. But some girls had already had enough. In March two brothels closed, leaving seven houses. "One of the gangs went to Cripple Creek," announced the *Iris* with satisfaction.[10]

There was also a very real attempt to ban liquor in Colorado City in 1906. In addition, mayor Ira Foote notified the girls of the row they had ten days to leave town. But the saloon keepers and bawdy girls refused to budge. Some of them had been there a long time, longer than many city officials and police, and they weren't about to be pushed around by new-comers. On January 18 officers Edward Rettinger and Webb raided a poker game in progress over the Hoffman Saloon. Fourteen people were present, though only eight were playing poker. Officer Rettinger, who had himself been accused of being drunk on the job six months before, lost no time in making arrests.

Sometimes prohibitionists handled the lawless in their own style. In January of 1907 a fire broke out from an unknown source, wiping out many beer halls on Saloon Row in Colorado City. During the fire, the Reverend Duncan Lamont of the Bethany Baptist Church appeared on the scene and watched as the firefighters turned their hoses on the flames. Lamont, a resident of Colorado City since 1902, had long been waging a battle against saloons and prostitution. His wife, Katherine, was now the president of the local WCTU. (Ironically, Lamont had officiated at the funeral of Laura Bell McDaniel's mother back in 1905.) In the midst of the conflagration, the Reverend Lamont began waving his arms and shouting, "Our prayers have been answered!" The firemen, many of whom patron-ized the saloons, turned their hoses on him. In the freezing night air,

Lamont literally became a sheet of ice and had to be carried back to his church.[11] Lamont resigned his position in May and escaped from the ridicule to Victor. By the spring of 1910, the embarrassing incident was mostly forgotten and the good reverend moved back to Colorado City, where he became postmaster in 1916.

For the Colorado chapter of the WCTU, the fire was a victory. And, they heard, Pueblo authorities had just succeeded in closing all wine rooms to women. In Colorado City the organization was headed by Mrs. Sue B. Chase at 105 Washington Avenue. At their afternoon teas, members talked of whether the houses of ill repute would return. Their gossip carried all over the city, but things had actually been quieting down. The red-light district was falling out of the limelight—until that respectable boy named Tucker Holland killed himself at Dolly Worling's brothel in 1908. The incident shed a new shady light on just what was going on in Colorado City's red-light district.

A few days later the Reverend F. W. Hullinger called a mass meeting at the Waycott Opera House just a block from the red-light district. Speakers at the meeting included Judge Cunningham, Senator Stephen, the Reverend Clark Bower, and saloon owners Byron Hames and J. H. Hamble. The speakers presented the pros and cons of the district, but Hames and Stephen managed to shift the main consideration of the meeting from prostitution to Judge Cunningham's actions, which included favoring annexation to Colorado Springs. Bower and Hullinger were also chastised for devaluating property in the decent parts of town by making such a public fuss over the red-light district.

In the end the resolution of the meeting declared that "the act of the mayor and city council in voting to abolish the red-light district and in cleaning up the city morally, be heartily endorsed and we do heartily pledge our support in such an action."[12] This time mayor Ira Foote carried out his promise with a vengeance. The Colorado City Council came up with a whole new petition:

Whereareas [sic] the laws of the state of Colorado and the ordinances of the city of Colorado City make the running of houses of ill fame unlawful, and; Whereareas the collection of regular stipulated monthly fines from the inmates of such resorts by the city of Colorado City is a violation of the status and the ordinances of our city, and, therefore, indefensible, legally and morally; therefore be it;

Resolved, That the city cease receiving from the prostitutes of the city any portion of their illegal earnings; and be it

Further Resolved, That the police be and they hereby are ordered and directed to at once close all houses of ill fame and arrest the inmates thereof."[13]

In February the *Colorado City Iris* and several chapters of the WCTU publicly commended Mayor Foote for his actions against the red-light district. The *Colorado Springs Gazette* was hinting that with the cleanup of Colorado City came talk of annexation to Colorado Springs. The news was enough to make most of the remaining prostitutes start packing their trunks. Only a few, including Laura Bell McDaniel and Mamie Majors, stayed put.

Down in Pueblo, summer plans were being made to close the red-light district and move the women out. Spuds Murphy and Pete Froney, whose saloon doubled as a brothel, were among those denied a liquor license. A January article in the *Colorado Springs Gazette* reported that saloons and gambling halls were "wiped out in Cripple Creek." As of November, the number of prostitutes in Colorado City had shrunk to twenty-four girls and eight madams, hardly down from the usual forty or so prostitutes.

This time it was serious. Mayor Ira Foote had had enough and notified the girls of the row once more that they had ten days to leave town. The point was emphasized by three fires in January of 1909. The first fire broke out around 11 P.M. on January 8, destroying five or six houses of ill repute on the south side of Washington Avenue between 5th and 6th streets. The second fire occurred on January 9 at 3 A.M. The north side of Washington Avenue between 5th and 6th streets and the entire south side of Washington between 6th and 7th streets were burned. The Red Light, of which Gus Heffner was allegedly the sole occupant, was among the casualties (Heffner survived). Police Chief McDowell estimated that close to $40,000 in damage had been done to the red-light district alone. Additional damage occurred throughout the city as high winds kicked up the cinders from both fires, sending flaming shingles and ashes for blocks and setting other fires. Those were extinguished quickly with buckets of water and garden hoses.

A police watchman was posted in the aftermath to watch for more fire dangers. The watchman could not prevent a third fire, however, which broke out within hours, mysteriously originating in the same area. This time the flames threatened the business district before being put out. The last fire, blamed on a vagrant trying to keep warm, started in the rear barn of Ridenhour & Rettiger's livery stable in the 400 block of West Colorado. Forty-three horses died, including Mayor Foote's own steed. The other forty-two horses had been slated for shipment to Alta Vista, a railroad stop outside the town of Victor. Fourteen carriages and hay also burned. Other casualties included Beyle & Company's warehouse and a one-story cottage on Washington Avenue. It took the combined efforts of the Colorado Springs Fire Department and the Colorado City Fire Department to put out the flames.

The red-light district was destroyed pretty much in its entirety. Among the brothels to go were the Mansions and the El Paso. In both cases, the buildings were insured. Other brothels to succumb to the fire were the Stone Fort, the Three Deuces, and the Trilby. All in all, nine houses burned. Most were insured, and much to the city's chagrin, the district slowly grew up again. As the ladies of the district struggled to regain their composure, the *Colorado City Iris* continued to complain.

In April of 1909, in yet another article crying out against prostitution, the *Iris* once again blasted city authorities. "But lo and behold, no sooner had the new officers held up the hands and taken the oath of office to support the laws of the land, than Laura Bell, the oldest and most influential sinner of them all, started a brick building said to cost $10,000. Mamie Majors, once sentenced to six months in the county jail and pardoned by Governor Buchtel, on the pleas that she had reformed, fitted up the old 'City Hotel' and opened up the house in full blast. Bessie Paxton followed, then Eula Hames, wife of Gus Hames, opened up an establishment."[14]

During May of 1909 Nellie White, Bessie Paxton, Mamie Majors, Eula Hames, and Laura Bell McDaniel were each fined $25 and costs. All pled guilty. All were represented by Samuel H. Kinsley, W. D. Lombard, and city attorney John Watt. The monthly fines were obviously back in effect. Judge Owen warned the madams that if he saw them in court again he would send them to jail. A total of nineteen inmates were arrested as well and placed under $100 bond. The madams each paid over $500 in total fines.

Authorities were frustrated and tired. What was the harm in having a red-light district if it meant additional income to the city? Denial was the best recourse. In July Alderman Kelly, after receiving several anonymous letters concerning the red-light district, replied publicly in the *Iris*:

[S]o far as I am personally concerned, I am unaware of the existence of such at the present writing. I naturally presumed that the fire of last December [*sic*] had forever wiped from existence this so called "Necessary Evil."

The police court of this city has at no time in the past 18 months, or possibly two years, assessed a fine upon a fallen woman. . . . I, like Senator John B. Stephen, believe that, if we are to be cursed with this evil, the best way is to confine it to certain quarters of the community, and there control it. . . . I am not now, nor have I ever at any time, been in favor of licensing the demi-monde.[15]

The ploy hardly worked, however, and throughout the summer city officials continued wrestling with the problem of red-light ladies as well as Colorado City's numerous saloons. In August of 1909 occupants of the Brunswick in Colorado City were given a deadline to move out. They did. In addition, a brothel at 7th Street and Colorado Avenue was ordered closed. Similar orders were given throughout the rest of 1909. Then, just a few days before Christmas, former madam Blanche Burton succumbed to burns received when a flaming curtain set her clothing on fire.

Blanche had lived an interesting life. Initially a resident of Colorado City and formerly hailed as the first madam of Cripple Creek, Blanche had retired back in Colorado City some years before. Blanche first appears on record in 1889, when she was already thirty years old and a seasoned professional. According to census records, she had been born in Ireland in November of 1865 and came to the United States in 1881. Blanche was once married to a prominent Kansas man who later moved back east. The couple had a son and a daughter. The boy died in an explosion, and the girl was placed in a convent.

Back in 1889 court records showed Blanche was accused of running a house of ill fame in Colorado City. The loophole Blanche dove through to gain her release was quite clever and amusing, as her defense successfully argued that she couldn't possibly run a "house" of ill fame because she actually lived in a tent. But such harassment was common in Colorado City, and so when word came of a gold boom in Cripple Creek, Blanche took the opportunity to move up there. She arrived with her tent in 1891 and immediately struck up a friendship with Bob Womack. The charming cowboy took Blanche under his wing and encouraged her to set up business near his cabin in Poverty Gulch. Almost right away Blanche discovered the value of being streetwise in Cripple Creek. One of her customers, aptly named Tim Hussey, had been paying for Blanche's services by giving her interests in his mining claims. An investigation by Womack revealed that the twenty-seven one-eighth interests were all from the same claim. Despite this and other gold camp frauds, Blanche appears to have done well during her first two years in Cripple Creek. Blanche had a limited education, but she could read and write. For several months she held the title of the first and only madam in town. By 1893 she had discarded her tent in favor of a parlor house over a saloon on Bennett Avenue.

Cripple Creek responded in kind by blossoming into a rough-and-tumble boomtown. Younger girls, some in their teens, came and set up business too. It is not unlikely that Blanche felt lost or even left out as newcomers poured into the city, and "old-timers" like herself were forgotten. When marshal Hi Wilson demanded that all ladies of the evening remove themselves from Bennett Avenue to more discreet quarters on Myers Avenue, Blanche had had enough. Upon departing from Cripple Creek in 1894, Blanche considered herself officially retired.

Or did she?

Back in Colorado City, Blanche took up residence at 812 Colorado Avenue, just around the corner from the northernmost part of the red-light district. But word of her reputation spread through town. Three years away, especially in an immensely popular town like Cripple Creek, did little to quell any rumors about her profession. Over time Blanche became a noted recluse with no visible means of income. In 1902 she moved one house over to 816 West Colorado. Also living at the house in 1902 was Miss Blanche Bell. On December 20, 1909, Police Chief McDowell and Patrolman Morse were on an evening stroll when they noted a person who appeared to be on fire running into the middle of Colorado Avenue. The men immediately grabbed the victim and used their overcoats and snow to extinguish the flames. Most of the clothing was burned off, and closer examination revealed it was Blanche Burton lying in their arms. Upon carrying her into the house the men discovered a hanging curtain, called a *portiere*, also in flames. Surprisingly, the fire was small and quickly extinguished. A broken oil lamp lay nearby, providing a clue to the mystery.

Two physicians, Dr. G. S. Vinyard and Dr. G. B. Gilmore, were called to the Burton home, but there was little to be done. Also at Blanche's side was Mamie Majors. Blanche lived long enough to tell everyone present that just a year and a half earlier her barn had burned. Her horse and two dogs had been killed, and in trying to rescue them she had almost died herself. The men tried to get her to reveal her true name (if there was one) as well as the address of the daughter she allegedly had. Supposedly, Blanche said on her deathbed that her daughter lived in Illinois, but she died just after 5 A.M. the next morning before she could give them any other information.

No doubt the men wondered why Blanche chose to mention her burning barn. They also wondered why a man was seen running west on Colorado Avenue shortly before Blanche's accident. The man was never identified, nor was there any cash in the house. Furthermore, authorities failed to find any bank accounts in Blanche's name. Blanche Burton probably would have been buried a pauper if it weren't for Mamie Majors. The bold Miss Majors paid for Blanche's funeral, which was conducted from Beyle Undertaking Rooms on Christmas Eve. Surely it was a sad and grief-stricken party that accompanied Blanche to her grave in Fairview Cemetery. Even the public and the press felt sympathy for the reclusive harlot. The presiding minister praised Blanche's good heart, explaining that the day before her death she had purchased a ton of coal for needy families in time for Christmas. Her obituary in the *Colorado Springs Gazette Telegraph* was headlined, "Did Much Good." The article stated that Blanche was a good nurse and always ready to respond to those in need.[16]

As the years went by, Blanche and her counterparts were all but forgotten until Bill Henderson came along. Henderson, formerly the mayor of Colorado Springs, took a special liking to the naughty (but deceased) ladies of Colorado City. Members of the Garden of the Gods Rotary Club were so moved by a speech Henderson gave they decided Blanche should have a proper gravestone. Accordingly, the group took up a donation. Richard Wilhelm of Wilhelm Monument Company carved the stone, which was erected in 1983 on the anniversary of Blanche's unfortunate death. It remains today, bearing an appropriately wise inscription based on a poem by Frank Waugh:

Pioneer Madam
Blanche
BURTON
1859–1909
The sins of the living
are not of the dead.

If the citizens of Colorado City and the *Gazette Telegraph* pitied poor Blanche Burton, the *Colorado City Iris* did not. In January the paper pointed out that after the fires of 1909 everyone thought it was the end of the red-light district. "But, lo and behold, not long after the city election and a change of administration, new houses began to appear in this abolished district." The *Iris* was seething. A month later came this further admonition: "The chief argument for maintaining a red-light district is that it is better to have it in one place than to have it scattered over town." Furthermore, the *Iris* openly accused the city of taking kickbacks from the madams.[17] The war continued to rage. In a January 1910 city council meeting, Alderman Kelly questioned the lack of fines for December of 1909. Police magistrate J. T. Brooks stated that it had been rumored the fines were "donated" as Christmas presents to the brothels, and that the madams had not paid. Subsequent exposés by the *Iris* revealed even more new construction and accused the police of "dividing their ill-got-gains with the city each month."[18] As usual, city authorities hustled—or pretended—to comply with the wishes of the WCTU and the *Iris*.

Colorado City's red-light district was not the only place to suffer under pressure from authorities. In 1910 Pueblo's red-light district was closed down again following a series of raids. One raid in particular, which took place on January 17, involved twenty-three arrests. Of them all, only Lena Garcia spoke in court—and then via an interpreter, because Lena could not speak English. She explained she had three children to support and no other way to make money. Judge Rizer fined her anyway. The following day, January 18, netted fifty-two arrests with one escape. Most of the offenders were released on $300 bail. Many of them claimed to have been inhumanely treated, insulted, neglected, and abused while in jail.

In the wake of the arrests four Pueblo officers, including Police Chief Sullivan, were accused in February of getting drunk earlier in the month and spending the night in a brothel. Among the bordellos the men had visited on their spree were the Tivoli, Pete Froney's Pleasure Saloon at 106 West 1st Street (which no longer stands), and Spuds Murphy's, where five or six rounds of beer were served. Witnesses to the officers' presence included Angelo Froney, piano player Louie Nevins, and prostitutes Margaret Ellsworth and Lucille Hall. Later, it was claimed, the officers went to the Quinn rooming house at 205½ Santa Fe and settled in prostitute Sarah (Sadie) Brown's room. Two other women besides Sarah were there: Helen Jackson and Aletha Brown. Another resident, Carrie Cromwell, was apparently absent. While there, Sadie Brown would later testify, detective Sam Shurtz almost tore her kimono off. The men even returned to the Quinn house on Friday night for more fun. In the end the officers, including Sullivan, were fired or demoted, as noted by the *Pueblo Chieftain*.

City officials continued in their quest to close down the brothels of Pueblo. Spuds Murphy simply moved from her place at 104 North Summit Street to the Grand Hotel at 8th and Santa Fe and operated there for a while (the Grand no longer stands). One source says Spuds had lost her house due to a drinking problem. The busts continued. Marie Noll spent ten days in jail in February for owning two cribs.

Then in March Pete Froney was accused of running a white slavery ring. Jennie Thompson testified that she refused to spy on the slaves and report their earnings. Jennie had already created a commotion ten years before, when a notorious fire in August of 1899 may have started at her dance hall in Victor. Shortly after her testimony against Froney, Jennie left and got respectable employment. More charges came against Froney from Mamie Lee, who attempted suicide in March. Mamie couldn't pay her rent at 262 River Street and claimed to have been seduced into prostitution by Froney, her landlord. Mamie also said she and her sister had worked as waitresses before falling victim to Froney.

Even with prostitutes testifying against their pimps, however, authorities still found cracking down a challenge. In April seven men and four women were indicted for prostitution-related offenses. In June forty prostitutes were told to leave Pueblo. The following day, prostitute Pearl Stevens and nineteen pimps were arrested and fined. As of July at least two women, Winnie Stephens and Blanche Bennett, were still in the brothel business in Pueblo.

Things were not as severe in Silverton, where brothel construction continued through 1910. Between 1910 and 1930 Silverton's largest brothels included the Laundry, the Diamond Bell, the Bon Ton, the Monte Carlo, the Tremount, and the National. Smaller brothels included the Tree Top, the Arcade, the Mikado, Nigger Lola's, Black Minnie's, Diamond Tooth Leona's, Sheeny Pearl's, Kate Starr's, Mayme Murphy's, and Tar Baby Brown's.

Such goings-on surely seemed like heaven to the naughty ladies of Pueblo and Colorado City, where the *Iris* triumphantly reported in 1911 that mayor P. J. Hamble, like his predecessor Ira Foote, had given the madams and their girls ten days to leave the city. Unfortunately, many prostitutes were forced to stand their ground for lack of a better place to go. Times were changing, mine production was slowly spiraling downward throughout the state, and Cripple Creek's population was dwindling by the day. Far-off places like Silverton made for an expensive trip, with no guarantee of work upon arrival. Besides, they reasoned, the city had issued orders like Hamble's so many times before, the whole thing had become somewhat of a joke.

In contrast to Colorado City, Cripple Creek appears to have fine-tuned its regulation of prostitution. Colorado City required its soiled doves to merely pay a monthly fine without benefit of health exams. Prostitutes were also allowed as much freedom in Colorado City as any law-abiding citizen, so long as they remembered their place in society and respected the higher class. Not so in Cripple Creek. During an election in 1909, voters overwhelmingly decided that Cripple Creek should remain "wet," voting down an ordinance to close all saloons. In answer, city authorities decided that regulating saloons and prostitutes was the only recourse. One ordinance ruled that prostitutes were allowed to do their shopping on Bennett Avenue one specific morning per week. Decent ladies dubbed this day as "wash day" and stayed home to do chores rather than risk running into "those other women." Long before, the City of Cripple Creek also stepped up on its requirement of shady ladies to receive monthly health exams. The girls then took their clean bill of health to city hall, paid their monthly fine, and received a "license" with which to operate for the next thirty days. On the average, dance hall and crib girls paid $4 per month. Wealthier parlor house girls paid $16 each, and the madams paid $40. Madams were required to display their license on the premises, just as in any other business.

In 1911, city officials began keeping a careful register of each girl, stating her name, known aliases, description, and physical condition. Where possible, authorities also ascertained where the girls were born, where they had last come from, where they were working or residing, and where they went when they left town. If they changed jobs or residence, the new address was also noted. Every scar and birthmark was recorded; in the case of Dorothy Dunn, the examiner noted "birthmark on right side of neck about size of a dollar." Many madams also kept registers, noting where the girls came from and why they had left their last place of employment. They had to, since madams were made responsible for their employees' conduct. If a girl was caught on Bennett Avenue during the wrong time, her madam was fined an additional $6.

A Sampling of Cripple Creek Prostitutes in 1911–13

Name	Date of arrival	Age	Birth-place	Notes
Ruby Ashby	May 1912	23	Kentucky	Arrived from Colorado Springs; worked at 373 ½ Myers.

Ethel Ayers	March 1912	23	Bolga, South Dakota	Arrived from Leadville; worked at 365½ Myers.
Marie Brady	January 1913	23	San Francisco	Arrived from Denver; worked at the Mikado, 341 E. Myers.
Leona Brown	April 1912	23	Joliet, Illinois	"Colored"; arrived from Pueblo; left after one week at 459 Myers; had been "sporting" six months.
Louisa Davis	March 1912	26	Virginia	French American; arrived from Central City.
May DeVine	January 1913	28	Sacramento	Arrived from Salt Lake City.
Theresa DeVine	April 1912	—	—	Arrived from Pueblo; worked at 341 Myers; left for Colorado Springs in June.
Rose Duprey	June 1911	28	—	Worked at 317 Myers through January 1912.
Kitty Hart	February 1912	24	Denver	Arrived from Casper, Wyoming; first worked at 373 Myers; left for Denver in May.
Alice Howard	May 1912	23	Detroit	Arrived from Denver; resided at 361 Myers; left for Denver in October.
Mattie Jones	November 1912	28	Amozina [sic], Missouri	Arrived from Denver; resided at 437½ Myers.
Mayme Marlowe	March 1913	25	Fort Worth, Texas	Arrived from Leadville; worked at 365½ E. Myers.

Name	Date	Age	Origin	Notes
Mattie Mathers	September 1912	28	New Orleans	Arrived from Chicago; resided at 441 ½ Myers.
Florence McCoy	May 1912	22	Butte, Montana	Arrived from Denver and went to work at 427 Myers; took a trip to Denver from May 10 to May 27; upon return worked at 425½ Myers.
Eveline Miller	March 1913	24	Galveston	Arrived from Denver; worked at 457 E. Myers.
Maud Osborne (alias Maud Williams)	June 1912	30	Michigan	Arrived from Colorado City; worked at 373 Myers.
Grace Rubby	February 1913	24	Cheyenne, Wyoming	Black; arrived from Denver.
Lilley Sampson	July 1911	28	—	French; arrived from Denver; worked at 433 Myers.
Maud Shafer	March 1913	29	Burmingham, Illinois	Arrived from Denver; worked at 369 E. Myers.
Florence Stokes	March 1913	22	Nashville	Arrived from Leadville; worked at 365 E. Myers.
Jennie Washington	December 1912	35	Arkansas	Black; arrived from Colorado Springs.
Willie Wellington	June 1911	34	Kentucky	Spent a short time in Victor before coming to Cripple Creek.
Dottie White	April 1912	22	Indiana	Arrived from Pueblo.
Babe Willison (alias)	August 1912	21	Jefferson County, Indiana	Arrived from Pueblo.
Pearl Winsfield	October 1911	23	Golden, Colorado	Arrived from Denver.
Elsie Winters (alias)	March 1913	23	Brown, Texas	Arrived from Denver.

More fines were assessed for such violations as fighting, being publicly intoxicated, or wearing skirts more than six inches above the ankles. The last-named ordinance was devised to keep dance hall girls from shortening their long cumbersome skirts to accommodate their jobs. Some dance hall dolls had hemmed their dresses to within four inches of their knees, creating quite a stir on the streets. Many girls countered the ordinance by wearing ankle-length pinafores or aprons, allowing them to appear decent in public with their short skirts covered.

As a result of these stringent policies, some girls were actually beginning to give in and give up their profession. The city register noted in July of 1911 that Viola Sellers was a former prostitute at 431 Myers Avenue. Viola was also working or residing on El Paso Street between 3rd and 4th as well as at 208 South B Street. At one time Viola had worked for Cripple Creek madam Frankie Mason but was noted as having "quit rustling." Sellers was thirty-seven years old at the time, and so probably opted to retire from the profession. Ada Fitzgerald was also listed as residing at 317 Myers. In January of 1912 the register notes she was "not on the row," indicating that while Ada was not currently doing business, she may have still been in the city.[20]

In contrast to Viola and Ada's apparent salvation, unfortunately, was the death of Nellie Smith. A Cripple Creek prostitute since at least 1907, Nellie was conducting business with miner Sam Vidler in room 213 at the prestigious National Hotel. Mrs. Vidler found out and burst into the room, shooting Nellie dead. Mrs. Vidler was acquitted of the murder in just ten minutes. And there were others: Jane Bernd, a forty-two-year-old who worked in the predominantly French 400 block through 1912; Bessie Belmont, a Springfield, Illinois, well-fed beauty who worked in Cripple Creek through 1913; and Edith Brooks, a twenty-two-year-old from Ogden, Utah, who moved around a lot before leaving town for destinations unknown in 1912. There was also Mamie Clark, formerly of Colorado City, who moved from her job at 369 Myers to a safer haven above the Combination Saloon in December of 1911. A year later, however, Mamie was back in a crib on Myers.

The Mikado, the Old Homestead's biggest competition, appears to have continued a booming business in 1912. Billie Lawrence, described as having a brunette complexion and perfect teeth, was one of the gals at the Mikado. Another was Florence Oakley, who had learned her trade in Deadwood and Denver. Competition was tough for a while between the Mikado and the Old Homestead, but the girls of both houses appear to have been pretty flighty at this point in time. Witness Babe Maxwell, who worked at the Mikado with frequent departures for Denver through 1913. In March of 1912 twenty-four-year-old Hazel Burns arrived in Cripple Creek and went to work at 310 Myers Avenue. After just one day of work Hazel left for Victor, but she returned to Cripple Creek in April. In June she left for Kansas but returned once more in August, finally settling down at the Mikado. Marill Danley was twenty-four years old when she first traveled from Denver to Cripple Creek in October 1911. Marill worked at the Mikado for a short time before moving to the Old Homestead. In August of 1912 she left for Victor, and in October she returned to Denver.

Traipsing between Cripple Creek and Victor seems to have been quite popular among prostitutes during this time. In October 1911 twenty-four-year-old Lillian Rogers left Cripple Creek for Victor after just one month in town. In February 1912 Cripple Creek prostitute Glyn Holmes, formerly of Kansas, moved to Victor. Margaret Walters also lasted less than a week in Cripple Creek before moving to Victor in June.

It seemed that despite a dying mining boom and fines at every turn, Cripple Creek's red-light ladies were still going strong. Even women of mixed nationalities could make it in a predominantly white, Irish, and Catholic place such as Cripple Creek. One such was Geroldine Dixon. Born in Oklahoma and having recently migrated from Salt Lake City, Dixon was described as being ¾ Indian and ¼ Negro. Another was Annie Brown, who was of Negro, Cherokee, and Spanish descent. In 1911, twenty-four-year-old Annie was working at 445 Myers. By January of 1912, however, she had disappeared. Yet another, Eva Marshal of South Dakota, was part Sioux Indian and English. And there was Lola Richards of Chicago, who was a mix of Spanish and Italian descent. One girl, Sadie Salome, was purebred Cherokee.[21]

The bad girls of Cripple Creek continued to experience success. Pauline Russell, for instance, was madam of the Old Homestead at the young age of twenty-three. After serving jail time in January of 1912, Pauline returned to her native town of Omaha. Pauline's competition at the Mikado was Nellie Johnson. Nellie's first job was at 341 Myers, but within six months she made the status of "landlady" at the Mikado. Nellie, of French and English descent, was just twenty-six years old when she took on her promoted duties. Another who escalated quickly was Margie Jones. In August of 1911 Margie had arrived from Denver and was also working at 341 Myers. She appears to have moved to the Mikado just before Nellie Johnson. Perhaps the arrangement was not comfortable; six months later Margie had moved again, this time to the more prestigious Homestead.

Other cities continued their attempts to control their prostitutes with a heavy hand. From April 1911 to March 1912 the city of Trinidad took in nearly $6,000 in fines from prostitutes while boasting one saloon for every 250 residents. In August of 1911 Pueblo County pursued another means of ridding the city of whorehouses by allowing road-houses in the county outside the city limits. Etta "Spuds" Murphy's house in Pueblo was raided in January of 1912, and she was fined $50. Two inmates, Blanche Warner and Hazel Hamilton, were fined $10 each. In March Etta was raided again and fined $100. Spuds finally gave up and moved to Casper, Wyoming.

Likewise, rough and rowdy Cripple Creek began slowing down in late 1912. Most of the remaining girls in town were taking refuge in the 300 block. French harlot Louisa Davis plied her trade at 341 Myers, for instance, rather than in the traditional "Parisian" 400 block. But the city was still not without its hard cases. Grace Howard, who came from Fort Collins in 1912, left for Salida in January "after picking man" (that is, select-ing a suitable traveling companion) but returned a month later. A month after that she was arrested for stealing money from a man in her crib. In April Grace was ordered by the chief of police to leave town for the crime.[22] Likewise, Belle Butler was denied her health certificate in 1912. In June Belle was living on North 1st Street, presumably not working in the red-light district.

Departures from Cripple Creek Prostitution in 1911–12[23]

Name	Date of departure	Age	Notes
May Alcemore	June 1911	23	Resided at 422 Myers; married and left.
Pearl Brooks	January 1912	25	From Kentucky; resided at 341 E. Myers; left for Glenwood Springs.
Grace Brown	July 1911	—	Left for Denver.
Dollie Buckley	July 1911	20	Possibly born in Wisconsin; moved from Denver to work at the Mikado; visited Denver several times throughout 1912 and 1913; finally settled in Denver.

Viola Carter	December 1912	34	Born Macon, Georgia; black; arrived from Denver November 1912; departed for Denver.
Lizzie Chambers	December 1912	—	Arrived from somewhere in Colorado six months before; "left for parts unknown."
Alice Dorman	January 2, 1912	—	Arrived June 1911.
Cliff Eldrig (a.k.a. Eldrid)	January 1912	34	Of French and Irish descent; resided at 445½ Myers in 1911.
Claret Grant	January 1912	23	Black; arrived from Denver July 1911; resided at 443 Myers.
Bessie Hyser	January 1912	24	Born South Dakota; resided at 317 Myers in 1911.
Johnny Jones	January 7, 1912	24	Born Oklahoma; resided at 310 Myers July 1911; moved to Antlers Rooms (not a brothel) January 2, 1912.
Anna Kelso	July 1912	28	Born Des Moines, Iowa; moved from Denver June 1911 and worked at 367 Myers; left for Denver October; returned to Cripple Creek December; left for Colorado City.
Marion Kente	March 1912	22	Born Iowa; arrived from Casper, Wyoming February 1912.
Myrtle Lynch	April 1912	22	Born Indiana; moved from Pueblo; departed for Leadville.
Florence Manning	August 1911	28	Arrived July 1911.
Lula Marshall	March 1912	25	Born Memphis; arrived from Leadville February 1912; worked at 441 Myers.
Alice McClellan	January 1912	26	Born Indiana; arrived July 1911.
Grace Miller (alias Grace Maycharm)	November 1912	—	Retired from the row, working at a novelty store on Bennett Avenue.

Name	Date	Age	Notes
Lucy Minturn	January 1912	—	Retired from the row.
Edith Mitchle	January 1912	—	Retired from the row.
Rose Price	January 1912	23	Born Ohio; worked at 349 Myers in 1911.
Ruth Price	January 1912	21	Born Texas; arrived from Cheyenne, Wyoming December 1911; worked at 337 Myers; departed for Pueblo.
Lucy Robinson	May 1912	30	Black; born Ranatomi, Kansas; arrived from Sacramine, Wyoming January 1912; operated under an alias at 443 Myers; departed for Colorado Springs.
Dorothy Sentry	January 1912	26	Worked at 343 Masonic (Myers) in 1911.
Dollie Shafer	April 1912	—	Arrived January 1912 from Raton, New Mexico; working at 425½ Myers Avenue; ordered off the row by police chief.
Jennett Shannon	January 1912	24	Arrived July 1911; worked in Poverty Gulch before moving to 310 Myers.
Vergo Smith	June 1911	22	Born Kentucky; briefly worked at 341 Myers.
Clara Stetson (alias Margaret Blake)	March 1912	22	Arrived October 1911 from Pueblo; resided at 365 Myers; married Earl Myers of nearby Goldfield.[24]
Fay Thomas	January 1912	27	Born Indiana; arrived from Denver June 1911.
Violet Walker	September 1912	23	Born Hannah, Wyoming; arrived from Denver October 1911.
Beatrice Watson (alias Andey Watson)	March 1912	28	Born Illinois; arrived from Illinois June 1911; worked at 369 Myers; moved to Victor September 1911; returned January 1912; married John C. Uhlby.

Julia Watson	January 1912	27	Born "Ohia"; black and Indian heritage; resided at 457 Myers.
Mamie Watson	March 1912	33	Born Little Rock, Arkansas; arrived from Pueblo.
Clara Winters	April 1912	35	Born Oregon; arrived 1907.

Cripple Creek was becoming so subdued compared to its younger days that there wasn't much for authorities to do. So when a prostitute named Mexican Jennie murdered her abusive boyfriend and fled the city in 1912, sheriff Henry Von Phul decided to go after her. Jennie was born to parents of German and Mexican descent in about 1881, in Trinidad. She had lived in Walsenburg before migrating to Cripple Creek sometime before 1904. Her maiden name was Benton, but in Cripple Creek Mexican Jennie acquired her colorful nickname while working as a barmaid and dance hall girl. In 1904 Jennie married Ray Wenner at the First Baptist Church in Victor. Both were actually residents of Cripple Creek, where it was probably difficult to find a minister to marry someone with Jennie's reputation. Jennie was twenty-three years old; Wenner was twenty-seven.

When Wenner left her, Jennie retained his name and became known as Jennie Wenner. In 1911 at the alleged age of twenty-one, Jennie married one of her customers, Edgar Keif.[25] For some time Jennie was known as Juanita Keif, but when Keif died Jennie once more was on her own. The city register in 1911 lists her at 447 Myers, age thirty. She could read and write but like many of her coworkers lacked the sophistication to seek employment in a fancy parlor house or even a decent dance hall. Soon she moved to Poverty Gulch.

Philip Roberts Jr., a blacksmith at the El Paso Mine, was Jennie's next patron-turned-lover. Roberts's visits to Jennie's cabin became more and more frequent until he moved in on a permanent basis. The two began a stormy four-year relationship. Jennie testified later that Roberts became her pimp, drinking constantly and beating her when she didn't make enough money. Even over the din and bustle of Poverty Gulch, neighbors could hear the two arguing often. On Christmas night, 1913 Roberts knocked Mexican Jennie to the floor one last time. This time Jennie pulled a revolver from her trunk and shot Philip Roberts. Then she gathered her things, closed the door, and left town. Roberts's frozen body was not found until New Year's Eve. He was shipped to Denver, probably to the same folks who paid $246 for his funeral expenses.[26] By that time Jennie had a

Fig. 40. Probably believing she would be declared innocent, Mexican Jennie smiled as her mug shot was taken at El Paso, Texas. Authorities scribbled her offense, "Murder," at the top of the picture.

(Courtesy Colorado State Archives.)

good head start toward her destination. Upon learning she was from Walsenburg, Cripple Creek sheriff Henry Von Phul headed south in pursuit on January 3. In Pueblo he discovered that one Juanita Keif had purchased a coach ticket to El Paso, Texas.

Had it not been for a delay in train service to Juarez, Mexico, Jennie might have never been found by the law. As it was, however, the delay required her to travel to El Paso, swim the Rio Grande River into Mexico, and join a group of army camp followers heading to Chihuahua City. Within this group she could ply her trade to make money to reach her destination. Two hundred and fifty miles later, Jennie arrived in Chihuahua City. Once there, she had no choice but to continue in her profession. What Mexican Jennie did not figure on was the determination of Sheriff Von Phul. After poking around in El Paso and Juarez, Von Phul learned of several celebrations going on in Chihuahua City. Within a matter of days the sheriff was in Chihuahua and successfully tracked Jennie down at the Capital Hotel. It is interesting to note that Jennie received Von Phul with a friendly greeting and did not resist arrest.

After keeping Jennie for a few days in a nearby military lockup, Von Phul transported her to Juarez and bribed the magistrate there into releasing her into his custody. But the legalities required two officials to escort the prisoner back across the border into El Paso. A willing prisoner, Jennie volunteered to walk across the border herself. Instead, Von Phul enlisted the help of Billy Dingman, former clerk of the district court in Cripple Creek. Sometime back Dingman had embezzled from the court and escaped with the money. Von Phul agreed to "lose" Dingman's file in exchange for his assistance in escorting Mexican Jennie across the border. It was more important, in Von Phul's eyes, to apprehend a murdering prostitute than to catch a thief who had absconded with government money.

At her trial in Cripple Creek, Jennie pleaded innocent by self-defense but was found guilty of first-degree murder and sentenced to life imprisonment. She began her sentence at the Colorado State Penitentiary in Canon City on May 4, 1914, at the age of thirty-two. For the next six years Jennie was known as prisoner #9178. Was Jennie surprised at her fate? Probably, since her scowling mug shot at the state pen differs substantially from that taken in El Paso, which depicts a lady showing no qualms about returning to Cripple Creek. Her prison record lists her occupation as "House-work." It was noted she drank liquor but did not smoke, and could read and write. Interestingly, Jennie listed her mother as a Mrs. O'Connor at 322 East Warren Avenue in Cripple Creek.

Jennie appears to have been a model prisoner. The only blight against her in her prison file came in 1919, when she was written up for refusing to do work assigned to her. She was also sick for two days, and it is this illness that probably prompted her parole on October 10, 1920. Jennie returned to Chihuahua, where she resumed her former profession. She died of tuberculosis in 1924, which she most likely contracted in prison. Mexican Jennie's story is a fascinating look at one prostitute's life. Her circumstances decided her destiny, but the law decided her fate.

Fig. 41. Jennie's prison photograph reveals an angry
victim of domestic violence and the justice system.

(Courtesy Colorado State Archives.)

In 1913 the American Federation for Sex Hygiene and the National Vigilance Association merged to form the American Social Hygiene Association. The new organization was divided between abolitionists looking to do away with prostitution and sanitariums hoping to promote health regulations among prostitutes. With their help, the WCTU successfully campaigned to vote Colorado City dry as a means of stopping prostitution once and for all. The red-light ladies were hardly fazed. They and their liquor-selling counterparts simply moved the brothels and bars to an area outside city limits, forming a town entirely devoted to liquor and prostitution. The saloon keepers of Colorado City gathered and bought $20,000 worth of land from Frank Wolff along 24th Street, a few blocks north of Colorado Avenue. They christened their new town Ramona after author Helen Hunt Jackson's romantic character from the book of the same name. The new city would be bordered by St. Vrain Avenue on the south, Cache La Poudre on the north, a half block west of 26th Street on the west, and 23rd Street on the east. Henry W. Abbey, a longtime bar owner in Colorado City, was among the first to open a place in Ramona, along with Harold C. Thompson and Marion Nickell.

Colorado City's citizens had more bones to pick. Allegedly, rowdy patrons of the new town were noisily entering the "annex" via what is now 24th Street. Transportation was provided by a truck. The truck bed was removed and replaced with chicken wire for a makeshift bus. This was the first cause of major concern, since respectable citizens lived on 24th Street and were no doubt unhappy with the nightly proceedings. Indeed, it was not long before complaints, like Ramona, ran amok. Nobody in Ramona listened, even when Colorado City's council members once more firmly upheld a decision in their petition not to supply Ramona businesses with water. As of January 1913, city employees were instructed not to supply water to anyone running a saloon, even though Ramona boasted only two at the time.

The *Colorado Springs Gazette* highly condoned the decision, commenting that Ramona had "turned out to be just what was predicted before the first shack was built—a degraded, besotted little sinkhole."[27] But Ramona's businessmen hardly took the matter lightly. In February saloon partners Abbey, Thompson, and Nickell sued for their rights to water. Both Abbey and Nickell reminded everyone that they had been residents of Colorado City for some time—Abbey since at least 1890 and Nickell since 1900. The men had joined up with Thompson after the closure of Abbey and Nickell's saloon in Colorado City.

The citizens of Colorado City were instantly enraged. The *Colorado City Iris* had something to say in the May 23 issue of 1913 after petitions were submitted to annex Ramona: "There is no secret that the purpose of the starting of the new town is to have a town given over wholly to the perpetuation of the liquor traffic and all its attendant evils, in the Pikes Peak region." The Women's Christian Temperance Union and the Anti-Saloon Club called an immediate joint session to discuss alleviating the foreseen problems. The result was a committee, consisting of A. W. Clark,

Percy Dunn, F. W. Kistler, and Mrs. A. K. Shantz. The committee's first goal was to circulate a written petition. The *Colorado City Iris* lost no time in publishing the petition, which read in part:

> Whereareas [*sic*], the city of Colorado City, after struggling with saloons for forty years, has recently by a vote of her people banished the saloons and wholesale liquor dealers from her midst, a feat accomplished only after a long struggle. . . . Whereareas, there is a movement on foot by certain liquor dealers to establish and incorporate a town on our very border, for the sole purpose of selling liquors with all the accompanying evils that those words mean.[28]

Few in Ramona listened to the accusation, but by early June forces were aligning to keep Ramona dry. The court petition published in the *Iris* listed eighty-six citizens of Ramona as the defendants. A court hearing was set for August 7, and the petition notified the citizens of Ramona that if they didn't come to court it would go in default, rendering Ramona dry.

Supporters of Ramona went right on with their plans. On July 17, 1913, the incorporation papers were filed. Within days, a protest against Ramona was filed on behalf of the Colorado City council by city attorney J. P. Jackson. The protest stated Colorado City had already started procedures to annex Ramona. Pro-Ramonans countered by threatening to abolish Jackson's position. The race was on, but the vote had really already been cast. A few days after the trial, the *Iris* published a single sentence, placed inconspicuously on a back page: "The election held yesterday in Ramona townsite to determine whether the residents wished to incorporate was a one sided affair, as was well known it would be, 37 votes being cast for incorporation and none against it."[29]

As usual, though, Colorado City didn't give up without a fight. On August 29 the *Iris* sneered, "Within three miles of the courthouse, a little band of men are now preparing to dedicate a few acres of whiskey, the greatest of all causes of the crimes that cost the taxpayer so dearly." Judge Cunningham of Colorado City wrote the piece, pleading with citizens to call another mass meeting. The Ministerial Association of Colorado Springs answered the call, arranging the meeting in September at Temple Theater to discuss Ramona. Churches were urged to cancel their evening services and attend, but the meeting was once more for naught.

By now the long-dry city of Colorado Springs was involved, with more money and power than little Colorado City. On September 5 the *Colorado*

City Iris applauded the Colorado Springs city council for denying water to Ramona. As it happened, Colorado Springs's water system also supplied water for Colorado City. "Ramonaites, or Ramonans, or whatever they want to call themselves, will have very little use for water," scoffed the *Iris*. "It may be useful if a fire breaks out or in case somebody feels the need of a bath, but as a factor in the scheme of nutrition it is nil. Ramona expects to live by, for and on booze."

By then Ramona already boasted at least four saloons as well as a cigar store and drugstore. The population had quickly grown to three hundred, but the city of Colorado Springs had instructed the water superintendent not to extend any mains, or to allow any new taps in Ramona. Only residents who were already supplied with water would continue to receive water. Throughout it all, Judge Cunningham complained that while taxes paid for liquor licenses would go to Ramona, court costs "created by this devilish grog" must be paid by property owners outside its borders. To make matters worse, judge John E. Little of the District Court upheld Ramona's right to elect town officers on September 9.

Elections were duly held. Robert McReynolds was named city clerk, treasurer, and police magistrate for a salary of $24 per month. L. C. Moats was hired as chief of police, city marshal, city detective, and jailer. His salary was $65 per month, good pay for a man who never appears to have arrested anyone. And despite these official titles, the first jail was really only a small tent. By November Ramona was ready for its "grand opening," but still lacked water. Another trial was scheduled.

This time the judge ruled against Ramona once more, saying Colorado Springs was under no obligation to supply water outside city limits. Ramona, which by now was also known as "Whiskeytown" and "Whiskeyville," was not to be foiled, however. Colorado Springs fire hydrants were secretly tapped at night by persons unknown and water piped through a fire hose to a Ramona water tank. February of 1914 was just one of many times Abbey, Thompson, and Nickell went to court to answer charges of stealing water from Colorado Springs and Colorado City. Authorities would shut the water main off, and the saloon men would turn it back on. Ultimately, the water decision was revoked when a man named Jordan asserted—and won—his right to water for a grocery store and barbershop he was building in Ramona.

At the time Abbey, Thompson, and Nickell's saloon was at 706 North 7th and they too were to enjoy water rights at long last. Naturally, the *Colorado City Iris* voiced its discontent at the city's failure to follow through. The paper published a sarcastic editorial about the water decision and the continuing ruckus on 24th Street. This article was followed by a comment in the *Gazette* that read, "The press reports of the opening of Ramona were deficient in that they failed to specify the number of drunks manufactured in the new town. Or tell of the noise, confusion and presence of women on that occasion."[30]

The population of Ramona was holding steady at three hundred souls. The town was clearly not going away. The only thing to do was to start making arrests. Mayor George Geiger was first. In March of 1914 Geiger was accused of allowing liquor to be sold to a sixteen-year-old girl at his saloon, the Heidelberg Inn. At the time the Heidelberg was the biggest saloon in Ramona and featured an elaborate hand-carved bar and furnishings. Across from the Heidelberg was a new brothel opened by Nellie White.

Fortunately, Geiger's popularity saved him. In spite of his support of saloons in Colorado City, Geiger had been a resident since 1899 and seems to have been well liked. He was mentioned often in both the *Colorado City Iris* and the *Colorado City Argus* newspapers. A month after his arrest, Geiger was reelected as mayor of Ramona. He celebrated his victory by opening the Ramona Athletic Club next door to the Heidelberg in August. Madam Laura Bell McDaniel was said to have been an investor in the club as well. Although it was no more than a small circus tent with a boxing ring and bleachers, the Ramona Athletic Club was a great success. Most evenings consisted of three matches featuring Cyclone Tucker and Kid Blackie—Jack Dempsey's original stage name. In an odd turn of camaraderie, the *Iris* itself predicted the matches would provide top entertainment. The *Colorado Springs Gazette*, however, criticized another boxing match in September, calling it "a most disgraceful affair."[31]

By October of 1914 Ramona was going strong. Not only were several dance halls, brothels, and saloons in business, but prizefights were taking place as well. Tents instead of buildings were used for many of the festivities—probably because they could be taken down in a hurry and moved in case of trouble. Sheriff Birdsall of Colorado City and his deputies were at a loss with the crazy proceedings and hesitant to interfere. In November the shoe was on the other foot when the prizefighters and the Ramona Athletic Club, confronted by the sheriff, could not show their licenses to box. The prizefight was moved to Leadville.

Despite the victory, the citizens of Colorado City were not pleased with the law's slow reactions, especially after the sheriff and seven deputies were held back by spectators while a small riot broke out at the fights one night. "The sheriff and the district attorney know or should know that liquor is being sold to minors and to women, that bawdy houses have been run there right along," the *Colorado City Independent* reported in disgust. "Drunks by the dozen swarm down here [in Colorado City] and . . . nine tenths of it comes from Ramona."[32] This time, to show some backbone, officers of Colorado City raided the red-light district in Ramona and apprehended several fast women. Arrests were made and fines were assessed. Another raid was made a year later. As in the ongoing war against the red-light district of Colorado City, however, most of the arrests and fines were in vain. At least the goings-on at Ramona gave prostitutes like Laura Bell McDaniel, who had stubbornly stayed right where she was in Colorado City, a brief reprieve.

So it was in cities where repeated attempts for decades to close down prostitution, gambling, and bars had been highly unsuccessful and indeed laughable. In fact, the general public got a great bang out of a 1914 interview between *Collier's Magazine* writer Julian Street and Mrs. Leola Ahrens, better known as the same Madam Leo who had chased Lil Powers out of Cripple Creek several years before. In 1911 Leo was listed along with the other girls in Cripple Creek's prostitute register. She was living at 461 Myers, of French descent, age forty, five feet six, 165 pounds with a medium build, medium complexion, blueish gray eyes, and brown hair. Three years after Leo appeared in the register, Street was sent up to Cripple Creek from Colorado Springs on the Midland Terminal train, with only an hour to spend in town. "I walked up the main street a little way, turned off and ran into Myers Avenue, the old red-light street, with a vacant tumble-down dance hall and a long line of tiny box-stall houses called 'cribs.'"[33] Among other things, Street noted some crib doors with the names Clara, Louise, and Lina on them, watched a prostitute cross the street wearing a pink wrapper, and saw a shabby-looking white man leave the crib of a "black negress." It was then that Madam Leo appeared.[34]

Back in more prosperous times Leo had once stood, naked and drunk, on the corner of Fourth and Myers shouting, "I'm Leo the Lion, the queen of the row!" When Street met her, however, she was a subdued middle-aged woman. Street described her in detail: "She wore a white linen skirt and a middy blouse, attire grotesquely juvenile for one of her years. Her hair, of which she had but a moderate amount, was light brown and stringy, and she wore gold-rimmed spectacles." She also appeared to be a half-wit, pointing to her name etched on the door glass and proclaiming, "Madam Leo. That's me. Leo, the lion, eh?"[35] Julian Street's scathing article ended up consisting entirely of his impressions of Myers Avenue in Cripple Creek and his chat with Madam Leo. As Street explained later, "I had not intended to write about Cripple Creek but the depressing place and the woman made such an impression on me that I described it in *Collier's Weekly*."[36]

Street made close observations of Madam Leo's crib, a tidy room containing a couple of chairs, a "cheap oak dresser," and an iron bed. On the wall hung a calendar with a picture of Cupid and Psyche; Leo claimed the latter was herself as a young girl. One last whiff of her "brutal perfume" and Street was back on the train to Colorado Springs, where he pounded out his account of Madam Leo on a typewriter. The resulting article even included encouragement by Madam Leo to "send some nice boys up here. Tell them to see Madam Leo . . . I been here for years."[37]

The published result caused no amusement at city hall chambers. When Street's article hit the newsstands, Cripple Creek mayor Jimmie Hanley sent a telegram to *Collier's* editor, Mark Sullivan. The telegram was followed by angry letters from "hundreds of citizens." Finally, Sullivan promised to publish a letter from Cripple Creek, as long as it fit the magazine's editorial standards. Mayor Hanley obligingly sponsored a contest for the best essay from Cripple Creek. The winner was submitted to *Collier's*, but Sullivan never published it.

Next a group formed at the Elk's Lodge and convinced the city council to change the name from Myers Avenue to Julian Street. The city council supposedly voted the ordinance in, but there appears to be no record of the action. Several Cripple Creek newspapers published editorials about Street's offense. Furthermore, the alleged name change of Myers Avenue to Julian Street made the Associated Press wire services and was broadcast across the nation.[38] Street's interview with Madam Leo in 1914 likely did little to improve her status in the dying boomtown. It certainly did nothing for Street's reputation in Cripple Creek, nor for the situation of the city's other prostitutes.

Alas, things were getting tough all over. In 1915 Denver's Market Street was officially closed down. It was said, however, that most of the hotels downtown adopted an unwritten policy allowing two prostitutes per hotel. Back in Colorado City, Sheriff Birdsall continued with his own miserable fight. In April of 1915 Birdsall accompanied a few of his deputies on a robbery complaint. A man allegedly named Dayton from Illinois claimed he had been robbed of approximately $400 in Ramona. While investigating the robbery, Sheriff Birdsall arrested one George F. Zeigler for running a gambling hall. The $400 mysteriously reappeared almost instantly, but

Zeigler was taken to jail on a $200 bond. Accompanying him were Eula Hames, Josie Parker, Bill English, and Lon Parker, "alleged frequenters of resorts of this kind."[39]

Undaunted, Eula Hames continued with her illegal activities for the next five years. She was charged and fined again in 1913 and 1914. But the arrests of 1915 were her final undoing—and the end as well of the town of Ramona. Three months after the raid in which Eula and her companions were arrested, Ramona's saloons closed their doors as quickly as they had swung them open. The state of Colorado was declaring the state dry, a feat that no amount of small and illicit districts could fight or deny. Many saloon owners were tired anyway, including Byron Hames. As early as February of 1913, Hames's assessment of the situation was more prescient than he knew: "The territory is not worth fighting for."[40]

Chapter Eleven

Closing Down for Good

❧

The Funeral of Madame Chase

A big black hearse; 'twas Dougal's hearse,
Creaked down through Union Street
And old, old echoes were aroused
By the horses' heavy feet
And all our town knew Dougal's hearse
Bore to some resting place
The last of her who once was known
As Madame Sarah Chase.

And all the old men of our town
Were on the street that day.
With senile stealth, it seemed to me,
They tried to hide away.
They did not meet, and stand, and gas
As old men love to do,
But seemed to slink, each by himself,
And why nobody knew.

One lone hack; 'twas Pitkin's hack,
With Pitkin on the seat,
Was all that followed Dougal's hearse
As it creaked through Union Street.

So slim, so gray, so very old,
He sat erect, and stern,
And glanced about from left to right
With eyes that seemed to burn.
And wagging tongues of gossip stopped,
And none that glance could meet,
As slowly passed the hearse and hack
Along through Union Street.

And my old man who hadn't bowed
To Hamerslough for years,
Stood at the curb, and bared his head,
And leaked some senile tears.
"I know him for a skunk," he said,
"And my hate'll never quit-
A liar, cheat, two-thirds a thief-
But, my God, he's no hypocrite!"

One lone hack; 'twas Pitkin's hack;
With Pitkin on the seat,
Was all that followed Dougal's hearse
As it creaked through Union Street.
One lone hack, and in that hack
Was one lone man, and he
Was Banker George S. Hamerslough,
For all the town to see.
—Damon Runyon

he "illegal" town of Ramona was not the only such place to suffer a quick and unceremonious demise. Efforts to close the houses of ill repute in Boulder began shortly after an 1894 flood did damage to the red-light district, with officers carrying several soiled doves and their pets to safety (Madam Kingsley, a pug dog in each arm, proved especially difficult to rescue due to her excessive weight). Ultimately, the Citizens' Reform League set about cleaning up Boulder in 1897. Somewhat surprisingly, the plan appears to have worked more than any other employed in Colorado even if it did take awhile to put into effect. In 1901 prostitutes were still

Fig. 42. Victor's Fortune Club sported no fewer than eight prominent prostitutes, according to present owner Mac McCormick. Most of these girls, however, fail to show up in city directories or census records.

(Courtesy Fortune Club.)

paying fines, but as of 1909 Boulder's red-light district had been closed down for good. Today most of Boulder's brothels have been replaced with apartment buildings and other modern structures.

Similar fates met most of Colorado's red-light districts, especially after 1910. Over the next several years, more districts closed as their soiled doves flocked to and from the fading boomtowns in search of work. Mayme Marlow, once a popular prostitute in Leadville, found herself migrating to Cripple Creek. Where she went after that is anyone's guess. The same went for Helen Moore, who made a late arrival at Cripple Creek in April 1913 but whose whereabouts after that are unknown.

Even the rowdy blue-collar city of Victor eventually gave in to pressure by temperance clubs and antisaloon organizations to take control over its red-light situation. A 1913 ordinance prohibited females "from entering or working at saloons and other places where intoxicating liquors are sold." Other new ordinances adopted prohibition in the city, but for good measure also defined alcoholic liquors as they related to penalties for selling booze.[1] Authorities began cracking down on the red-light ladies with a vengeance in 1915. According to Victor business owner Mac McCormick, present owner of the Fortune Club, Red Stocking Lee was among those whose actions were not tolerated. Her alleged affair with the mayor of Victor at the time inspired city authorities to run her out of town. Red Stocking Lee went on to Kansas, where she opened a saloon.

Other prostitutes, many of whom had seen prostitution in its heyday and were now in their golden years, made the papers as they met their demise. Molly Foley of Silverton died at age seventy-eight in 1914. She had worked through at least 1910, charging only 50¢ for her favors versus the $2 younger girls on the line charged. In the last years of her life, Molly and another retired prostitute named Denver Kate did laundry and cleaning for younger prostitutes. It was said that Denver Kate had put two daughters through the University of Colorado and that the girls never knew their mother's true profession. Kate died in 1925.

By 1915 the Old Homestead and its inhabitants disappear entirely from Cripple Creek city directories. Most sources say the Homestead continued to maintain fine tradition in men's entertainment until at least 1918, and certain old-timers remembered seeing girls there as late as the 1930s and 1940s. The next time the building appeared in property records at the Teller County Courthouse was in April of 1935, when a Mrs. W. F. Peterie purchased it from the county treasurers for back taxes dating back to 1928. The amount owed was only $7.50. Long before then, however, most of the soiled doves of Myers Avenue had already flown elsewhere. A few were able to marry and settle in Cripple Creek, taking back their real names and fading into obscurity. Dickie Grater of Victor recalled a prostitute who married a miner and lived across the street from his childhood home. As her husband worked the night shift, the woman would often come to visit with Mrs. Grater for the evening. Dickie recalled escorting her back across the street late at night, because she was afraid of the dark.

In Victor, Harry Lang closed the Fortune Club in 1916 in anticipation of nationwide Prohibition. The state of Colorado had officially become a dry state as of January 1, and twenty-nine saloons in the district—sixteen in Cripple Creek, eleven in Victor, and two in Goldfield—closed their doors. Newspapers decried the move, especially since it put over 150 men out of jobs and cost the city of Cripple Creek alone $11,700 in annual liquor licenses. Undaunted, city authorities also voiced their intent to sweep Cripple Creek's Myers Avenue clean of its soiled doves and to make sure they left the county. As one might guess, such efforts were not totally successful: one of Harry's employees, Violet Long, allegedly moved to Cripple Creek and opened a café. By going straight, Violet could hardly be persecuted. Within two years, however, the illicit businesses disappeared from Victor's city directories altogether.

The notorious chapter in Victor's wild nightlife closed with the alleged 1918 death of Hattie May Jordon, former madam of the Fortune Club. Even the *Victor Daily Record* gave a decent epitaph to the respected lady as hundreds of other people continued moving away from the Cripple Creek District. The red-light districts naturally dwindled with the population. Because of the town's quick evolution into near ghost town status, at least a few soiled doves were able to marry and remain in Cripple Creek, banking on time to erase their former reputations. A few others moved to outlying areas.

Some women, like Nigger Mollie, lived in Poverty Gulch and continued servicing miners as the camp declined and other prostitutes moved on. Once, it was said, Mollie was on a drunk and stepped in front of a streetcar, which knocked her down. She stood up, dusted the snow from her dress, and declared, "It'll take more than that big black son-of-a-bitch to keep me down."[2] Then she took a long drink from the bottle she carried and went on her way. Eventually, Mollie took a job cleaning the Midland Terminal depot in Cripple Creek. One day she took down her blouse and showed a local woman the scars left from beatings she had received as a child slave during the Civil War. It was said that Liverlip, who had suffered an arrest near Leadville as early as 1896, finally retired from prostitution and worked as a bootlegger in Cripple Creek during Prohibition. For the most part, however, the onslaught of nationwide Prohibition halted almost all the illicit activity in Cripple Creek and surrounding towns—at least for a few years.

Likewise, Silverton's fallen women continued operating as best they could, offering bootleg whiskey as part of their services. When the women were discovered, city authorities merely required them to pay a weekly fine right along with the bootleggers. Even at this late date, the girls could shop only along Green Street and were not allowed to linger there. One local merchant on Green Street prospered well from the sales of his fine ladies' wear.

The authorities of Silverton may have been encouraged by the actions of Gen. John "Black Jack" Pershing in New Mexico. The military wrestled with the presence of brothel camps as U.S. involvement in World War I approached in 1916. Pershing opted to legalize prostitution in Columbus, New Mexico. A district was established with segregated houses. Alcohol and firearms were forbidden. All other brothels in town were closed, and prostitutes who did not pass their health exams were run out of town. The women were examined once a week by two doctors, one of whom was mayor T. H. Dabney. The physicians received $50 a week for performing the exams. As a result of Pershing's actions, the incidence of venereal disease fell, although some infected women still freelanced in the saloons and managed to elude the law.

But with the state of Colorado officially going dry, it seemed as though the jig was up for good in every red-light district left. By 1916 Denver's Market Street bordellos were virtually gone, with only a handful of prostitutes continuing to ply their trade. Throughout the year, a mere fifteen women were arrested for keeping "disorderly houses" in Denver. Four others were arrested for keeping houses of prostitution, and only ten girls were arrested for being inmates of brothels. By the time national Prohibition hit in 1919 there were hardly any bars left to close. Mattie Silks simply converted one of her houses at 1916 Market Street into the Silks Hotel. Likewise, Verona Baldwin opened a discreet tavern called the Baldwin Inn. Whether Mattie and Verona's services included prostitution is unknown.

Farther south, the closing down of Ramona's bars came in a rather sad announcement published by the *Colorado City Independent*. Black crepe was tied on the doors of the saloons as the barkeepers and prostitutes in the tiny hamlet packed their trunks and headed for new horizons.[3] The news came hard to people like Byron Hames, who left Colorado City in

January of 1916, old and broken down. Hames made the rounds of Colorado City and said his good-byes before departing for Denver, where the once powerful saloon owner is said to have died in poverty. Longtime barkeeper Jake Schmidt committed suicide. Mr. and Mrs. George Geiger hosted a turkey dinner at their Heidelberg Inn for all of their former employees. The couple planned to stay in Colorado City, but George announced he would also be spending time in Cheyenne.[4] In March of 1916 one last attempt was made to hold a prizefight at Ramona. Only a couple hundred people showed up, and most left before the fight was over.

Arrests naturally dropped dramatically. When Sheriff Weir and night watchman Martin broke up a card game at Ramona in May of 1916, it seemed like a half-hearted attempt. Seven were arrested, but several dozen others escaped. Still, authorities worked Colorado's new prohibition law to their advantage. An ordinance to annex Colorado City to Colorado Springs had been drawn up on April 6, 1917 and passed on April 18. Colorado City was officially annexed on June 11, presumably along with what was left of Ramona. The annexation meant new laws, more police, and a whole different way of life. Colorado City's red-light district was finally defeated, once and for all.

Well, almost.

Mamie Majors gave up and quietly disappeared, but Laura Bell McDaniel stayed right where she was, discreetly advertising herself as the "keeper of furnished rooms." Inside, the business was the same. Up to that time, Laura Bell had managed to live a fairly easy and decent life for a woman in her career. The worst that had happened recently was in 1913, when the red glass globes in front of her brothel were stolen.[5] In fact, Laura Bell had been advertising herself as a keeper of furnished rooms since 1912, even though the smokescreen did little to keep the law from her door. Despite the antics going on in nearby Ramona, continued fines, and the death of her husband, Herbert Berg, in 1916, Laura Bell persevered. In October of that year she again paid $52.50 for keeping a disorderly house, while one of her "inmates," Alice Harper, paid $27.50. And the newspapers left her alone, save for when the *Colorado City Independent* noted her as a new subscriber in December. Throughout 1917 Laura Bell paid her fines and minded her own business.

But if Laura Bell looked to her future with an open heart and positive mind, fate did not. The authorities were determined to do away with her. On November 20, 1917, a final distressing blow was dealt. The police appeared at Laura Bell's house at 2612 West Cucharras with a search

Fig. 43. Laura Bell's red lamps, stolen in 1913,
were eventually recovered and donated to the Old Colorado
City History Center, where they are on display.

(From the author's collection.)

warrant and scoured the place. Thirty-four bottles of high-grade liquor, purported to be stolen from the home of Comstock millionaire Charles Baldwin in the elite and wealthy Broadmoor area of Colorado Springs, were found. Laura Bell, the cultured and kind-hearted proprietress of the richest house in the tenderloin district, was arrested for harboring stolen liquor in her home. Authorities took her into custody. She had been known so long as simply "Laura Bell" that her legal surname had to be added later.[6] Bail was set at $1,500, and Laura Bell's court date to answer charges for "Receiving Stolen Goods" was set for January 18, 1918.

The day of the trial, Laura Bell's attorneys, James Orr and W. D. Lombard, were granted a continuance to January 24. Orr and Lombard were experienced lawyers in the red-light district. In previous years Lombard had worked for Mamie Majors and other notorious madams. Proceedings that morning began at 10 A.M. Witnesses against Laura Bell were listed as city detective John Rowan, I. B. Taylor, Martin Logsden,

I. Bruce, Alexander Day, Frank Hufnas, Louis Kam, Charles Baldwin, and Walter Goukenour. The prosecuting witness was J. R. Girling. Not surprisingly, most of the witnesses were employees of the police department. The court alleged that on November 12, 1917, Laura Bell had purchased stolen liquor, consisting of sixteen bottles of Gordon's gin, seven bottles of Pol Roger [*sic*] Champagne, and eleven bottles of whiskey. Ironically, Charles Baldwin was not even at the trial, despite receiving a summons. The paperwork simply noted, "Out of town. Won't be back soon."[7]

That Baldwin's absence was truly a coincidence is doubtful. Either way, the defense jumped on the opportunity to tell the truth about where the liquor came from. In the end, it was none other than Dusty McCarty, Laura Bell's friend from long ago, who came forth to testify on her behalf. In actuality, McCarty stated, two men had stolen the liquor from Baldwin's and planted it at Laura Bell's. How the liquor was planted is unknown, although frozen pipes had recently been replaced at the house. Perhaps the guilty parties accomplished the dirty deed then. Dusty, who at one time owned the Tenderfoot Saloon in Colorado City and lived just a few doors down from Laura Bell's brothel, pointed the finger at the real wrongdoers.[8] The case was dismissed.

Stories vary about why Laura Bell chose to drive to Denver the day after her acquittal. Some say she was celebrating. Others say she was taking blind Dusty McCarty to Denver for eye treatment. She may also have been giving her niece, twenty-seven-year-old Laura Pearson (a.k.a Pierson), a ride to her home at 1200 California Street in Denver. What is known for sure is that Laura Bell invited her niece and Dusty on a trip to Denver. It was also said that Laura Bell was training "Little Laura" to follow in her footsteps, and that the two women spent much time together. Given that Little Laura was already twenty-seven years old, however, odds are that she was already well experienced in the profession. Little Laura's father, James, lived in Oklahoma. Records are scant as to whether he knew what his daughter was up to, even though Little Laura had lived with her aunt since at least 1910. What is known is that at the time, Laura Bell and her sister Birdie both had children who were residing in Denver: Pearl Kitto, Eugene Moats, Harry Hooyer Jr. The other children of James Hooyer do not appear to have lived in Colorado. In all probability, Laura Bell, Little Laura and Dusty expected to join their relatives upon reaching Denver.

In anticipation of the trip, Laura Bell had her beloved Mitchell touring car serviced in Colorado City. It was no secret that Laura Bell considered the car one of her most prized possessions, having it washed and serviced often. For the drive to Denver she purchased fifteen gallons of gas, one-half gallon of oil, and six spark plugs from Baty Motor Company in Colorado Springs.[9] With the car in tip-top shape, Laura Bell, Little Laura, and Dusty took off with Little Laura at the wheel. Fate, however, intervened in the most tragic fashion. Roughly a quarter mile south of the town of Castle Rock, the car inexplicably left the road at 40 miles per hour and overturned. Little Laura was crushed and died instantly. Dusty was knocked unconscious, receiving bruises and cuts on the head. Laura Bell, also unconscious, was taken to Beth El Hospital (now Memorial Hospital) in Colorado Springs. She had received massive injuries to her ribs, chest, and lungs. The presiding physician, David F. Law, held little hope for her. That evening, Laura Bell McDaniel died at the age of fifty-six years and three months. Harry Hooyer, the husband of Laura Bell's sister Birdie, signed the death certificate.

The type of accident that killed the Queen of the Colorado City Tenderloin was commonplace in the days before seatbelts and speed limits. What makes this particular accident interesting, however, is who witnessed it. Three men were situated just two hundred yards ahead of Laura Bell's car when it crashed. One was Jack Caruthers, a deputy district attorney from Colorado Springs. With Caruthers were Carl Blackman and George Curtis.[10] Whether these three men merely witnessed the accident or had something to do with it is debatable and probably lost to history, since the courthouse at Castle Rock burned some years ago and no records appear to exist regarding the incident. Dusty McCarty, Laura Bell's blind friend who never saw what really happened, returned to Colorado City. What Dusty knew and what he told authorities is also unknown.

The untimely death of Colorado City's reigning madam no doubt had a very big impact on the town. Although Laura Bell left no will, her estate paid for a costly and grand funeral for herself and Laura Pearson. Laura Bell's daughter, Pearl, who may have been living in Casper, Wyoming, was summoned. Boone Undertakers at 8 South 25th Street, which advertised the only female mortician in town, hurried to handle the arrangements. The double ceremony included two copper-lined steel caskets, two hearses (one of which made the sad trip to Castle Rock to retrieve the body of Little Laura), eight bouquets of flowers, five limousines, a soloist and pianist, and services. Two pairs of silk stockings were also purchased, but only one silk dress—presumably for Laura Pearson. The total cost? A hefty $1,856, a small fortune for that time. Laura Bell was buried in the lot she had already purchased at Fairview Cemetery at Colorado City. Little Laura was buried next to her. Cemetery records discreetly listed Laura Bell as a divorced housewife.[11]

Pearl was the sole heir of Laura Bell McDaniel's estate, estimated at $22,700. Pearl had married Charles Kitto in 1912, a marriage attended and witnessed by her mother and Birdie Hooyer. She does not appear to have chosen prostitution as a career. Rather, she pursued an education and settled down as a housewife. Despite exercising her option not to take up prostitution, Pearl indicated to others she was proud of her mother, whose success enabled her to receive a good education. Laura Pearson had perhaps acted in Pearl's stead, coming under Laura Bell's wing to learn the tricks of the trade.

Upon her arrival in Colorado Springs, Pearl Kitto was established as Laura Bell's only living child and therefore sole heir and administratrix of the estate. Pearl promptly posted a $15,000 bond with the Fidelity and Deposit Company of Maryland and filed papers in Colorado Springs to claim Laura Bell's estate.[12] Notice of the estate was published in February and March in the *El Paso County Democrat*.

Laura Bell McDaniel's Estate Totals[13]

Assets

4 promissory notes from Alice Bouton @ $25 each	$100
Household furnishings	$487
Cash deposit at Colorado Springs Bank	$11,388.10
5 diamond rings	$1,000
Rent of house in Colorado City to September 11, 1918	$81.35
Rent of house in Colorado City and "junk" to 2/26/1919	$86
15 lots of property on Cucharras and Vermijo, as well as property in Washington State and Manitou Springs	$10,000

Liabilities

August 1917 to February 1918 to Frank Priess, plumber on Colorado Avenue	$33
December 3, 1917 to Dr. O. N. Williams, D.D.S., for extraction and treatment	$5.50
January 25, 1918 to Baty Motor Co., Colorado Springs, including storage	$216.16
January 25, 1918 to Dr. George E. Alexander, Castle Rock	$100

January 25, 1918 to Dr. E. L. Timmons,	
Beth El Hospital	$15
January 25, 1918 to Beth El Hospital	$2.50
January 28, 1918 to Dr. D. S. S. Fuller,	
for visit to attending family at funeral	$15

Estate Fees

| Total fees, including attorneys, funeral expenses, | |
| & taxes | $3,634.66 |

All told, Pearl received $8,194.77 in cash and her mother's properties.[14] The properties consisted of a house on three lots at 2416 West Vermijo, another house (containing two stories and nine bedrooms) on two lots at 2422 West Vermijo, yet another house on two lots at 310 24th Street, one and one-half lots consisting of Laura Bell's last brothel at 2612 Cucharras, and a lot at 132 South Path in Manitou Springs.[15] After the settlement of Laura Bell's estate in March of 1919, Pearl resided in Denver. She and Charles Kitto lived a quiet and unassuming life until their deaths. The couple never had children.[16] Nothing more of note really happened to the family, save for a decision to move Laura Bell to a different plot at Fairview Cemetery. Initially, Laura Bell had been buried in lot 7, block 20, a plot she herself had purchased in advance before her death.[17] In 1921, for reasons unknown, her family moved her to addition 2, to a spot right next to the caretaker's house and nearly at the entrance to the cemetery.[18] Possibly Laura Bell's family sought to protect her grave from vandals and robbers.

Laura Bell's death was indeed the end of Colorado City's red-light districts. Her demise was still fresh in people's minds when nationwide Prohibition became official in 1919. Liquor was to be dispensed to county clerks for medicinal purposes only and would be illegal everywhere else except in private homes. Finally, the longtime survivors of Colorado City's red-light district were forced to bow to this law of laws. City directories for 1918 show that of seven buildings on the north side of Cucharras Street's 2600 block, only three were occupied. In the 2700 block, only one of five buildings shows a resident. She was Mary Jones, who had been working in the red-light district since 1900. Of Laura Bell's many friends, only Prairie Dog O'Byrne left any trace of his whereabouts. By 1918 Prairie Dog had returned from Denver to his Colorado Springs home at 427 East Bijou. He later wrote a book, *Pikes Peak or Bust and Historical Sketches of the Wild West*, discussing his life in Colorado Springs and Colorado City. Included in the book is a fitting tribute to Laura Bell:

In Old Town I cut quite a dash.
I took many pains to spend all my cash, and
I drove through the street with Laura Bell by my side—
A span of elk, how fine we did ride.
We drove down to Byron Hames' old place,
And says I, "Let's go in and see what's the muss,
For I feel just at present like having a fuss . . ."
And there stood Soapy Smith with three cards in his hand,
And each word he uttered he spoke with command:
"Now gents," he would say, "there is the ace and it is
plain to be seen."
And that's where I lost all my money on the Ace and the Queen.[19]

Laura Bell's last house, the Trilby, is still partially intact under the facade of a nursing home on West Cucharras. Several alterations were made to the building between 1952 and 1973 after the property was purchased by Norton Nursing Home. In 1986 the building was purchased by

Fig. 44. For many years after her death, Laura Bell's last house of ill repute remained mostly intact. These days the brothel is a nursing home.

(From the author's collection.)

LTC Care Centers, which in turn sold it to Beneficial Living Systems in 1990. Further remodeling in the mid-1990s destroyed some of the original exterior. Next door, Mamie Majors's old place at 2616 West Cucharras, now an apartment house, remains virtually untouched on the outside. Ironically, a large portion of the remaining red-light district is now owned by Grace Tabernacle Church and the Mennonites. The buildings that once housed Colorado Avenue's rowdy saloons now serve as quaint boutiques, restaurants, apartments, and other businesses.

Aside from the brothel queen's former home, little else survives of Laura Bell's past. A beautiful painted portrait of Laura Bell at the Old Colorado City Historical Society has been authenticated by family photographs, although an actual picture of the lady herself has never surfaced. Decades after the demise of Ramona, a bar with Laura Bell's name opened near the site of the old Ramona Athletic Club. The original owner of Laura Bell's Bar had the madam's likeness rendered in stained glass from the artist's imagination. It reposes above the bar.[20]

Today Laura Bell's grave is still highly accessible at Fairview Cemetery near her mother and stepfather, Anna and John Kistler. For thirty years after her death, someone placed flowers on her grave each Memorial Day.[21] Even today fresh flowers appear occasionally at the base of the aging headstone.

Of the men who had worked so hard—and possibly so illegally—to do away with Laura Bell for good, only the fate of city detective John Rowan is known. In September of 1918 Rowan died in a shoot-out with four Kansas train robbers in Colorado City.[22]

When Colorado Springs successfully annexed Colorado City, street names and addresses were changed accordingly. But because nobody wanted to buy property there due to its shady past, much of the 2600 and 2700 block of West Cucharras in the old red-light district remained vacant for many years. Only two homes were occupied in the 2700 block. One occupant was Joseph Muso, a longtime resident of the area. The other was Mary Jones, who in 1900 ran a brothel at 615 Washington. The census in 1900 noted that Mary was white, born December 1868, age thirty-one in 1900, single, born in Indiana, employed as a housekeeper, and could read and write.

Not all of Colorado City's prostitutes came to a bad end. Millie Arnold, a.k.a. Mrs. Robert L. Arnold, died a peaceful death in August of 1921 in Colorado Springs. Pearl Livingston, who arrived in Colorado City in 1903, was still there in 1927. Belle Dedrick, in the profession since 1896, remained with her husband, William, at 618 Washington Avenue through

Fig. 45. Today Laura Bell McDaniel's headstone has a prominent place at the entrance to Fairview Cemetery. Bill Henderson, who erected the stone, also paid tribute to Laura Bell's immediate family.

(From the author's collection.)

1928, when William died. Belle, who was also known as Mamie and at one time had worked in Victor, had her home in the very brothel she had worked in at the time of her death in the 1940s. By then, the place was an apartment house for the elderly. Other brothels have found new life as private homes and even churches. In April of 1921 it was announced that the Heidelberg Inn in Ramona would be sold and razed at once. After Ramona closed down, the building had fallen into disrepair "except for one summer when it was used by a motion picture company." A number of westerns were made using the barroom.[23]

Although the main source of Ramona's livelihood was lost, the town somehow managed to hang on for a number of years despite the closing of its saloons. In 1922 a $25 tax on bachelors was proposed to boost the economy. The town treasury contained only $100 and no longer supported its own police force or other necessities. Until 1947, however, Ramona kept its incorporation, with a population of seven residents. Finally, however, the tiny town voted to revert to El Paso County's jurisdiction. Colorado City welcomed the downfall of the town with open arms and professed a desire to renovate and reintroduce the beautiful assets of the area, which included building a park. In accordance, Ramona was annexed to Colorado Springs in 1955 and evolved into just another neighborhood on the west side. By 1962 not one of Ramona's notorious commercial buildings existed. Many had been torn down, while others were moved to places unknown to make room for a new housing development. For those who know about it, however, the Ramona annex remains a historic and picturesque area.

Over in what was fast becoming known as Old Colorado City, the rest of the red-light district eventually became home to a park and a small Mennonite community. Along Colorado Avenue, SnoWhite Laundry now sits in place of the gambling hall where Frank James, brother of Jesse, dealt faro.[24] The occasional old-timer of Colorado Springs's charming west side might remember stories about the past. In the present, Laura Bell's old haunt has melded into a quiet, comfortable historic place. At last, one of the West's wildest places had a fitting end.

Chapter Twelve

A Memory Slowly Fades

Think of her mournfully;
Sadly, not scornfully—
What she has been is nothing to you.
No one should weep for her,
Now there is sleep for her—
Under the evergreens, daisies and dew.

Talk if you will of her
But speak not ill of her
The sins of the living are not of the dead.
Remember her charity
Forget all disparity
Let her judges be they
Whom she sheltered and fed.

Keep her impurity
In dark obscurity,
Only remember the good she has done.
She, to the dregs has quaffed
All of life's bitter draught—
Who knows what crown her kindness has won?

Though she had been defiled;
In the tears of a little child
May wash from the record much of her sin;
Whilst others weep and wait
Outside of Heaven's gate,
Angels may come to her and lead her in.

When at the judgement throne,
The Master claims his own,
Dividing the bad from the good and true.
There pure and spotless,
Her rank shall not be less
Than will be given, perhaps, unto you.

Then do not sneer at her
Or scornfully jeer at her—
Death came to her and will come to you.
Will there be scoffing or weeping
When like her you are sleeping
Under the evergreens, daisies and dew?
　　　　　　　　　　　—Frank Waugh

News of Laura Bell McDaniel's death in 1918 likely spread to the other red-light districts throughout the state. The year also saw the most devastating influenza epidemic in U.S. history and other illnesses that took their toll on Colorado's prostitutes. In Silverton madam Matilda "Big Tilly" Fattor died of pneumonia at age forty-two in 1918. Her large body was transported for burial in a double coffin to Springfield, Massachusetts. Big Tilly's last brothel went through a series of owners after her death. In 1929 Gio Bari owned it. In a loan he got from a Mrs. Corazza, a clause in the paperwork stipulated the property "is not to be used for prostitution." The upstairs was converted to boarding, although a liquor store and bar still functioned downstairs.[1]

Big Tilly's death notwithstanding, Blair Street remained very much active throughout the 1920s, with most bordellos and gambling dens remaining open twenty-four hours a day. Operating brothels included one run by Mr. and Mrs. Kloster, who took over Dottie Watson's parlor house in 1900 after Dottie was declared insane and sent to the state mental asylum at Pueblo. She was diagnosed with "softening of the brain," a condition often associated with syphilis. She never recovered. Dottie's house and furnishings reverted to Mrs. Kloster, who had lent Dottie money.[2]

As late as 1923 Silverton continued to receive an influx of prostitutes. One was Leona Wallace. She wasn't very good looking, but they did call her Diamond Tooth because of the diamond she had set in her front tooth.[3] In December of 1928 Leona was still in business, and records of her phone bills show she made calls to other prostitutes in Durango, Leadville, and Telluride. Durango, where gambling had been successfully shut down in 1905, was experiencing a resurgence in prostitution and illegal poker games, but Telluride's red-light business had trickled down to practically nothing. Of Telluride's twenty-six houses of ill repute, only three cribs remain today, at 121, 123, and 125–127 East Pacific. Most of them were small two-room brothels, and the surviving buildings are now private homes. Like Leona Wallace, Ollie Kelly was another prostitute still working in Silverton during the 1930s. Ollie's first job was at the National Hall. In the 1930s she was working at the Mikado. Ollie had a son in Kansas to whom she often sent money.

Ultimately, many of Silverton's prostitutes were moving away or simply dying off by the late 1930s. In 1939 Lola Daggett was one of the last fallen women to die in Silverton. Born in northern Colorado and raised at Pueblo, Lola first came to Silverton around 1904. With her was her half sister, a mulatto named Freda. Lola's nickname became Nigger Lola. After Freda died in 1912 Lola continued working. In 1922 she purchased a house on Blair Street, moving up the street a few years later. Her new brothel sported several girls and a female piano player. Interestingly, Lola's chauffeur was a white man named Bud Martin. She lived out her life with the means to purchase several nice cars and coats, dying at the age of fifty. Silverton's last brothel closed in 1948. It was operated by Jew Fanny, who had opened for business back in 1935.

During the 1920s the former taverns of Victor underwent several makeovers. The Fortune Club was purchased by Mr. and Mrs. Ivan Harshbarger, who opened a confectionery and stationery store in 1925. Other places followed suit, and when Prohibition was repealed during the Depression era a new, smaller series of bars replaced the old ones.

In the metaphorical sense, many red-light districts continued dying off little by little. Their dwindling was accompanied by a slight surge in domestic disputes, a small percentage of which was likely caused by husbands having no choice but to face their own issues at home rather than running to the arms of fallen women. Members of Denver's newly reformed society found themselves having to deal with their problems within their own families, and many an unhappy couple were forced to come to terms with their marriage without the benefit of outside influences. In 1910 Gertrude Gibson Patterson shot her abusive husband in the back but was found not guilty for the murder. And in 1911 a love triangle between married socialite Isabel Springer, Frank Henwood, and Tony von Phul, which resulted in von Phul's death in Denver, was the scandal of the new century. "The moral uplift movements of the present day prompt men to accuse other men of crimes on the slightest pretext," commented one Denver judge. "The courts of the land have nothing to do with regulating the morals of the people."[4]

Denver authorities seemed to be at a loss regarding what to do about their newfound moral dilemmas, but there was no choice but to continue the assault against the dying red-light district. During the year 1918 a mere eighty-two women were arrested for practicing prostitution in Denver. A year later the notorious Mattie Silks sold the House of Mirrors at 1942 Market Street to the Buddhist Temple, which used it as a church until 1948. Throughout the early 1920s Denver arrests of prostitutes fluctuated. In 1920 the number of arrests had dwindled to thirty-five. The following year they were back up to fifty-seven. In 1922 the arrests topped out at ninety-five. As for Mattie, she was presumably retired, living at 2636 Lawrence Street with her beau, John Dillon Ready, a.k.a. Handsome Jack Kelley.[5]

It was said that in his prime the six foot three, 220-pound Handsome Jack could throw a drunk halfway across Market Street. He also adored diamonds to the extent he had one set in his front tooth. Jack and Mattie appear to have been much more subdued by the 1920s. Mattie apparently moved out of the couple's residence in 1923, when John Ready is listed in the city directory as living alone at 1922 Market Street. The couple must have reconciled, for by 1924 they are listed back at their Lawrence Street address. It was said that Mattie later married John Ready, when she was between seventy-six and seventy-eight years old. She died after a bad fall on January 7, 1929 at the age of eighty-three.

When all was said and done, Mattie's final estate amounted to only $1,922. The money was left to Jack Ready and Cort Thomson's granddaughter. Mattie is buried in Denver's Fairmount Cemetery under the name Martha A. Ready. Allegedly, an unmarked grave beside her is the final resting place of Cort Thomson. Mattie's sisters of the underworld numbered about fifty-six the year of her death, according to Denver arrest records. Mattie Silks's and Jennie Rogers's old House of Mirrors is now a fancy restaurant adorned with photos from the district's past. Certain male employees of the restaurant claim that Mattie is still present and occasionally tickles the backs of their necks.

Mattie's death was followed by that of Anna or Annie Ryan, a matronly madam who was said to have gone into business with her daughter and a niece back at the turn of the century. The only clues to Anna's past lie in the census records for 1930. They state she was born in

Massachusetts to Irish parents in 1870 and said she was a retired teacher. She was living in a boardinghouse at 1420 Logan Street. At some point Anna and Sadie Doyle moved to more stately quarters at 1939 Curtis Street. There, on August 8, 1930, Anna shot and killed former police officer Maurice Lyons. By then Sadie had gone blind, so although she was there during the shooting she could not attest to what happened. Anna served fifty-two days in jail at Canon City, but was allegedly set free for lack of evidence.

Soon after Anna passed away, Sadie moved to 1923 Arapahoe Street. Despite her loss of sight, Blind Sadie, as she became known, continued running a house of ill repute known as the Lucky Strike Rooms until 1949. Her caretaker, Frank "Toughy" Keith, had been renting Sadie's bed to one Anne O'Neil for prostitution. In August of that year the court put an end to Sadie's bed renting. District judge Joe Cook deemed Sadie mentally ill and ordered the eighty-six-year-old woman committed to a convalescent home. There Sadie died on October 1, 1950. Even then, fifty friends and acquaintances attended her funeral services.

The repeal of Prohibition in 1933 seemingly brought about a whole new rash of prostitution in Denver, if only for a little while. As late as 1934, Denver newspapers were still reporting prostitution, including a "Love Market" that was raided on Marion Street. The *Rocky Mountain News* referred to that address as "the most publicized house in Denver." After a burglary at the house, police talked to the *Rocky Mountain News* about an investigation involving a statutory rape against a fifteen-year-old runaway called Sondra. The girl and two other women, Vera Davis and Dorothy Regan, told police that Sondra had accompanied madam Mrs. Vera Brinkerhoff, Simon A. "Sherlock" Holmes, and another man to a Denver nightclub. The next morning Holmes came to the Marion Street house and violated Sondra. Afterward he sent her a box of candy before departing for Raton, New Mexico. Later, garage owner John Richardson was also charged with rape. In the meantime, the women of the house were accused of hampering the investigation.

In the excitement, nobody even seemed to notice when Anna "Gouldie" Gould quietly passed away in December of 1936. In its day Gouldie's place on 24th Street between Larimer and Market Street had served as a discreet resort for many of Denver's wealthier men. Before she got to Denver in the 1880s, Gouldie had married a half brother of Billy the Kid in New Mexico and had become known for the long black cigars she was so fond of smoking. Gouldie was one of Denver's wealthiest madams; her services included sending photographs of her girls by courier to elite hotels, where her clients could pick their own companion for the evening. Gouldie remained open until World War I, when she retired.

Others like Gouldie were forgotten as more and more districts closed down. In 1917 Pueblo built a new city hall practically right on top of the old red-light district. The move hardly deterred ladies from taking advantage of the 1911 law allowing roadhouses in the county. During the 1920s the once-elite Fountain Lake Hotel outside of Pueblo became known as a speakeasy, where bootleggers hid their illegal whiskey. The Wolpert Mansion along Riverdale Road in Adams County experienced the same fate. In 1939 the city of Grand Junction appointed a special grand jury to investigate local crimes that included gambling and prostitution. Other information about the investigation is unknown, but Grand Junction's red-light district near 2nd Street had certainly been no secret for decades. In Salida, only Laura Evens appears to have continued in the profession wholeheartedly.

Laura Evens's Employees in 1920 Census[6]

Name	Relation to household	Occupation	Age	Marital status	Birthplace
Laura Evens	Head	Lodging house	47	Single	Alabama
Ruth Clark	Lodger	None	25	Married	Colorado
Margaret Colgin	Lodger	None	24	Single	Missouri
Dollie Dawson	Lodger	None	22	—	Oklahoma
Rosa James	Lodger	None	30	Divorced	Colorado
Pearl LaNell	Lodger	None	23	Single	California
Dora Wellington	Lodger	None	25	Single	Tennessee
Cort Anderson	Lodger	Cook	61	Widower	Alabama
Adella Chavez	Lodger	Cook	32	Divorced	New Mexico
Dudley O'Danile	Lodger	Auto mechanic	33	Widower	Kentucky

Laura Evens was shut down for good in about 1950. Accordingly, she converted her house of ill repute into a boardinghouse for railroad workers. A sign out front read "No Girls." Laura willingly talked about her past with anyone who asked. She also enjoyed playing poker, rolled her own cigarettes, and refused to give up her habit of keeping her money stashed in her stockings. Laura passed away in 1953. Witnesses claimed that on her deathbed, Laura spread her arms wide and called, "Mother, come and take me." She was buried in a lavender casket and her funeral was reported as quite lavish, but only twenty-six people attended the service.[7]

After Laura's death her daughter, Lucille Sneddon, tried to give her building away, but no one wanted it due to its racy past. The Mon-Ark Shrine finally agreed to use the building as a lodge. The property did not include a wooden garage nearby, which contained five of Laura's cars. Lucille Sneddon removed the cars and rented out the garage for $75 per month. When she died in 1992, Lucille left the garage to the Shriners and they tore it down. Laura Evens's building has changed significantly over the years. The building has been stuccoed, and several windows were covered over. Only the interior of the second floor remains similar to Laura's original decor.

In the once elite and allegedly brothel-free city of Colorado Springs, at least one brothel was known to exist in the 1920s. This was the Cheyenne Canon Inn at 2030 West Cheyenne Boulevard. Built in 1920 as a bordello, the inn catered to what was left of Cripple Creek's millionaires and other wealthy men from the nearby and newly built Broadmoor Hotel. Lillian Kneisser reigned as madam. When the brothel failed, Kneisser sold to Grace Casey, who reopened the place as an illegal casino. The building was abandoned in the 1930s and was renovated into a bed-and-breakfast in 2001.

In 1922 the city of Trinidad opted to stop using the Madam's Trolley just eight months before its contract with the city trolley line was up. Gilbert Sanders sued the city on behalf of the madams, and the matter was settled out of court. The Madam's Trolley was no more, and notorious Santa Fe Street was renamed Country Club Drive. Further evidence of the red-light district's dwindling came in 1927, when several elderly madams in Trinidad decided to establish a Madams' Rest Home. The new home was built just west of town, near farmlands on the way to the town of Sopris. It was a two-story, square, brick building with a kitchen, four bedrooms on each floor, and a balcony. The endeavor was short-lived, however, and the Madams' Rest Home closed sometime between 1934 and

1936. During World War II, it is said, nearby military camps caused authorities to bring even more pressure to Trinidad, and the district closed down for good.

As late as 1924 raids were still taking place in Pueblo at such places as the Verona Rooming House at 312½ North Union. By 1926 prostitution was not so visible in Pueblo, but it had become a problem in the county due to the 1911 law allowing roadhouses. In 1926 the law was repealed. The roadhouse owners moved across the county line to Custer County. In addition, prostitution continued operating above former saloons and in hotels in Pueblo for several more years. In May 1929 gangster Pretty Boy Floyd made the papers when he was arrested with three prostitutes at 322½ North Union Avenue. All were arrested for vagrancy and prostitution. The women were Betty Curtis, alias Bettie Golden; Alta Jackman, alias Alta Wells and Alta Duffy; and Mary Douglass, alias Alice White. By then,

Fig. 46. The former West Hotel on West 3rd Street in Pueblo is now a popular tavern known as the Irish Pub. The structure is about the only remaining brothel from Pueblo's racy past.

(From the author's collection.)

hotels with such prostitutes were discreetly referred to as places with "French Ladies." A black maid at the West Hotel at 108½ West 3rd Street was once reprimanded for innocently telling male clients she knew nothing about any French ladies at the hotel.[8]

During World War II prostitution actually received yet another new lease on life. Pueblo's Union Avenue reverted back to a smaller, more discreet red-light district for about ten years, with girls soliciting from their windows or the doorways of bars. The girls typically charged between $5 and $10. After the war, however, the houses of prostitution faded once more. By 1954 Esther Baldwin's place at 3rd and Court in Pueblo had evolved into part of the downtown district. The nearest bar was the Gold Rail Tavern at 219 3rd Street. The Stranger's House on the east side of Santa Fe Avenue was in the midst of car lots and auto parts stores and is now part of Pueblo's elite Center for the Arts. The former Pueblo saloon district, on 1st Street between Santa Fe and Albany, had evolved into a Hispanic neighborhood.[9] A brothel at 232 Union had become Johnnie's Place Liquors with a residential apartment upstairs. The building has since been replaced with a modern apartment building and senior center. The Verona Rooming House at 312½ North Union was still functioning as a flophouse known as the Union Avenue Hotel. The West Hotel at 108½ West 3rd was still in operation and is now a popular tavern known as the Irish Pub. And the scene of Pretty Boy Floyd's arrest at 322½ North Union was being rented as furnished rooms by a Mrs. Lucille E. Marshall.

Pueblo's fluctuating success was not at all unusual for the shrinking red-light districts of Colorado. A 1928 letter from a prostitute in Leadville to "Big Billie" Betty Wagner in Silverton illustrates the plight of prostitutes everywhere:

Dear Billie,

No doubt you will be surprised to hear from me but I heard you were there and I'm writing to ask how business is and is there a chance for an old lady to come over and go to work? There is absolutely nothing here and I want to get away from here as soon as I can for I will drive my car out of here and I want to leave before the snow gets too deep. If I can get a crib or go to work in one of the joints let me know. I wrote to Garnett and she said there wasn't any place there I could get so I guess I can still work a bit

myself. Please answer at once and let me know. Must close now and put this in the mail, so by-by and answer soon.
P.S. If you call you can get me at 351 after 6 P.M.

Mamie G.
200 N. 3rd Street.[10]

Women like Mamie G. and Big Billie were unsure not only of their futures but also of what punishment they would have to bear for the sins they had committed. A woman in Tin Cup recalled that as a child she met a prostitute known as Tin Can Laura. The infamous lady had come to collect her lacy laundry from a Mrs. Bley. "To Elsie and me, Laura said, 'Be sure and mind your mothers. Your mothers know best. Mind everything your mothers tell you.'"[11] Shortly after the chance meeting, Tin Can Laura left Tin Cup and allegedly married, settling near the tiny community of Granite. But the children remembered her speech and later said it did more for them than any lecture from their own mothers. Salvation of children, in Tin Can Laura's mind, no doubt made up for some of her past sins.

Sometimes going straight wasn't enough to wipe out the past. Clarence Wright recalled a woman he knew in Lake City named Edith. As a young orphan, Edith had come to Lake City looking for work and had fallen victim to the red-light district madams. Eventually she married and began teaching school. Her husband was on the school board. One day a friend asked Edith, who was fond of children, why she had no kids of her own. "What, and have someone tell an innocent child some day that his mother was a wanton woman?" she said.[12] The shame of her past life kept Edith from having children.

Elizabeth Enderlin, a.k.a. Cockeyed Liz of Buena Vista, once made a poignant confession to her housekeeper. "I'll have to pay for the awful things I've done, won't I?" she said. "I couldn't help myself when I was young, but, oh, all the little lives I've destroyed—that's what I'll have to pay for—all those little young lives." Liz died at age seventy-two in 1929 of a heart attack. Even then, with all of her remorse and after thirty years of respectable marriage, it is said the churches in town refused to hold services for her.[13]

Another well-known prostitute who died in 1929 was Etta "Spuds" Murphy. A good friend of Laura Evens as a young prostitute, Etta spent many years in Pueblo before being run out of town in about 1912. In its time, Murphy's Resort Saloon in Pueblo was a leading brothel in town, but Etta ended up in the much less attractive Sandbar District of Casper, Wyoming. In Casper Spuds spent her retirement washing clothes for other prostitutes. Laura Evens went to visit Etta at Casper to offer her a home in Salida, "but she was ashamed and wouldn't even see me. Poor little Spuddy."[14]

It is said that the Old Homestead in Cripple Creek stayed in business as late as the 1930s. Various old-timers in recent years have also claimed that as many as a dozen prostitutes worked in Cripple Creek into the 1940s. Cripple Creek native Minnie Zimmerman bought the house from Mrs. Peterie in 1935. Minnie was once crowned "Last Madam of the Homestead," though it may have been a title associated with Minnie merely because she was the newest owner of the building. A turn of the century church cookbook features recipes from Minnie, a privilege she would not have enjoyed as a Myers Avenue harlot. In 1943 Minnie changed the ownership to include her paramour, Charles Daniels. Three years later Minnie and Charlie sold to Herman and Elva Conrow, who used the house as their private home. The Conrows sold to Aurelian G. "Bob" and Mable Ragle in 1952; they made some improvements to the house, which they also used as a private residence. During this time, the Homestead remained pretty much as it had been during the gold boom. Just behind the Homestead was a smaller brothel that had once housed black prostitutes. In the 1950s the building still contained stoves and furnishings, and the original wallpaper was still visible on the walls.[15]

In March of 1958 the Ragles sold the house to Fred and Pat Mentzer. It was the Mentzers who decided to renovate the house to its original turn-of-the-century condition. Some of the original furnishings were still present, including a full-length mirror predating the 1896 fires. Living in a former brothel appears to have pleased the Mentzers immensely, and the couple lost no time in throwing the occasional party and dressing in period costumes. They also decided to make the Old Homestead a museum and began giving tours. Allegedly, it was Minnie Zimmerman who came forth, anonymously, and provided much valuable information about what the house had been like during its heyday.[16] Minnie's secret was kept for many years not only by the Mentzers but also by Harold and Lodi Hern, who purchased the museum in about 1964.[17]

Of the literally thousands of prostitutes that passed through the Cripple Creek District during a fifty-year period, the fates of only a few are known. Cripple Creek prostitute Ethel Ayers may have migrated to Florida, where she died in 1975. Viola Carter died in Denver in 1980. A few others married and left, and some married and stayed. But the vast

Fig. 47. In 1958 Pat and Fred Mentzer purchased and revived
the spirit of the Old Homestead. The couple dressed in
costume and threw fancy parties on a frequent basis.

(Courtesy Denver Public Library.)

majority of them took their secrets with them to the grave. Today, the
places of Myers Avenue have evolved from dilapidated buildings to empty
lots to parking garages. The only exception is the Old Homestead Parlor
House Museum.

Fortunately, not all of Colorado's bad girls disappeared into the mist for-
ever. Of all the forgotten soiled doves in the Cripple Creek District, French
Blanche's story is one that bears mention. Born Blanche LeCoq in France,
French came to America at the age of eighteen. Although it was thought she

was kidnapped and brought to America to work in New Orleans, Blanche later stated that she was hired by Morris Durant to come to Cripple Creek. A saloon owner in Cripple Creek and Victor, Durant apparently commissioned several girls from France to work on Myers Avenue.

French was quite beautiful in her youth, and Durant fell in love with her. Before long she was pregnant with Durant's child. When French's daughter was born, the proper women of the town tried to take it away from her. French was defended by Daisy Barbee, a female attorney from St. Louis whose clients were nearly all prostitutes. Barbee succeeded in winning French's case, but a celebration party that turned into a drunken brawl caused French to lose the baby for good and it was given up for adoption. Matters turned even worse when Morris Durant's wife heard about the child. Mrs. Durant accosted French and threw acid in her face. The wounded harlot retreated to the nearby town of Midway, between Cripple Creek and Victor, where for many years she concealed her scarred face behind a veil. At Midway she could still service miners coming to the Grand View Saloon along the High Line Railway.

For years, according to French, her only company at Midway was a handsome man who lived next door. The two had a brief courtship until French discovered he was seeing another woman. Despite his being her only neighbor in Midway, French never spoke to the man again, and he eventually moved away.[18] During her remaining years at Midway, French Blanche lived a quiet life. No one is certain when she ceased doing business. After a time she would accept groceries delivered to her door, and people of the district later recalled seeing her sitting in the window with the evening sun on her face. She waved at folks passing by, but if someone happened to knock at her door, French never answered without her veil in place. "She kind of scared people," recalled Steve Mackin, who grew up in the district.[19]

As she grew older, wrinkles disguised her scars, and French stopped wearing the veil. Steve Mackin remembered visiting her as a child with his friends. "She made the most incredible cookies," Mackin recalled.[20] Her tiny cabin was wallpapered and clean, with a green and white porcelain cookstove. Perhaps the children gave French Blanche courage, for she began making monthly trips to Victor for groceries. Before long, a Mrs. McCready of Victor began giving her rides back to Midway, and in the late 1950s French moved into a cabin next to the McCready home in Victor. Mrs. McCready also talked the city authorities of Victor into giving French $35 per month because she wasn't a U.S. citizen and had nothing to live on. By then French was in her eighties.

Fig. 48. French Blanche was among the last surviving prostitutes in the Cripple Creek District. This, the only known photograph of French, shows her standing in front of the old Midway Saloon.

(Courtesy Evelyn Trenary.)

Over time French Blanche and the McCreadys became close. Mrs. McCready's daughter, Sally Johnson, described French as "nice and very quiet."[21] When Sally gave birth to her daughter, French Blanche gave the child a baby doll. In the early 1960s French contracted pneumonia. Her condition worsened, and a neighbor named May Dunn took her to Hilltop Clinic, located in the old St. Nicholas Hospital in Cripple Creek. Blanche died, and per her instructions, Sally Johnson and her mother found $200 stashed in a drawer for her burial. The women ordered a special plate meant to identify one's name and house address, using it instead as Blanche's grave marker.

French Blanche's story doesn't end here. Two years after she died, the daughter she had been forced to give up years ago came looking for her. The woman, now in her thirties, said she had been taken by a doctor in Kansas who revealed her adoption and her mother's true identity on his deathbed. She received a photograph and a few of French's belongings,

Fig. 49. French Blanche's pauperlike grave is still visible at Victor's Sunnyside Cemetery. Fortunately, the grave was marked, thanks to Sally Johnson and her mother.

(From the author's collection.)

then disappeared. All that remains of French Blanche is the small metal sign that marks her grave at Victor's Sunnyside Cemetery.

Throughout World War II more and more districts closed down or faded into obscurity. One of Colorado's best-known prostitutes in the 1940s was still Lillian Powers. Tiger Lil, as she was also known in Florence, was finally closed down by Fremont County district attorney John Stump Witcher in 1950. Witcher in fact closed down all prostitution in and around Florence, including private clubs such as the one at Fawn Hollow, outside of town. Lil died in a nursing home on October 22, 1960 at the age of eighty-seven. Shortly after her death, Lil's house was sold and divided into apartments. It now serves as a private home in its entirety.

Likewise, many of Breckenridge's soiled doves moved away, but a good number also moved in with former customers and became wives. May Nicholson, a former madam who claimed to have led a Fourth of July parade through town carrying the American flag, died in the 1960s. The very last of Colorado's madams to pass on just may have been Hazel

Gillette "Ma" Brown. Hazel ran the Pioneer Bar at 118 West 2nd Street in Leadville. Built in 1882 as the Pioneer Billiard Hall, the building had allegedly continued to operate as both bar and brothel up until 1970. A bar and dance floor was located below, with a separate entrance leading to private upstairs rooms. Hazel, who wore cat's-eyes spectacles set with genuine diamonds, acted as proprietress until her death in 1970, although it was said she quit doing business in the 1950s. The Pioneer Bar was converted to apartments in 1998, but the tavern on the bottom floor is open once more.

In the years since Hazel Brown's death, a number of events have commemorated the madams of Colorado's past. During the 1950s Dick Johnson of the Cripple Creek District Museum had a new marble headstone installed at Pearl DeVere's grave after the old wooden one was found rotting in the cemetery. In 1977 Cripple Creek resident Myke Minnow organized the *Pearl DeVere Affair*, a play of sorts that included a reenactment of Pearl DeVere's funeral. Minnow hoped to make the occasion an annual event, but her idea never came to fruition.

Even so, admirers make the trek to Cripple Creek each year to visit Pearl's grave and leave tokens of love. For well over a decade one poem in particular, encased in plastic, has withstood winter snows and wind to stand like a sentinel on the cement slab covering the grave:

> *Goodbye Pearl, Goodbye*
> *My dear Friend,*
> *Never will I forget*
> *The sparkle in those beautiful brown eyes;*
> *Nor the radiance of your smile.*
> *The generosity that came so freely,*
> *Your kindness that knew no bounds.*
> *Though your own life was sad*
> *And left much to be desired,*
> *You always made sure*
> *That others were comfortable.*
> *Though your life here was ended*
> *Before its time,*
> *And grieving for your loss*
> *Makes me ill,*
> *I see you in the rain;*
> *I feel you when the sun*

Dances on the water;
I hear your laugh
In the breeze;
I smell your perfume
In the yellow roses;
I keep you
In my heart.
And I promise you
You will never be forgotten.
Goodbye Pearl, Goodbye.

Lovingly,
JMS

These days, Pearl's Follies is a benefit held each year to raise money for the Old Homestead, which celebrated its forty-fifth year as a museum in 2003. The museum, however, now in the ownership of casino and lodging

Fig. 50. Cripple Creek District Museum founder Richard Johnson replaced Pearl's wooden tombstone with a marble stone in the 1950s. Even today admirers still leave flowers, poems, and other tokens of love at Pearl DeVere's grave.

(From the author's collection.)

Fig. 51. Most appropriately, this piece of sheet music was found in an abandoned brothel at Crystola, a tiny community located between Colorado Springs and Woodland Park.

(From the author's collection.)

conglomerates, has been in danger of closing for several years.[22] Another event is Madam Lou Bunch Days in Central City. Each June the three-hundred-pound madam is honored in a weekend long event that includes a parade, bed races, and a variety of other fun and silly games. In addition, Ed Nichols of the Central City Opera House Association hopes to restore a former brothel in Central City at some time in the future.

By all accounts, women like Hazel Brown, French Blanche, Pearl DeVere, and Lou Bunch were respected and loved even after their deaths. How sad that for too many decades society regarded them as disgraceful, snickering at the sins these "naughty ladies" committed rather than honoring the contributions they made to their societies and the West. Their true identities have been covered up. Thousands of their photographs remain unidentified, perhaps forever. Those who knew them have refused to talk about them, and many of their descendants have no idea of their ancestry. The brothels are gone or serve some other use, with no clue as to what happened there. Invaluable documents and memorabilia have been destroyed, lost, or sold to private collectors. Writers of western lore and Hollywood glitter have portrayed these women as merely sexual objects, ignoring their humanity and their courage.

In more recent years, thankfully, prostitutes are finally getting the recognition they deserve. In Butte, Montana, city officials dedicated a park across the street from the 1890 Dumas Hotel Brothel in memory of the red-light ladies of that town. Contemporary organizations such as New York City's Museum of Sex and the International Sex Worker Foundation for Art, Culture, and Education, founded by a former prostitute, are working to educate the general public about prostitution both then and now. Western writers are delving deeper in their research to find out more about the lives prostitutes led—resulting in more stories, more ancestry leads, and more heroic harlots than we ever knew existed. Indeed, it is hard to imagine a history of Colorado without them. If only they knew that.

Appendix One

✵

A Sampling of Cripple Creek Prostitutes in 1900, by Address[1]

333 Myers (the Harem)

Name	Race	Age	Birthplace	Marital status	Owns/ rents	Literate
C. Addy	White	20	South Dakota	Single	—	Yes
Gladys Coplyle	White	21	Ohio	Single	—	Yes
Celia Hoggett	White	27	Illinois	Widow	—	Yes
Nettie Powell	White	29	Maryland	Married 7 years	—	Yes
E. Prince	White	33	Georgia	Single	Owns	Yes
Jessie Strong	—	22	Iowa	Widow	—	Yes[2]
May Wade	White	21	Missouri	Single	—	—

354 Myers

Name	Race	Age	Birthplace	Marital status	Owns/ rents	Literate
Rosie Lee	White	21	Maine	Single	—	Yes
Fannie Smith	White	22	Minnesota	Single	—	Yes
May Taylor	White	20	Missouri	Single	—	Yes

361½ Myers

Name	Race	Age	Birthplace	Marital status	Owns/ rents	Literate
Sheron	—	—	—	—	—	—

Name	Race	Age	Birthplace	Marital status	Owns/ rents	Literate
F. Musan (housekeeper)	White	55	Pennsylvania	Divorced	—	Yes

375 Myers

Name	Race	Age	Birthplace	Marital status	Owns/ rents	Literate
Cynthia Bomer	White	22	New Jersey	Married	—	Yes
Hellen Fowler	White	21	Tennessee	Widow	—	Yes
Madeline Hoyt	White	30	Kentucky	Widow	—	Yes

437½ Myers

Name	Race	Age	Birthplace	Marital status	Owns/ rents	Literate
Maud Edwards	White	26	Kansas	Widow	—	Yes
Ginger Hailes	White	26	Pennsylvania	Single	—	Yes
Bell LaMont	White	21	Missouri	Widow	—	Yes
Julia Maher	White	34	France; came to U.S. 1890	Single	Rents	No
Alice Vincent	White	32	Minnesota	Single	—	Yes

449 E. Myers

Name	Race	Age	Birthplace	Marital status	Owns/ rents	Literate
May Bell	White	29	New York	Widow	Owns	Yes
Maggie Hill	—	—	—	—	—	—
Annie Laurie	—	—	—	—	—	—

451 E. Myers

Name	Race	Age	Birthplace	Marital status	Owns/ rents	Literate
May Bell	White	29	New York	Widow	Owns	Yes
Marie Clayton	White	20	Missouri	Single	—	Yes
Mrs. Irene Tobin	—	—	—	—	—	—

459 Myers

Name	Race	Age	Birthplace	Marital status	Owns/ rents	Literate
Ellen Dixie	White	29	Germany; came to U.S. 1880	Single	Rents	Yes

501 Myers

Name	Race	Age	Birthplace	Marital status	Owns/ rents	Literate
Victoria Bosmburn	White	31	France	Single	Rents	No; does not speak English
Rossa Dock	—	21	Georgia	Single	—	No
Bell Ellis	White	33	France; came to U.S. 1900	Single	—	No; does not speak English
Teo	White	26	Japan; came to U.S. 1897	Single	—	No; does not speak English

512 Myers

Name	Race	Age	Birthplace	Marital status	Owns/ rents	Literate
Millilen	Black	21	Kentucky	Single	—	—

526 E. Myers

Name	Race	Age	Birthplace	Marital status	Owns/ rents	Literate
Anna Belle	Black	—	—	—	—	—

Appendix Two

A Sampling of Traveling Gals in Cripple Creek[1]

Name	Notes
Lyda Caypton	Aged 26; arrived in Cripple Creek 1911 from Missouri; worked at 341 E. Myers; June 1911 left for Glenwood Springs; July 1911 returned to Cripple Creek; August 1911 left for Denver
Nadine Conkle	Born Quincy, Illinois; aged 25; 1911 worked at 1925 Market, Denver; September 1911 arrived in Cripple Creek, worked at 339 Myers
Pud Couch	Aged 22; alias Don-Edith; arrived July 1911 at 363 Myers but left same day for Victor; January 1912 had returned to Cripple Creek but departed for Colorado City; undated note reads: "Now in Junction City"
Ethel Doyle	Born Illinois; aged 26; moved from Victor to Cripple Creek October 1911 and worked at 310 Myers; departed Cripple Creek January 1912; returned in May and went to work at 371 Myers; departed Cripple Creek again in June
Lucille Hall	Born Sedalia, Missouri; aged 26; resided in Pueblo 1910; came to Cripple Creek March 1913 and resided on E. Myers

Dorothy Hytt	Born Iowa; aged 23; arrived in Cripple Creek June 1911; noted as "not in Cripple Creek" January 1912, but working at 341 Myers in April; left for Colorado City July 1912
Mabel Joe	Born Illinois; aged 25; resided at 310 Myers in Cripple Creek in July 1911; departed for Denver
Dottie Kirk	Born Des Moines, Iowa; aged 19; arrived in Cripple Creek November 7, 1911 from Kansas City, Missouri, and began working at 367 Myers; traveled to Denver October 15, 1912; left on the 7 A.M. train for Pueblo January 23, 1913
Marrie Smith (alias Marrie Ashby)	Born Kansas City, Missouri; aged 24; arrived in Cripple Creek from Colorado Springs October 1911 and worked at 431 E. Myers; taken to court under alias October 18; moved to 310 E. Myers October 28; went back to work at 431 E. Myes January 2, 1912; left for Salida January 14; returned to Cripple Creek July 5; departed for Telluride July 24
Maud Turpin	Aged 28; came from St. Louis, Missouri; arrived in Cripple Creek June 1911 and worked at 365 Myers; went to Pueblo June 14; returned to Cripple Creek October 6; left town January 1912
Sue Williams	Aged 24; mulatto; arrived in Cripple Creek July 1911 and worked at 445½ Myers; left for Leadville August
Lilly Willison	Born Belgium; aged 28; arrived in Cripple Creek from Denver August 1911; gone by 1912
Annie Wilson	Formerly of Denver; migrated to Cripple Creek; moved to Kansas City 1904

Pearl Wins

Born Lawrence, Kansas; aged 27; arrived in Cripple Creek from Pueblo October 1912; left for Colorado Springs November

Jennie Wolf

Born New York; aged 27; came to Cripple Creek from Denver June 1911; gone by January 1912

Notes

❦

Chapter One

1. Thomas J. Noel, *The City and The Saloon: Denver 1858–1916* (Lincoln: University of Nebraska Press, 1982), 86.
2. Caroline Bancroft, personal papers, Denver Public Library, box 30, FF59.
3. *The Real West* (A & E Television Network, in association with the History Channel, produced by Greystone Communication, 1994).
4. "Georgie Burnham was the black sheep of the God-fearing Mormon Burnhams of Utah and New Mexico. When she died, Georgie's family refused to claim her body. George Burnham, a great uncle, finally did come forward and Georgie was buried in an unmarked grave near the Navajo Reservation near Bluff, Utah. Georgie's story was later told by the New Mexico Burnhams during the 1950s." Eleanor Smith, interview by author, Los Osos, California, April 2003.
5. Erik Swanson, interview by author, Cripple Creek District Museum, Spring 2002.
6. Lawrence Powell, "Early California Society," *Westways Magazine*, August 1965, 17.
7. Allan G. Bird, *Bordellos of Blair Street* (Pierson, Mich.: Advertising, Publications & Consultants, 1993), 67.
8. Sanford C. Gladden, *Ladies of the Night*, Early Boulder Series 5 (Boulder: privately published, 1979), 31.
9. Clark Secrest, *Hell's Belles: Denver's Brides of the Multitudes* (Denver: Hindsight Historical Publications, 1996), 219.
10. Ibid.
11. *Ouray Times*, August 20, 1881, 2.

Chapter Two

1. An 1859 survey of 2,000 prostitutes asking why they took up the profession revealed that 525 were destitute; 258 were seduced or abandoned; 164 were treated badly by parents, relatives, or husbands; and 71 were persuaded to come

to work by other prostitutes. The rest simply succumbed to the various vices at hand. *Trail's End Magazine*, December–January 1998, 21.

2. Clark Secrest, *Hell's Belles: Prostitution, Vice, and Crime in Early Denver*, rev. ed. (Boulder: University of Colorado Press, 2002), 233.

3. Ibid., 108.

4. *The Real West* (A & E Television Network, in association with the History Channel, produced by Greystone Communication, 1994).

5. Allan G. Bird, *Bordellos of Blair Street* (Pierson, Mich.: Advertising, Publications & Consultants, 1993), 47.

6. Although the author is unknown, this traditional song is said to be a parody of Charles Graham's melody "Picture That Is Turned toward the Wall." Courtesy of Erik Swanson, Alma, Colorado.

7. City of Cripple Creek, register of prostitutes, 1911, BPOE Elk's Lodge #316, Cripple Creek, Colorado.

8. Joanne West Dodds, *What's a Nice Girl Like You Doing in a Place Like This?* (Pueblo, Colo.: Focal Plain, 1996), 11.

9. Lizzie Beaudrie, *Lizzie Beaudrie, Dance Hall Girl, 1882–1960*, edited by Joanne Tankersley and Mary Schroder (Creede, Colo.: Creede Historical Society, 1992), 21.

10. Dodds, *What's a Nice Girl Like You Doing in a Place Like This?*, 22.

11. Beaudrie, *Lizzie Beaudrie*, 21.

12. Dodds, *What's a Nice Girl Like You Doing in a Place Like This?*, 6

13. Sandra Dallas, *Colorado Ghost Towns and Mining Camps* (Norman: University of Oklahoma Press, 1985), 124.

14. Darlene Leslie, Kelle Rankin-Sunter, and Deborah Wightman, *Central City, "The Richest Square Mile on Earth," and the History of Gilpin County* (Black Hawk, Colo.: TB Publishing, 1990), 32.

15. Richard Erdoes, *Saloons of the Old West* (Avenel, N.J.: Gramercy Books, 1979), 196.

16. Dodds, *What's a Nice Girl Like You Doing in a Place Like This?*, 27.

17. Incidentally, Art's grandmother was Lelia Loveless, a performing actress who lived just a block below Myers Avenue on South 3rd Street. After the death of Art's paternal grandmother, Lillie, in 1919, his grandfather, Franklin Wicks, married Lelia. Although Lelia was successful in her career, Art speculated that she may have dabbled in prostitution on occasion. Regardless, she was accepted and loved without prejudice by Art's family even though Art's mother obviously disapproved of the girls on Myers Avenue. "She was a fine person," Art said of Lelia. "We all got along. She was family." Frank Wicks passed away in 1938, and Lelia moved to Colorado Springs where she died in the 1940s. Interviews with Art Tremayne (Encore Video Productions, in conjunction with the City of Cripple Creek, 1999 and May 16, 2003).

18. Ed B. Larsh and Robert Nichols, *Leadville, U.S.A.* (Boulder: Johnson Books, 1993), 28.

19. Ibid., 36.

20. Dodds, *What's a Nice Girl Like You Doing in a Place Like This?*, 23.

21. Ibid., 23.

22. Ibid.

23. Fred Mazzulla and Jo Mazzulla, *Brass Checks and Red-Lights* (Denver: privately published, 1966), 38.

24. Marshall Sprague, *Money Mountain* (Lincoln: University of Nebraska Press, 1953), 316.

25. Sanford C. Gladden, *Ladies of the Night*, Early Boulder Series 5 (Boulder: privately published, 1979), 11, 15.

26. When two such masks were found in a brothel from Butte, Montana, lipstick stains were still visible on them. eBay.com.

27. Secrest, *Hell's Belles: Prostitution, Vice, and Crime*, 233.

28. Beaudrie, *Lizzie Beaudrie*, 23.

29. Anne M. Butler, *Daughters of Joy, Sisters of Misery: Prostitutes in the American West, 1865–90* (Chicago: University of Illinois Press, 1985), 30–31.

30. Beaudrie, *Lizzie Beaudrie*, 2.

31. Ibid., 8.

32. Ibid., 9.

33. Ibid., 20.

34. Ibid., 21.

35. *Criminal Record of the Western Federation of Miners, Coeur d'Alene to Cripple Creek, 1894–1904*, Denver Public Library.

36. Bird, *Bordellos of Blair Street*, 65.

37. Vardis Fisher and Opal Laurel Holmes, *Gold Rushes and Mining Camps of the Early American West* (Caldwell, Idaho: Caxton, 1968), 200.

38. Sadly, this poor child appears not to have escaped life as a prostitute. In 1884 The *Boulder County Herald* reported on a man "charged with fornication with Maggie Wells, the colored cripple who has but one leg and no arms." Gladden, *Ladies of the Night*, 15.

39. Dodds, *What's a Nice Girl Like You Doing in a Place Like This?*, 7.

40. Gladden, *Ladies of the Night*, 28.

41. *Cripple Creek Citizen*, December 7, 1899, 3:4.

42. Clark Secrest, *Hell's Belles: Denver's Brides of the Multitudes* (Denver: Hindsight Historical Publications, 1996), 107.

43. Murielle Sybell Wolle, *Stampede to Timberline* (Boulder: University of Colorado, 1949), 93.

44. Kay Reynolds Blair, *Ladies of the Lamplight* (Leadville, Colo.: Timberline Books, 1971), 4.

45. Secrest, *Hell's Belles: Prostitution, Vice, and Crime*, 106.

46. Blair, *Ladies of the Lamplight*, 4.

47. Ibid.

48. *Durango Herald-Democrat*, October 10, 1938, 6:3.

49. Caroline Bancroft did not find any record of a smallpox epidemic in this region from 1861 to 1863. Secrest, *Hell's Belles: Prostitution, Vice, and Crime*, 106.

50. Blair, *Ladies of the Lamplight*, 7.
51. Ibid.
52. Secrest, *Hell's Belles: Prostitution, Vice, and Crime*, 106.
53. Max Evans, *Madam Millie: Bordellos from Silver City to Ketchikan* (Albuquerque: University of New Mexico Press, 2002), xiii.
54. Fisher and Holmes, *Gold Rushes of the Early American West*, 205.

Chapter Three

1. *The Real West* (A & E Television Network, in association with the History Channel, produced by Greystone Communication, 1994).
2. Clark Secrest, *Hell's Belles: Prostitution, Vice, and Crime in Early Denver*, rev. ed. (Boulder: University of Colorado Press, 2002), 75.
3. Darlene Leslie, Kelle Rankin-Sunter, and Deborah Wightman, *Central City, "The Richest Square Mile on Earth," and the History of Gilpin County* (Black Hawk, Colo.: TB Publishing, 1990), 34.
4. *James Thomson's Colorado Diary 1872*, with introduction and notes by K. J. Fielding, *Colorado Magazine*, July 1954, 113.
5. Leslie, Rankin-Sunter, and Wightman, *Central City*, 33.
6. *Daily Denver Tribune*, February 28, 1874, clipping files at Denver Public Library.
7. Richard Erdoes, *Saloons of the Old West* (Avenel, N.J.: Gramercy Books, 1979), 182.
8. Fairmount Cemetery, *Distinguished Women Walking Tour* (Denver, undated pamphlet).
9. Max Miller, *Holladay Street* (New York: Signet, 1962), 72.
10. Dodds, *What's a Nice Girl Like You Doing in a Place Like This?*, 40.
11. Secrest, *Hell's Belles: Prostitution, Vice, and Crime*, 237.
12. Mike Flanagan, *Out West* (New York: Harry N. Abrams, 1987), 157.
13. The definition of the term *mikado* is a real enigma. There was a Mikado parlor house in both Cripple Creek and Silverton, and the frequent use of the word with respect to prostitution is truly puzzling. The only clues as to its origin lie with the *Oxford American Dictionary*, which defines a mikado as "a Japanese emperor." In 1885 Gilbert and Sullivan produced *The Mikado*, a highly popular opera about the Japanese son of a mikado who falls in love with a young girl. Finally, a game of "pick-up sticks" originating in Europe was alternately called mikado, but this was not introduced to America until 1936, long after the term was in use in the prostitution industry. At best guess, a mikado parlor or parlor house was one that was decorated very lavishly, probably patterned after Japanese decor. Such a place would have been deemed special, a cut above the rest. Many madams studied parlor house decor in France and other places and implemented what they saw into their own bordellos. More than likely, especially considering the success of Gilbert and Sullivan's opera, Japanese decor influenced the ladies' taste as well.

14. Clark Secrest, *Hell's Belles: Denver's Brides of the Multitudes* (Denver: Hindsight Historical Publications, 1996), 232.

15. In 1984 the angel was pulled down and severely damaged but has since been remounted and repaired. Fairmount Cemetery, *Walk through Historical Riverside Cemetery* (Denver, 1991 and 1996).

16. Ronald Dean Miller, *Shady Ladies of the West* (Los Angeles: Westernlore Press, 1964), 96.

Chapter Four

1. Over time Doc Garvin's cabin also served as a Chinese laundry with an opium den, among several other uses. At one time the cabin reposed on the golf course at Colorado Springs's elite Broadmoor Hotel and occasionally served as a float in parades at both Colorado City and Denver. During the year 1959 the cabin had a prominent spot on the grounds of Denver's state capitol in celebration of the "Rush to the Rockies" Centennial. Today the cabin is preserved in Colorado City's Bancroft Park and is used by the Old Colorado City Historical Society for special events.

2. *Colorado Springs Gazette*, November 26, 1887, 4:1.

3. *Colorado Springs Gazette & Telegraph*, March 9, 1924, 4:7.

4. *Westword* (Colorado Springs: Old Colorado City Historical Society, May 1990).

5. *Colorado Springs Gazette Telegraph*, August 3, 1893, A6:1.

6. Colorado City Board of Trustees, *Ordinances of the Town of Colorado City*, compiled by John R. Watt, city attorney (Colorado City: W. P. Epperson, Iris Printers, 1896).

7. Ibid.

8. Colorado City directory, 1900 and 1901.

9. The Central Hotel, a large two-story structure taking up two lots at 708 Washington, led a long and varied life. In 1890 the place appears to have been a legitimate hotel, but by 1892 it was noted as a place of "female boarding." By 1897 the name of the hotel had changed to the Lincoln, and it was still noted as a brothel. In 1902 the place was called the Union; although there is no use listed, several sources point to its continued use as a borello. In 1904–5 the city directory lists the City Hotel at 710 Washington, run by Mrs. Minnie Tebow. This was probably the old Central. Sanborn Fire Insurance maps for 1890, 1892, 1897, and 1902.

10. Beginning in about 1902, the Colorado City Council decided to change the names of certain streets, for reasons unknown. Hence the reader will note that in 1902, the name of 1st Street was changed to 6th Street, 2nd Street was renamed 7th Street, and 3rd Street was renamed 8th Street. There was also a change in street numbers, making certain addresses extremely difficult to identify. Between 1907 and 1917, when Colorado City was annexed to Colorado Springs, the names of Washington Avenue and Grand Avenue were changed to Cucharras Street and Vermijo Street, respectively. In the interest of simplicity, the addresses

referred to in Colorado City from here on out are recorded as they were found in the research. Colorado City and Colorado Springs Sanborn Fire Insurance Maps for 1890, 1892, 1897, 1902, 1907, 1950, 1957, 1962, and 1970.

Chapter Five

1. Sanford C. Gladden, *Ladies of the Night*, Early Boulder Series 5 (Boulder: privately published, 1979), 5.
2. Joanne West Dodds, *What's a Nice Girl Like You Doing in a Place Like This?* (Pueblo, Colo.: Focal Plain, 1996), 30.
3. Mary Ellen Gilliland, *Summit: A Gold Rush History of Summit County, Colorado* (Silverthorn, Colo.: Alpenrose Press, 1980), 51.
4. Allan G. Bird, *Bordellos of Blair Street* (Pierson, Mich.: Advertising, Publications & Consultants, 1993), 17.
5. Freda Carley Peterson, *Over My Dead Body! The Story of Hillside Cemetery* (Norman, Okla.: Levite of Apache, 1996), 122.
6. Allan G. Bird, *Silverton Gold* (Silverton, Colo.: privately published, 1986), 121.
7. Ibid., 96.
8. Kay Reynolds Blair, *Ladies of the Lamplight*, rev. ed. (Ouray, Colo.: Western Reflections, 2002), 91.
9. Richard Erdoes, *Saloons of the Old West* (Avenel, N.J.: Gramercy Books, 1979), 194.
10. Ibid.
11. Ibid., 197.
12. Vardis Fisher and Opal Laurel Holmes, *Gold Rushes and Mining Camps of the Early American West* (Caldwell, Idaho: Caxton, 1968), 98.
13. Dodds, *What's a Nice Girl Like You Doing in a Place Like This?*, 7.
14. Max Miller, *Holladay Street* (New York: Signet, 1962), 191.
15. Dodds, *What's a Nice Girl Like You Doing in a Place Like This?*, 22.
16. Ibid.
17. Doris H. Gregory, *Ouray's Era of Bars and Brothels* (Ouray, Colo.: Cascade, 1982), 13.
18. Erdoes, *Saloons of the Old West*, 188.
19. Eleanor Perry, *I Remember Tin Cup* (Littleton, Colo.: privately published, 1986), 17.
20. FourteenerNet, Colorado History, "The Story of Cock-Eyed Liz," www.fourteenernet.com.
21. Anne M. Butler, *Daughters of Joy, Sisters of Misery: Prostitutes in the American West, 1865–90* (Chicago: University of Illinois Press, 1985), 90.

Chapter Six

1. Joan Swallow Reiter, ed., *The Women* (New York: Time-Life Books: 1978), 70.

2. Joanne West Dodds, *What's a Nice Girl Like You Doing in a Place Like This?* (Pueblo, Colo.: Focal Plain, 1996), 4.

3. Ibid., 18.

4. Ibid., 33.

5. Ibid., 53.

6. Gertrude Edman, a.k.a Gertrude Eastman and known to her friends as Gertie, was the subject of this ditty written by Margaret Richter. Gertie was a Trinidad prostitute who operated along Main Street at a place called the Reo Rooms. Dodds, *What's a Nice Girl Like You Doing in a Place Like This?*, 78.

7. Ibid., 53.

8. Ibid., 71.

9. Ibid., 44.

10. Ibid., 88.

11. City of Cripple Creek, register of prostitutes, 1911, BPOE Elk's Lodge #316, Cripple Creek, Colorado.

12. "Lillian Powers of Florence," Canon City (Colorado) Public Library.

13. Roy Pray, interview by author (Encore Video Productions, in conjunction with the City of Cripple Creek), Florence, Colorado, 2000.

14. Arthur Mink to Caroline Bancroft, April 4, 1964, Caroline Bancroft Papers, box 30, FF59, Denver Public Library.

15. "Reporter Spoke Last Words over Grave of 'Creede Lily,'" Undated news clipping, Penrose Public Library, Colorado Springs.

16. Clark Secrest, *Hell's Belles: Prostitution, Vice, and Crime in Denver*, rev. ed. (Boulder: University of Colorado Press, 2002), 74.

17. Anne Ellis, *The Life of an Ordinary Woman* (Boston: Mariner Books, 1999), 40.

18. Dodds, *What's a Nice Girl Like You Doing in a Place Like This?*, 27.

19. Betty Lynne Hull, *Cobwebs and Crystal: Colorado's Grand Old Hotels* (Boulder: Pruett, 1982), 20.

20. Dodds, *What's a Nice Girl Like You Doing in a Place Like This?*, 77.

Chapter Seven

1. Missouri Marriages, www.ancestry.com.

2. *Salida Semi-weekly Mail,* May 20, 1887, 2:1.

3. Ibid., May 27, 1887, miscellaneous clipping supplied by Donna Nevins, Salida.

4. Ibid., May 20, 1887, 2:1.

5. Ibid.

6. Ibid., May 27, 1887.

7. Ibid.

8. Ibid.

9. "Sporting Houses," undated manuscript, Penrose Public Library, Colorado Springs. Amusingly, this revealing article is typed on official City of Colorado Springs stationery.

10. Colorado census for 1900, National Archives, Denver.

11. City of Colorado Springs, *Here Lies Colorado Springs,* edited by Denise Oldach (Colorado Springs: Fittje Bros., 1995), 108.

12. Teller County Treasurer's Office, tax records for 1904, Teller County Courthouse, Cripple Creek, Colorado.

13. *Colorado City Iris,* April 15, 1909, 1:4.

14. The name "the Mansions" appears to have figured prominently in Colorado City's red-light district. In 1903 it was the name of Mamie Majors's place. Others sources state the Mansions was under the care of Bessie Paxton when it burned in 1909. After the fire, Laura Bell McDaniel named her newly built brothel the Mansions. Whether these three businesses were the same or even on the same site is unknown.

15. *Colorado City Iris,* May 7, 1909, 2:3.

16. Marriage license of Laura McDaniel and Herbert N. Berg, El Paso County Clerk and Recorder, Colorado Springs, Colorado.

17. City of Cripple Creek, register of prostitutes, 1911, BPOE Elk's Lodge #316, Cripple Creek, Colorado.

18. Beyle Brothers Funeral Home ledger, 1897–1914, Penrose Public Library, Colorado Springs, Colorado.

19. According to author Cathleen Norman, Mamie Majors was also known as Mamie Rogers when she operated a brothel now located at 2616 West Cucharras. Cathleen Norman, *In and Around Old Colorado City* (Lakewood, Colo.: Preservation Publishing, 2001).

20. "Sporting Houses."

21. *Colorado City Iris,* September 20, 1907, 2:2.

22. Ibid.

23. Ibid., April 15, 1909, 1:4.

24. Joanne West Dodds, *What's a Nice Girl Like You Doing in a Place Like This?* (Pueblo, Colo.: Focal Plain, 1996), 35.

25. Clark Secrest, *Hell's Belles: Denver's Brides of the Multitudes* (Denver: Hindsight Historical Publications, 1996), 279.

26. Colorado census for 1900.

27. Ibid.

28. Ibid.

29. *Colorado Springs Gazette Telegraph,* January 16, 1903, 8:1.

30. *Colorado Springs Gazette,* January 20, 1908, 1:2.

31. Ibid. Interestingly, a recap of the incident in the *Gazette* on January 21 records a different dialogue between Dolly and Tucker: "'Look Tucker,' she said, 'He's going to shoot my dog.' 'Here's for me, too' was the answer, and the man fell back unconscious, still grasping the pistol with which he had shot himself." The January 21 article also gives other variations of the first story, such as where Dolly was standing when she first saw the boy on the sidewalk.

32. *Westword* (Colorado Springs: Old Colorado City Historical Society, 1998).

33. *Colorado Springs Gazette Telegraph,* January 18, 1906, 3:1.

34. Colorado census for 1900.

35. www.ancestry.com

36. "Sporting Houses."

Chapter Eight

1. Marshall Sprague, *Money Mountain* (Lincoln: University of Nebraska Press, 1953), 202.

2. Ibid.

3. Jackie Matz, interview by author, Cripple Creek, Colorado, December 10, 2003.

4. *Rocky Mountain News*, August 19, 1898, 10.

5. Thomas J. Noel and Cathleen M. Norman, *A Pikes Peak Partnership: The Penroses and the Tutts* (Boulder: University Press of Colorado, 2000), 36.

6. Gene Fowler, *Timber Line* (Garden City, N.Y.: Halcyon House, 1933), 118.

7. Ibid.

8. Ibid.

9. Regina Elizabeth Peck Andrus, *The Peck Family Book* (Salt Lake City, Utah: Brigham Young University Print Services, 2002), 186.

10. There has been much speculation about the true identity of Isabelle Martin and about her subsequent marriages, especially because a definitive record of her has yet to be found. One Sarah Isabella Donegon, for example, married a James Hamilton Martin in 1882 near Colorado City, a time when Pearl is not believed to have yet come to Colorado. A woman named Isibell Powers married Marion G. Martin in Denver in 1896, by which time Pearl was living in Cripple Creek. Several Ed Martins are listed in the Colorado marriage records, but the names of their wives, the dates, or the locations don't seem to match up. One theory is that Isabelle's actual maiden name could have been Martin, but there is not enough evidence to substantiate this. Colorado marriage records, Denver Public Library.

11. Clark Secrest, *Hell's Belles: Prostitution, Vice, and Crime in Early Denver*, rev. ed. (Boulder: University of Colorado Press, 2002), 226.

12. When visitor Eleanor Smith toured the Old Homestead in the 1980s, she recalled that one of the docents told the group that Pearl's room may have been where the dining room now is. More likely, however, a small room in the back of the house adjacent to today's dining room was Pearl's boudoir. This room appears to have been altered and is probably much smaller than Pearl's original bedroom; given its present dimensions, it could hardly have held all the furnishings listed in Pearl's probate record. Eleanor Smith, interview by author, Los Osos, California, May 2003; Probate case #M-79 of Isabelle Martin, El Paso County Courthouse, 1897.

13. Probate case of Isabelle Martin.

14. *Cripple Creek Times*, June 10, 1897, 1:1.

15. Ibid.

16. Curiously, one of Pearl's physicians, Dr. Kerr, submitted a bill for $25 to her estate. For reasons unknown, however, the good doctor then disappeared from Cripple Creek and never claimed his money. Probate case of Isabelle Martin.

17. Ibid.
18. Sometime after the Cripple Creek District Museum opened in 1953, Pearl's wooden grave marker was found lying on the ground at her grave. Museum founder Richard Johnson replaced the old marker with a marble heart-shaped tombstone. The original marker is on display at the museum.
19. Myke Minnow, *The Pearl DeVere Affair* (play program, Cripple Creek, Colorado, 1977).
20. Howard quickly deposited Pearl's valuables with the Colorado Finance and Safe Deposit Company at 269 East Bennett Avenue and set to work administering her estate. Ironically, the notary who signed his petition and other documents pertaining to Pearl's probate record was none other than Ethel Frizzel, who later married Albert Carlton shortly before he became one of Cripple Creek's wealthiest and best-known millionaires. Probate case of Isabelle Martin.
21. Ibid.
22. Colorado census for 1900, National Archives, Denver; Cripple Creek City directory, 1900.
23. On March 7, 1900, thirty-year-old Mary Kennedy, a.k.a. Mary Samuels, officially married Ashmore Samuels. Teller County Clerk and Recorder, marriage records, Teller County Courthouse, Cripple Creek, Colorado.
24. Sandra Dallas, *Colorado Ghost Towns and Mining Camps* (Norman: University of Oklahoma Press, 1985), 10.
25. Leslie Doyle Spell and Hazel M. Spell, *Forgotten Men of Cripple Creek* (Denver: Big Mountain Press, 1959), 67.
26. City of Cripple Creek, register of prostitutes, 1911, BPOE Elk's Lodge #316, Cripple Creek, Colorado.
27. Quote from Cy Martin, *Whiskey and Wild Women* (New York: Hart, 1974), 171.
28. Lowell Thomas, *Good Evening Everybody* (Boston: Hall, 1980), 230.
29. Report from Cripple Creek Police Department to City Council, October 1, 1906. Cripple Creek District Museum.
30. Dorothy Aldridge, *A Peek into the Past* (Colorado Springs, Colo.: Gowdy Printcraft Press, 1991), 123.
31. *Cripple Creek Times*, November 12, 1907, 3.

Chapter Nine

1. *Cripple Creek Morning Times*, January 23, 1897, 1:3.
2. *Weekly Cripple Creek Times*, January 11, 1900, miscellaneous news clipping, Cripple Creek District Museum.
3. Doris Gregory, *Ouray's Era of Bars and Brothels* (Ouray, Colo.: Cascade, 1982), 9.
4. Joanne West Dodds, *What's a Nice Girl Like You Doing in a Place Like This?* (Pueblo, Colo.: Focal Plain, 1996), 16.
5. Helen's plight was not unusual. The *Boulder County News* in 1876 reported on a disgruntled soiled dove who wished to reform but was being kept from doing so by lack of public sentiment and aid. The paper ended its commentary by encour-

aging the Christian ladies of the town to do the right thing. Sanford C. Gladden, *Ladies of the Night*, Early Boulder Series 5 (Boulder: privately published, 1979), 34.

6. Turner Entertainment, *Arsenic and Old Lace* (MGM/United Artists, 1944).

7. Lawrence Powell, "Early California Society." *Westways Magazine*, August 1965, 17.

Chapter Ten

1. Joanne West Dodds, *What's a Nice Girl Like You Doing in a Place Like This?* (Pueblo, Colo.: Focal Plain, 1996), 2, 3.

2. Anne M. Butler, *Daughters of Joy, Sisters of Misery: Prostitutes in the American West, 1865–90* (Chicago: University of Illinois Press, 1985), 67.

3. Cynthia J. Pasquale et al., *100 Years in the Heart of the Rockies* (Salida, Colo.: Arkansas Valley, 1980), 25.

4. Dodds, *What's a Nice Girl Like You Doing in a Place Like This?*, 9.

5. Ibid., 48.

6. Kay Reynolds Blair, *Ladies of the Lamplight*, rev. ed. (Ouray, Colo.: Western Reflections, 2002), 91.

7. Sanford C. Gladden, *Ladies of the Night*, Early Boulder Series 5 (Boulder: privately published, 1979), 35.

8. *Colorado City Iris*, February 2, 1906, 2:2

9. Ibid., February 9, 1906, 3:4.

10. Ibid., March 23, 1906, 3:2.

11. Jim Easterbrook, "The Saga of Old Colorado City: The Golden Years," miscellaneous news clipping, Penrose Public Library, Colorado Springs, Colorado.

12. *Colorado City Iris*, January 21, 1908, 3:3.

13. Ibid., January 24, 1908, 1:3.

14. *Colorado Springs Sun*, August 11, 1970, 3.

15. *Colorado City Iris*, July 16, 1909, 3:2.

16. Ibid., December 24, 1909, 5:3.

17. *Colorado Springs Sun*, August 11, 1970, 3.

18. Ibid.

19. City of Cripple Creek, register of prostitutes, 1911, BPOE #316, Cripple Creek, Colorado.

20. Ibid.

21. Ibid.

22. Ibid.

23. Ibid.

24. Clara's marriage certificate indicated that neither she nor Earl Myers had been married before. Marriage certificate of Clara Stetson to Earl Myers, Teller County Courthouse, marriage records, Cripple Creek, Colorado.

25. Jennie's marriage certificate states she was twenty-one in 1911; the city register that year states she was thirty, and her prison record at the Colorado State Penitentiary records her as being thirty-four years old in 1914. Teller County Courthouse, marriage records, Cripple Creek, Colorado; register of prostitutes;

Canon City State Penitentiary records, Canon City State Penitentiary Museum, Canon City, Colorado.

26. Cripple Creek mortuary records, November 7, 1910 to August 17, 1913. Cripple Creek District Museum, Cripple Creek, Colorado.

27. *Westword* (Colorado Springs: Old Colorado City Historical Society, February, 1989).

28. *Colorado City Iris*, May 1913, miscellaneous news clipping, Penrose Public Library.

29. Ibid., August 22, 1913, 3:3.

30. *Colorado Springs Gazette*, February 1914, miscellaneous news clipping, Penrose Public Library.

31. Ibid., September 1914, miscellaneous news clipping, Penrose Public Library.

32. *Colorado City Independent*, September 25, 1914, 1:3.

33. *Cripple Creek Gold Rush*, June 11, 1976, 2.

34. *Pioneer Courier*, September 2001, 4.

35. *Cripple Creek Gold Rush*, June 11, 1976, 2.

36. Ibid.

37. Ibid.

38. Ibid.

39. Jan MacKell, *The Black Sheep of El Paso County* (Old Colorado City History Center newsletter, 1993).

40. Ibid.

Chapter Eleven

1. By slip of memory, these ordinances remained on the books in Victor until just recently. The ordinances were officially repealed by mayor Kathy Justice on October 25, 2002. When asked if he planned to uphold the laws until they were officially repealed, Police chief James Mason replied, "Of course not. Both of our bars are owned by women, so that would be kind of hard." *Gold Rush Newspaper*, August 14, 2002, B2; James Mason, interview by author, Victor, Colorado, September 30, 2002.

2. Leland Feitz, *Myers Avenue: A Quick History of Cripple Creek's Red-light District* (Colorado Springs, Colo.: Little London Press, 1967).

3. *Colorado City Independent*, April 2, 1915, 1:1.

4. Ibid.

5. Some decades later, the lamps resurfaced as a donation to the Old Colorado City Historical Society, where they are on display today.

6. Case #6599, *State of Colorado v. Laura Bell*, January 1918, El Paso County Courthouse, Colorado Springs, Colorado.

7. Ibid.

8. The original court documents do not reveal the names of the two men who stole the liquor. Jim Easterbrook, *The Time Traveler in Old Colorado* (Colorado Springs, Colo.: Great Western Press, 1985), 16.

9. Probate file #M-311, Estate of Laura Bell McDaniel, El Paso County Courthouse, Colorado Springs, Colorado.

10. Blackman is listed in Colorado Springs directories as early as 1907 as a student at Colorado College. Little is known of George Curtis's background. Two men by that name are listed in the 1907 directory. One was a rancher, the other a secretary at the Rapson Coal Mining Company. One George L. Curtis also served six years at the Colorado State Reformatory in Buena Vista. Colorado State Reformatory prisoner records, Denver Public Library.

11. Most interestingly, nearly all of the documents referring to Laura Bell's court case, as well as her mysterious death, have disappeared from El Paso County records. The only reference to Laura Bell's case #6599 at the El Paso County Courthouse shows the date was changed in the ledger from January 1918 to September 1918. In addition, the courthouse at Castle Rock burned in 1977, destroying any records about the accident.

12. Probate file #M-311, Estate of Laura Bell McDaniel.

13. Ibid.

14. Ibid.

15. El Paso County Assessor's Office, Colorado Springs, Colorado.

16. And what of the rest of the clan? In 1919 Harry and Birdie Hooyer were still residing in Cripple Creek, where Harry Jr. was two years away from entering high school (he graduated in 1925). Birdie's son Cecil Eugene by Ed Moats was residing in Denver, near Pearl. In 1920 Cecil took a brief trip to Los Angeles, where he was noted as living in the census that year. The 1930 census lists the Hooyer clan twice. The first listing finds them at their home on West Eaton in Cripple Creek. Occupants of the house were Birdie, Harry, and Harry Jr. The latter was working at a hardware store; his father was employed as an interior decorator. Shortly after the census was taken the family must have relocated to Colorado Springs, where only Harry Sr. and Birdie are shown living at either a large boarding house or a hotel on North Tejon.

   Birdie Hooyer died in 1948 and was buried at Fairview Cemetery in Colorado City. Today Birdie shares a tombstone with Laura Bell, as well as their mother and stepfather. The stone was in fact placed there by Bill Henderson, who in 1983 also paid for a tombstone for prostitute Blanche Burton. Harry Hooyer's brother, Royal, continued attending annual Cripple Creek reunions through 1959. In 1951 he was living at the Shirley Savoy Hotel in Denver and does not appear to have ever married (Cripple Creek Reunion Annual Journal, 1951–59, Penrose Public Library, Colorado Springs, Colorado).

   In 1955 Pearl's husband, Charles, finally located his long-lost son from a former marriage. The boy, originally named Charles Alcorn Kitto, had been adopted and given the new name of Charles K. Nichols. Charles was working as a sales manager for the Stanley Works in New Britain, Connecticut. The reunion was apparently rocky; when Charles died in January 1957 in Denver, "Under the terms of his will Kitto directed that his son, Charles Alcorn Kitto 'who was taken to New York at the age of three by my former wife' and whom he 'had never seen nor heard of again' be disinherited" with the exception of $1,000. The remainder of Charles's $89,000 went to Pearl (*Rocky Mountain News*, February 8, 1957, miscellaneous clipping, Denver Public Library).

It appears that Pearl did maintain contact with her cousin Cecil Moats and her uncle Royal Hooyer. Cecil and Pearl lived within just a few blocks of each other until Cecil's death in March of 1961. Royal died in January of 1963. Pearl died the following December after an illness, leaving an estate estimated at an amazing $221,330.58. Among her personal possessions were a diamond brooch, a diamond dinner ring, a three-carat diamond ring, and a two-carat diamond ring. (Pearl's rings may very well have been inherited from Laura Bell's estate, which listed five diamond rings with a total value of $1,000. Probate file of Eva Pearl Kitto, #32509, Denver County Courthouse.) In addition, there were stocks in such well-known corporations as American Sugar, Chrysler, General Motors, and 20th Century Fox.

Only a few descendants of Laura Bell's nephews or nieces survive today. By the time Harry Jr. graduated from Cripple Creek High School in 1925, his mother had not appeared in Cripple Creek records since 1918 (*Cripple Creek/Victor High School Alumni: 1897–1996* [Cripple Creek, Colo., 1996]). Harry Sr., however, continued living in Cripple Creek for quite some time. In 1930 he sold property to Anna C. Strauss and conducted another real estate transaction with her in 1931 (Teller County Clerk and Recorder, Teller County Courthouse, Cripple Creek, Colorado). Shortly afterward, in May of 1931, Harry died, but for reasons unknown he was buried at Evergreen Cemetery in Colorado Springs (Evergreen Cemetery records, Penrose Public Library, Colorado Springs, Colorado).

Pearl's will and probate record are the only known documents to reveal other relatives of Laura Bell McDaniel. They were Cecil Eugene Moats, to whom Pearl intended to leave $10,000; cousin Harry P. Hooyer Jr., who was living in Maryland and received $2,500; cousin Buelah H. Chilton of Houma, Louisiana, the daughter of Laura Bell's brother James; and another relative named Nell H. Bennett whose exact relation to Pearl remains unknown. That Nell was also residing in Louisiana encourages speculation that she was a daughter of Beulah. A number of institutions, including the Shriner's Hospital for Crippled Children and the Denver Orphan's Home, were also listed as beneficiaries (probate file of Eva Pearl Kitto). It is assumed that these cousins have long since passed away, but only one is documented. In 1973 Buelah Chilton Heuston passed away. Her daughter Wanda was raised by grandparents and died in California in 1987 (ancestry.com).

17. Fairview Cemetery records, Penrose Public Library, Colorado Springs, Colorado.
18. Ibid.
19. John O'Byrne, *Pikes or Bust and Historical Sketches of the Wild West* (privately published, 1922), 22.
20. Lee Michels, interview by author, Colorado Springs, Colorado, April 13, 1993. Ms. Michels, an avid fan of Laura Bell McDaniel, says the rendering does not accurately represent the way Laura Bell looked or the clothes she wore.

21. City of Colorado Springs, *Here Lies Colorado Springs*, edited by Denise Oldach (Colorado Springs: Fittje Bros., 1995), 108.

22. Miscellaneous brochure, distributed by the Old Colorado City Historical Society, 1993.

23. J. Juan Reid, *Growing Up in Colorado Springs: The 1920s Remembered* (Colorado Springs, Colo.: Century One Press, 1981), 17.

24. *Westword* (Colorado Springs: Old Colorado City Historical Society, February 1989).

Chapter Twelve

1. Allen G. Bird, *Bordellos of Blair Street* (Pierson, Mich. Advertising, Publications & Consultants, 1993), 152.

2. Ibid.

3. Diamond Tooth Leona wasn't the only one to sport such a nickname because of her diamond tooth. There was also Evelyn Hildegard, a.k.a. Diamond Tooth Lil. Allegedly married and divorced thirteen times, Lil sang and played piano at the 1903 World's Fair and ran several successful brothels throughout the West, including in Denver.

4. Dick Kreck, "'I Will Be There': Prelude to Murder at the Brown Palace," *Colorado Heritage Magazine* (Spring 2003): 3.

5. Clark Secrest, *Hell's Belles: Denver's Brides of the Multitudes* (Denver: Hindsight Historical Publications, 1996), 237.

6. Joanne West Dodds, *What's a Nice Girl Like You Doing in a Place Like This?*, (Pueblo, Colo.: Focal Plain, 1996), 50.

7. Unidentified, undated newspaper article about Laura Evens's death, Salida Public Library, Salida, Colorado.

8. Dodds, *What's a Nice Girl Like You Doing in a Place Like This?*, 81.

9. In fact, Albany now ends at 5th Street. The portion that would have extended to 1st Street is now buried under Interstate 25. Locals say that the street was realigned after a flood in 1921 that buried Pueblo's downtown district under water, including the first stories of many buildings.

10. Bird, *Bordellos of Blair Street*, 160.

11. Eleanor Perry, *I Remember Tin Cup* (Littleton, Colo.: privately published, 1986), 24. Mrs. Bley was just one of many respectable women who did laundry for prostitutes. In 1882 the *Boulder County Herald* reported on a woman in Mrs. Bley's position whose fourteen-year-old daughter assisted her by picking up and delivering laundry in the red-light district, as well as by cleaning house for one or two madams. On several occasions, the paper reported, the girl had been approached by men looking for sexual favors.

12. Carolyn Wright and Clarence Wright, *Tiny Hinsdale of the Silvery San Juan* (privately published, 1964), 58.

13. FourteenerNet, Colorado History, "The Story of Cock-Eyed Liz," www.fourteenernet.com.

14. Dodds, *What's a Nice Girl Like You Doing in a Place Like This?*, 23.
15. Steve Mackin and Bonnie Mackin, interview by author, Cripple Creek, Colorado, 2000.
16. Ibid.; Grantor/grantee records and property transactions, Teller County Courthouse, Cripple Creek, Colorado.
17. In 1995 exorbitant taxes forced Lodi and Harold Hern to sell to a national corporation. Over the past several years, the Old Homestead has balanced precariously on the edge, with several new owners and various threats to close the museum, turn it into a casino, build over it, or tear it down. The Old Homestead is currently still operating as a museum; its new owners have expressed an interest in maintaining the museum and possibly selling it to Homestead House, Inc., a nonprofit established by Mrs. Hern and Charlotte Bumgarner.
18. Interview with French Blanche, miscellaneous news clipping from the *Gold Rush* newspaper, February 18, 1988, Cripple Creek District Museum.
19. Steve and Bonnie Mackin, interview.
20. Ibid.
21. Sally McCready Johnson, interview by author, Cripple Creek, Colorado, March 1996.
22. The Old Homestead's current owner as of 2004, Walsh-Rivera Investment Partners, has expressed much interest in preserving the old brothel and maintaining it as a museum. In January the corporation installed offices in a dining room that was part of the tour as well as in three rundown and unused rooms, including Pearl DeVere's bedroom suite. Walsh-Rivera has opened a new casino in an adjacent modern building; spokesmen have stated that when the company relinquishes the rooms in the Old Homestead, it intends to restore them all to their original historic splendor.

Appendix One

1. Cripple Creek City directory, 1900; Colorado federal census, 1900. Unusually, since many census takers shied away from listing the true occupation of residents, the census for Cripple Creek boldly listed prostitutes as "sporting women."
2. It is possible that Jessie Strong reigned as madam before or after E. Prince (Eva Prince, early partner of Pearl DeVere's), since the latter is listed as owner of the house.

Appendix Two

1. City of Cripple Creek, register of prostitutes, 1911, BPOE #316, Cripple Creek, Colorado.

Glossary

⁂

Abandoned woman—A sympathetic term for a prostitute, possibly relating to the fact that many women were abandoned by their husbands or family.

Amazon—From Greek mythology; a woman who is tall and strong or athletic; used to refer to prostitutes.

Bagnio—A house of prostitution.

Bar girl—A girl who works at a bar and sometimes in rooms upstairs as a prostitute. This term appears to have been used almost exclusively in Trinidad.

Bawd, bawdy house—A *bawd* is identified by most dictionaries as a procuress, a female pimp. The original meaning of the word *bawdy* is something that is humorous in an indecent way, much like a dirty joke.

Belladonna—Another name for deadly nightshade, a poisonous plant. The leaves of the plant can be dried and used as a narcotic stimulant. When placed on the eyelids the leaves will cause the pupils to dilate; thus the plant was very popular among prostitutes who wanted to achieve those "bedroom eyes."

Blowen—An early 1800s term for prostitutes or women who cohabited with men without the sanctity of marriage.

Bordello—A house of prostitution.

Boric acid—A substance derived from the chemical boron that is resistant to high temperatures and can be used as a mild antiseptic. Boric acid can be made into suppositories to cure yeast infections; in larger doses, the substance can induce an abortion.

Brothel—A house of prostitution.

Cancan—A popular dance of the 1800s and early 1900s, wherein female dancers kick high enough that spectators can see under their skirts and turn around to show their backsides to the audience.

Carbolic acid—A poisonous acid used by prostitutes to commit suicide; death was agonizing but quick.

Carogue—A harlot who takes revenge on the men who have corrupted her by corrupting them in return.

Cathouse—A house of prostitution.

Ceremonial husband—A man who marries a prostitute strictly for business purposes relating primarily to prostitution.

Chicken ranch—A house of prostitution, usually used to describe houses in rural areas.

Courtesan—From seventeenth-century France, a highly paid prostitute who keeps company only with wealthy or prominent men.

Creeper—A thief who stealthily creeps along the floor and steals a customer's belongings while he sleeps or is having sex with a prostitute.

Crib—A small, one-room apartment where a prostitute can conduct business. Usually cribs are built like row houses with adjoining walls.

Dance hall—A place where men may pay women to dance, drink, and sometimes have sex with them.

Demimonde—A French term, literally translated as *half-world*, for a red-light district.

Ergot—A fungus known to grow on rye and other cereals; the fungus could be dried into powder form and used to induce an abortion.

Erring sister—A prostitute; a fellow woman who has "erred" in her ways.

Fainting couch—Specially designed lounges made so that one may lie back on them. Fainting couches were especially popular among women who wore tight corsets and felt the need to lie down often.

Fair Cyprian—A prostitute.

Fair sister—A prostitute.

Fallen angel—A prostitute; a formerly good woman or girl who has fallen from the graces of God, the church, and society.

Fallen woman—A prostitute; a woman who has fallen from the graces of proper society.

Fancy girl—Sometimes used to refer to a dance hall girl or parlor house girl with regards to the fancy clothes she wore.

Female boarding—Noted on most maps as a place where houses of prostitution exist.

Fille de joie—A French term for a prostitute; literally a young girl of joy.

Frail sister—Another sympathetic term for a prostitute, given her harsh and unhealthy lifestyle.

Fresh meat—A term usually employed to announce the arrival of new prostitutes in town.

Giddy girl—A prostitute who is giddy, usually from alcohol or drugs.

Good-time Daisy, good-time girl—A prostitute or woman with loose morals.

Gray Bar Hotel—Jail.

Harlot—A woman of easy virtue.

Harridan—A bad-tempered old woman, but also a term applied to prostitutes.

Hog ranch—A term used to identify rural and lower-class houses of prostitution, such as on the plains or in remote areas. More popular in Wyoming, Utah, and Nevada where such places are more prominent.

Hook artist—A thief who steals a man's clothing via a rod and hook while he has sex with a prostitute.

Hooker—A prostitute.

House of ill fame—A house of prostitution.

House of ill repute—A house of prostitution.

Hurdy-gurdy girls—An early term for dance hall girls; based on a musical instrument originating in Europe, called a hurdy-gurdy or barrel organ, that was played by turning a handle.

Hustling—The act of soliciting sex in exchange for money.

Inmate—A woman who lives or works at a house of prostitution.

Jewelled bird—A prostitute.

Lady of easy virtue—A prostitute.

Lady of the evening—A prostitute.

Lady of the lamplight—A prostitute. See *Red light.*

Lady of the night—A prostitute.

Landlady—In the prostitution industry, a madam.

Laudanum—A strong liquid form of opium that was once available over the counter at drugstores. The drug was usually sold in quart bottles and administered by the spoonful.

Line, the—Another term for a place where several houses of prostitution exist.

Love market—A house or area where prostitution is practiced.

Madam—The female owner or manager of a house of prostitution.

Moll—A term usually used to describe the female companion of a gangster or criminal. The word became especially popular during the Depression when referring to gangsters such as Pretty Boy Floyd or Bonnie and Clyde, but was also used earlier.

Monterey, the—A popular dance practiced at dance halls but also at other bars, theaters, and taverns.

Norrel woman—A term of unknown origins for a prostitute.

Nose paint—Liquor or perhaps cocaine.

Nymph du pave—A French term for a prostitute.

Oil of tansy—The oil of a plant with yellow flowers that can be used to induce an abortion.

Old-timer—A prostitute who has been in town too long, has outlived her usefulness as a working girl, or is older and more experienced in the profession.

Painted cat, painted hussy, painted lady—A prostitute or dance hall girl; someone who paints her face. The origin of makeup will shock some women today; it was originally used by prostitutes to mask their identities. Early in its debut, makeup was applied in the form of "pancake" powder and rouge to make prostitutes look almost like clowns or mimes. In decent society, proper women were not permitted to use makeup.

Panel house—A house of prostitution with a hidden panel in the bedrooms, used to access the room and rob customers while they slept or were otherwise engaged. Sometimes there was merely a sliding panel in the back of a closet. "Panel workers" could then remove the man's wallet and steal just enough money from it not to be noticed before putting it back.

Parlor house—The fanciest and most expensive of houses of prostitution.

Pimp—A person, almost always a man, who controls prostitutes by running their businesses and sometimes their personal lives in exchange for money.

Prussic acid—Also known as hydrocyanic acid, a weak acid that is extremely poisonous. Prostitutes could use it for abortions or to commit suicide.

Red light—The most common symbol of prostitution, dating from the days when railroad men left their red signal lanterns outside the brothels while paying a visit to a prostitute. In this manner, the men could be found in an emergency. The romantic shade of red was used by many a prostitute in her decorating schemes.

Row, the—Another term for a place, such as a row of houses, where prostitution is practiced.

Rustling—The act of soliciting or engaging in prostitution.

Saffron—A common household herb that can be used in large doses to induce an abortion.

Scarlet woman—A prostitute, relating to the use of red lights and the color red in prostitution. See *Red light*.

Shady lady—A prostitute.

Signboard gal—One of the lowest forms of prostitute who, for lack of a house or crib to work out of, conducts business behind signboards and other discreet outdoor places.

Skin dive—An early term for a bar, gaming house, or other place of questionable character where sex may be sold.

Soiled dove—A prostitute; the symbolism is of a once white and wholesome dove that is now dirty.

Sporting girl, sporting house—A prostitute or house of prostitution.

Streetwalker—Another low form of prostitute who has no other choice than to walk the streets looking to sell sex.

Strumpet—An older term for a prostitute.

Tannic acid—A derivative of tannin, made from oak and other tree barks and primarily used in tanning and dying. It could also be made into a tea and used to induce abortion.

Tenderloin—An early term, originating in New York, for a district where prostitution is practiced.

That other woman—A term mostly used by decent women to identify a prostitute, probably in reference to the prostitutes their husbands did business with.

Tongue oil—Liquor; the term implies that the oil may make the tongue work faster, thus causing a person to reveal more than is discreet.

Tonsil varnish—Liquor.

Trick—The customer of a prostitute; also used to refer to the act of purchased sex itself.

Two-bit house—A cheap or low-priced house of prostitution (two bits was equal to a quarter).

Variety artist—A person known to perform in theaters but also in houses of prostitution, where the entertainment might include sexual services.

White slave—A prostitute who pays for her transportation and placement in a brothel by paying off a pimp or madam.

Whorehouse—A house of prostitution.

Woman of the town—A woman with loose morals or a prostitute.

Wrapper—A bathrobe; often worn by prostitutes during their time off during the day.

Additional Reading

Books

Aldridge, Dorothy, *Historic Colorado City: The Town with a Future.* Colorado Springs, Colo.: Little London Press, 1996.

Armstrong, Helen, *The Walking Tour: A Guide to Historic Old Colorado City.* Manitou Springs, Colo.: TextPros, 2000.

Beebe, Lucius, *The American West.* New York: E. P. Dutton, 1955.

Benham, Jack, *Ouray.* Ouray, Colo.: Bear Creek, 1976.

Black, Celeste, *The Pearl of Cripple Creek.* Colorado Springs, Colo.: Black Bear, 1997.

Breckenridge, Juanita L., and John P. Breckenridge. *El Paso County Heritage.* Colorado Springs, Colo.: Curtis Media, 1985.

Brown, Robert L., *Colorado Ghost Towns Past and Present.* Caldwell, Idaho: Caxton, 1981.

City of Colorado Springs, *Old Colorado City Historic Inventory.* Colorado Springs, Colo.: privately published, 1974.

———. *The Westside.* Colorado Springs: Great Western Press, 1986.

Donachy, Patrick L. *Echoes of Yesteryear,* vol. 3. Trinidad, Colo.: Inkwell, 1984.

Eberhart, Perry. *Ghosts of the Colorado Plains.* Athens: Ohio University Press, 1986.

———. *Guide to the Colorado Ghost Towns and Mining Camps.* Chicago: Swallow Press, 1959.

Eddleman, Sherida K. *Missouri Genealogical Records and Abstracts.* 3 vols. Bowie, Md.: Heritage Books, 1992.

Fetter, Richard. *Frontier Boulder.* Boulder: Johnson Books, 1983.

Goodstein, Phil. *The Seamy Side of Denver.* Denver: New Social Publications, 1993.

Hetzler, Rosemary, and John Hetzler. *Colorado Springs and Pikes Peak Country.* Donning, 1989.

Hughes, David R. *Historic Old Colorado City,* vol. 1. Colorado Springs, Colo.: Old Colorado City Historic District, 1978.

Hunt, Inez, and Draper, Wanetta. *To Colorado's Restless Ghosts.* Denver: Sage Books, 1960.

Johnson, Fred J., and Bowman, George. *The Fabulous Cripple Creek District.* Privately published, 1954.

Luzier, Athlyn. *Evergreen Cemetery Records, Colorado Springs, El Paso County, Colorado, 1856 to 1972.* Colorado Springs: Pikes Peak Genealogical Society, 1993.

Mazzulla, Fred, and Jo Mazzulla. *First 100 Years in the Cripple Creek District.* Victor, Colo.: Barbarossa Press, 1956.

Meixsell, Tara. *Silver Heels.* Montrose, Colo.: Western Reflections, 2002.

Noel, Thomas J. *Buildings of Colorado.* Chicago: Oxford University Press for Society of Architectural Historians, 1997.

———. *Colorado: A Liquid History and Tavern Guide to the Highest State.* Golden, Colo.: Fulcrum, 1999.

Porter, Rufus. *Gold Fever.* Privately published, 1954.

———. *Pay Dirt.* Privately published, 1961.

Rees, Sian. *The Floating Brothel.* New York: Hyperion, 2002.

Seagraves, Anne. *Soiled Doves: Prostitution in the Early West.* Hayden, Idaho: Wesanne, 1994.

Sneed, F. Dean. *The Phantom Train and Other Ghostly Legends of Colorado.* Lakewood, Colo.: Dream Weavers, 1992.

Sprague, Marsahll. *Newport in the Rockies.* Chicago: Swallow Press, 1971.

Swift, Kim, *Heart of the Rockies: A History of the Salida Area.* Woodland Park, Colo.: Johnson Printing for Poppin' Wheelies Multimedia Productions, 1980.

Westerners. *The Brand Book.* Denver: State Museum Building, 1952.

City Directories

Canon City, 1905
Colorado Springs, Colorado City, and Manitou Springs, 1879–1921
Cripple Creek District, 1893–1918
Denver, 1885–1960
Pueblo, 1954
Salida, 1890–1950

Documents

Advertisement for Belle Birnard's, Denver. Amon Carter Museum, Fort Worth, Texas, box 48A, ff2.

Advertisement for Palace of Pleasure. Amon Carter Museum, Fort Worth, Texas, box 48A, ff2.

The Blue Book, New Orleans, 1936. Photocopy of front cover and correspondence. Provided by the Amon Carter Museum, Fort Worth, Texas.

Chaffee County births and deaths records. Chaffee County Courthouse, Buena Vista, Colorado.

Chaffee County marriage records. Chaffee County Clerk and Recorder, Chaffee County Courthouse, Buena Vista, Colorado.

Church of Jesus Christ of Latter-Day Saints Family History Library, Salt Lake City, Utah.

Colorado census for 1880, 1885, 1900, 1910, 1920, and 1930. National Archives, Denver, Colorado.

Denver probate index. Denver County Courthouse.

Dozier, Otis. "Business Houses of Colorado City." 1944. Penrose Public Library, Colorado Springs.

Ellinwood, L. E. "Memories of Old Colorado City." Undated. Penrose Public Library, Colorado Springs.

Englert, Lorene Baker. "First Three Plats of Colorado City." Undated. Penrose Public Library, Colorado Springs.

Fortune Club Ladies, photos and history compiled by Wayne "Mac" MacCormick, the Fortune Club, Victor, Colorado.

Greenwood Cemetery records. Canon City Library History Center, Canon City, Colorado.

Invitation to the Red-light. Amon Carter Museum, Fort Worth, Texas, box 48A, ff2.

Marriage license for Jennie Benton and Edgar Keif. Teller County Clerk and Recorder, Teller County Courthouse, Cripple Creek, Colorado.

Mathews, Carl F. "Colorado City, Its Peace Officers, Notes (and Notorious) Characters, etc." 1944. Penrose Public Library, Colorado Springs.

Miscellaneous documents regarding brass checks. Things: Tokens, box 42 ff4, Amon Carter Museum, Fort Worth, Texas.

Report from police department to Cripple Creek City Council, August 1, 1902. Cripple Creek District Museum, Cripple Creek, Colorado.

Report of J. W. Bruister, police magistrate, August 1894 and October 1894. Cripple Creek District Museum, Cripple Creek, Colorado.

Salida cemetery index. Salida Regional Library, Salida, Colorado.

Films

Treasure of the Cripple Creek Mining District. Encore Video Productions in association with the City of Cripple Creek, Colorado Springs, 2000.

Voices of Cripple Creek. Encore Video Productions in association with the City of Cripple Creek, Colorado Springs, 2001.

Internet Sources

Browning Genealogy. browning.evcpl.lib.in.us/.

Butte Montana Dumas Brothel Masks. Item #203812138. eBay.com.

Cyndislist.com.

Familysearch.org.

Hurst, James W. *Columbus, New Mexico's Soiled Doves.* zianet.com.

Rootsweb.com.

Social Security death index. ssdi.com.

Maps

Plat maps:
Cripple Creek, Teller County, Colorado, 1901.
Ramona, El Paso County, Colorado, #690, 1910.
Sanborn Fire Insurance maps:
Colorado City, 1890, 1892, 1897, 1902, 1950.
Cripple Creek, 1896, 1900, 1907, 1918.
Pueblo, 1904.
Salida, 1886, 1888, 1890, 1893.
Trinidad, 1890, 1900.

Periodicals

Aspen Evening Chronicle
Colorado Gambler Magazine
Colorado History News
Colorado Prospector
Colorado Springs Cheyenne Edition
Colorado Springs Free Press
Colorado Springs Independent Magazine
Colorado Springs Kira Magazine
Denver Republican
Durango Herald-Democrat
Fruita Historian
Old Colorado City Bullsheet
Pikes Peak Journal
Salida Downtown Walking Tour
Salida Mountain Mail
Travel America (September–October 1995)
Victor Record
Westways Magazine

Index

CPSIA information can be obtained
at www.ICGtesting.com
Printed in the USA
FSHW021948210620
71414FS

9 780826 333438